Living Law

Gender, Culture, and Politics in the Middle East
miriam cooke, Simona Sharoni, and Suad Joseph, *Series Editors*

Select Titles in Gender, Culture, and Politics in the Middle East

The Best of Hard Times: Palestinian Refugee Masculinities in Lebanon
Gustavo Barbosa

Fatema Mernissi for Our Times
Minoo Moallem and Paola Bacchetta, eds.

The Funambulists: Women Poets of the Arab Diaspora
Lisa Marchi

The Hammam through Time and Space
Julie Peteet

Istanbul Appearances: Beauty and the Making of Middle-Class Femininities in Urban Turkey
Claudia Liebelt

Quest for Love in Central Morocco: Young Women and the Dynamics of Intimate Lives
Laura Menin

Sexuality in the Middle East and North Africa: Contemporary Issues and Challenges
J. Michael Ryan and Helen Rizzo, eds.

Sumud: Birth, Oral History, and Persisting in Palestine
Livia Wick

For a full list of titles in this series,
visit https://press.syr.edu/supressbook-series
/gender-culture-and-politics-in-the-middle-east/.

LIVING LAW

Women and Legality in Marinid Morocco

Rosemary Admiral

Syracuse University Press

First Edition 2025

25 26 27 28 29 30 6 5 4 3 2 1

For a listing of books published and distributed by Syracuse University Press, visit https://press.syr.edu.

ISBN: 9780815611844 (hardcover)
9780815657446 (e-book)

Library of Congress Cataloging-in-Publication Data

Names: Admiral, Rosemary, author.
Title: Living law : women and legality in Marinid Morocco / Rosemary Admiral.
Description: Syracuse : Syracuse University Press, 2025. | Series: Gender, culture, and politics in the middle east | Includes bibliographical references and index.
Identifiers: LCCN 2025010808 (print) | LCCN 2025010809 (ebook) | ISBN 9780815611844 (hardback) | ISBN 9780815657446 (ebook)
Subjects: LCSH: Married women—Legal status, laws, etc.—Morocco—History. | Married women (Islamic law)—Morocco—History. | Husband and wife—Morocco—History. | Husband and wife (Islamic law)—Morocco—History. | Divorce (Islamic law)—Morocco—History. | Paternity (Islamic law)—Morocco—History. | Women (Islamic law)—Morocco—History. | Morocco—History—647–1516. | Beni Marin dynasty.
Classification: LCC KSW550 .A93 2025 (print) | LCC KSW550 (ebook) | DDC 346.6401/630902—dc23/eng/20250318
LC record available at https://lccn.loc.gov/2025010808
LC ebook record available at https://lccn.loc.gov/2025010809

The authorized representative in the EU for product safety and compliance is Mare Nostrum Group B.V.
Mauritskade 21D, 1091 GC Amsterdam, The Netherlands
gpsr@mare-nostrum.co.uk

For Mohamed Amine

Contents

Tables and Charts

Tables

Charts

Acknowledgments

This book came together from two separate interests, one in Islamic family law and one in women's legal scholarship in premodern Morocco. These interests evolved into an inquiry on women's engagement with Islamic law in Morocco under the Marinid dynasty; however, partway through the research process these interests split off again into two separate projects. The research here is an overview of ordinary women's lives through a legal framework, and I put aside the study of women's engagement with the law at the level of advanced scholarship and interpretation (*faqihat*) for a future project. I owe my gratitude to many people who have helped me over the years to complete this research.

My dissertation committee was a dream team who brought important perspectives to my work. Their insight, support, feedback, and expertise at every stage of the process made this work possible. I cannot thank them enough. Ken Cuno was an exemplary advisor, dissertation supervisor, and mentor, who guided this project, and my development as a historian, from start to finish. Antoinette Burton was an inspiration on many fronts, and I appreciate her patience in pushing me to think more theoretically about gender and law, make meaningful connections, and refine my arguments. D. Fairchild Ruggles was a constant advocate, resource, and support, insisting on precision and challenging me to see the bigger picture. Mauro Nobili encouraged me to see the broader regional and thematic context, as well as pay more attention to detail, and his feedback on the structure of the dissertation helped shape the final product. I can never thank these mentors enough for the huge amount of time they invested in my studies and research.

I initially conducted research for this project in Morocco from September 2012 to December 2013. People were incredibly generous with their time, ideas, and advice throughout my stay in the country and I am grateful to all of them. More people than I can mention here gave me books, journals, reality checks, and pointed me in the right direction. As I was struggling through a manuscript by one of the most important scholars in my research, Abdullah al-Abdusi, I found out that Dr. Hicham Mohammadi had just completed compiling and editing al-Abdusi's fatwas for his dissertation. He not only invited me to attend his dissertation defense but also gave me a copy of his impressive dissertation (now published as a book), which was a huge help and saved me months of work. Professor Abd al-Latif al-Jilani's encyclopedic knowledge and wise counsel, in addition to his generous sharing of resources, made this a better project. The shortcomings in all cases are my own and I hope I have at least partially lived up to the trust people placed in me.

A number of distinguished historians shared my interest in women's history in medieval Morocco. Professors Mohamed Yassir al-Hilali, Mustapha Nachchat, Hamid Titaou, and Latifa Elbouhsini gave their insights, guided me to resources, compiled bibliographies, and allowed me access to impressive dissertations. Their work provided the foundation for my work. Professors Said Ennahid, Khalid Saqi, and Mohamed Dahbi offered advice, assistance, and facilitated connections. Dr. Abdelhadi Tazi was an early inspiration for my interest in learned women in medieval Morocco and I am so grateful that I had the opportunity to share my project with him before his passing.

In Rabat, I benefited from the tutoring of Hanane Eljed, and later Roots Academy, in Arabic. Dris Soulaimani's expertise in Arabic grammar and manuscripts helped to resolve many questions and translate complex language. Research, and life in general, was made better by the friendship and professional support of Aziza Ouguir, Sabahat Adil, Khadija Soulaimani, Asma Sayeed, Josie Hendrickson, and Ghizlane Bentaouzer. In Spain, Professor María Jesús Viguera generously shared her notes on Marinid historiography and her impressive research resources. Professor Francisco Vidal Castro's incisive advice on the project's direction came at a crucial time and helped me reframe my questions and ultimately finish the dissertation. Professor Rachid El Hour was generous with both books and advice.

The institutional support I received made this research feasible. Librarians at the University of Illinois at Urbana-Champaign (UIUC), the Royal Library (*al-Khizana al-Hasaniyya*) and National Library (*al-Maktaba al-Wataniyya*) in Rabat, the Fondation du Roi Abdul-Aziz in Casablanca, the Qarawiyyin Library in Fez, and others helped to locate sources and suggested additional resources. Financial support from Fulbright (IIE), the Social Sciences Research Council's International Dissertation Research Fellowship (SSRC-IDRF), and the American Institute for Maghrib Studies (AIMS) allowed me to take the time in Morocco to carry out the research. James Miller and The Moroccan-American Commission for Educational & Cultural Exchange (MACECE) in Rabat provided helpful research support, while the Social Science Research Council (SSRC) Fellows Workshop was a valuable opportunity to consider my work in a broader interdisciplinary context. Funding from the UIUC Department of History and the Graduate College gave me time to write the initial research. I'm grateful to the friends and fellow graduate students who made Urbana-Champaign a community.

In my new institutional home at the University of Texas at Dallas (UTD), the friendship and mentorship of colleagues, especially Mike Farmer, Michael Wilson, Kimberly Hill, and Songyao Ren, kept me going as I completed revisions for the book. In times of crisis, the support of Ben Wright, Ali Alibhai, Whitney Stewart, Ravi Prakash, Anne Gray Fischer, and Nomi Stone helped restore my faith in the institution. Professional and financial support from the Bass School of Arts, Humanities, and Technology and Deans Dennis Kratz and Nils Roemer was invaluable. My students became my intellectual community, reading through my sources with me and offering insight. UTD students continue to inspire me with their intelligence and bravery. The UTD McDermott Library was generous in buying books and their InterLibrary Loan department was endlessly resourceful in tracking down the resources I needed.

As the book took shape, Charlotte Weber's incisive editing skills took my text to the next level. At Syracuse University Press, Laura K. Fish's exceptional guidance kept me on point. Her support, along with the early interest of Peggy Solic, made this book possible. Lisa Goodrum's copyediting improved all aspects of the book. Thanks also to the editorial board and the anonymous reviewers, whose excellent feedback helped strengthen the manuscript.

Thank you to my parents and siblings for their love and support and for always being there. Most of all, I would not have started my degree (and book) if it weren't for my husband, and I definitely would not have finished it. Thank you for your constant support and always believing in me. More recently, my son has brought new joy and motivation to this project, and I write this book for him.

Parts of chapter 4: "Women, Men, and Legal Knowledge," were originally published in Rosemary Admiral, "Finding the *Faqihat:* Women's Legal Scholarship and Biography in Premodern Morocco," *Journal of North African Studies* 29, no. 1 (2024): 37–61. Used with permission of Taylor & Francis Informa UK Ltd; permission conveyed through Copyright Clearance Center, Inc. Parts of chapter 8: "Transgressions and Legal Accommodation," were originally published in Rosemary Admiral, "Transgressing the Boundaries: *Zina* and Legal Accommodation in the Premodern Maghrib," in *The Routledge Handbook of Islam and Gender*, ed. Justine Howe (London: Routledge, 2020): 299–309. Used with permission of Taylor & Francis Informa UK Ltd; permission conveyed through Copyright Clearance Center, Inc. Parts of chapters 7 and 8 were originally published as Rosemary Admiral, "Living Islamic Law: Women and Legal Culture in Marinid Morocco," *Islamic Law and Society* 25, no. 3 (2018): 212–34. Thanks to Brill for permission to reuse this material.

A Note on Transliteration and Dates

The approach used here for identifying Arabic terms loosely follows the *International Journal of Middle East Studies* (*IJMES*) system. It aims for readability by non-specialists and assumes specialists will have no trouble discerning the correct Arabic term. It avoids using diacritical marks in transliteration and notes only medial ʻayns (ʻ) and hamzas (ʼ). Wherever possible, after the introduction of a term, it uses an equivalent English term instead of the original Arabic term.

Dates are provided only in the Common Era calendar to make reading this work more accessible for non-specialists.

Prelude

A Scandal in Taza

In the middle of the fourteenth century in a small town near Fez, Morocco, a young woman ran away from her father's home and married her neighbor with the help of the local qadi, or judge.[1] This event was not the start of the scandal, but it was the spark that ignited a larger regional dispute that drew in the local community, regional jurists, and the ruler himself, Sultan Abu al-Hassan (r. 1331–48) of the Marinid dynasty. Marriage overwhelmingly defined the lives of women in the premodern Islamic world. It generated wealth accumulation for wives, who received a dower from their husbands and often other financial gifts from their parents. It also enabled families to form strategic alliances and safeguard inherited wealth within extended genealogies. Fathers, acting on behalf of the family, negotiated partnerships for their daughters that would secure their future stability. So, when Iysa al-Turjali, the qadi of Taza, allowed the daughter of Ibrahim al-Anbaki to marry Ibn al-Turjuman against her father's wishes, he was appropriating her father's fundamental right.

Many of the details of the case remain lost to history. The timeline is a bit fuzzy. We cannot be certain how things ended. The judge and the father presented conflicting versions of events, and their narratives agree on very little. Either the daughter ran away to force her father into allowing her to marry Ibn al-Turjuman, or she had been seduced. Ibn al-Turjuman was either a young man in love, or a powerful and well-connected manipulator. Maybe the young woman had committed fornication, or had simply confessed to this crime to improve her legal standing. The father had beaten and humiliated his daughter, or the witnesses had lied, and the judge himself manipulated the legal proceedings. Perhaps the father had refused to marry his daughter to Ibn al-Turjuman because the latter was a scoundrel, or because he denied his daughter the right to marry any man. In Qadi al-Turjali's version of the story, a portrait emerges of a tenacious young woman who went to great lengths to escape an abusive father and utilized her advanced knowledge of Islamic law in order to marry the man that she chose herself. From the father's perspective, he was the victim of a rogue judge who had circumvented his paternal authority and abused his position to oppress Ibrahim al-Anbaki and ruin his naïve young daughter's future.

The documentary evidence for the case from Taza presents a rich text, showing how ordinary people interacted with the law and how communities intervened to resolve disputes.[2] It also sheds light on the instability of gendered identities, such as the basic category of woman, as gendered rights were negotiated as part of people's encounters with the law. The case was a battle over disputed facts and questionable legal reasoning, and a clear example of the sometimes contentious relationships between local legal officials and central legal authorities. And, at a most basic level, it reflects a power struggle on the part of a young woman who challenged her father's authority and insisted on marrying a man he detested. In short, the case encapsulates the larger argument of this book: that the legal system functioned in premodern North Africa as an integral part of social networks and that women's engagement with Islamic law was routine and demonstrated clear agency. Women regularly used legal tools to limit men's authority over them. In areas where the law was gendered, law, in practice, often served to increase women's rights as defined in the doctrine, while at the same time limiting men's rights. Women's relationship to Islamic law transformed in the modern period as colonial and postcolonial regimes gutted the legal system and the social networks that supported it.

Overall, this book tells the story of a young woman struggling against paternal authority to marry the man of her choosing and of other women who engaged with Islamic law on a daily basis in their lives and in their disputes. The stories of these women show the historical production of

Islamic law in premodern Morocco and provide an alternative perspective to the vision of both modern supporters and detractors of Islamic law, who see law as outside of history, static texts relegated to legal books, never adapting or changing, and always restricting and regulating women.

Living Law

I

Introduction

This book tells the history of ordinary (and some not-so-ordinary) women living in Marinid Morocco, like the young woman from Taza, through their interaction with the law. Taking Islamic law as its archive, it explores the social world of Marinid Morocco (mid-thirteenth to mid-fifteenth century) as reflected in these texts, focusing on women's relationships with the people around them, and with the law. At the same time, it investigates the implementation of the Maliki school of Islamic law through its encounters with women. This study builds on recent scholarship on law, gender, and history to complicate current understandings of the historical relationship between Muslim women and Islamic law, understandings which are often based on ahistorical assumptions drawn from encounters with postcolonial hybrid legal systems, and projected back onto the past. This work challenges notions of the Muslim woman's passivity and inability to act on her own behalf, while also contesting the pervasive idea that agency can only be recognized when women are resisting or fighting patriarchal systems.[1] Islamic law certainly laid out clear gender norms, with men having greater rights than women in some areas or having control over women, particularly within the family. As Judith E. Tucker notes, "We are not dealing here with the hidden discrimination of western legal thought, but rather with a law and set of legal institutions that are forthright in the privileging of men in certain areas of economic and social life."[2] In her ethnography of pious Islamist women in Egypt who embrace education through the mosque, Saba Mahmood deconstructs the Western liberal "belief that all human beings have an innate desire for freedom, that we all somehow seek to assert our autonomy when allowed to do so, that human agency primarily consists of acts that challenge social norms and not those that uphold them, and so on."[3] Mahmood's approach is useful here in understanding women who challenge or seek to renegotiate aspects of Islamic law while at the same time embracing that same legal system and the larger system of belief in which it is embedded. Simplistic and narrow feminist readings of agency erase the stories and devalue the experiences and actions of women who worked within systems that did not treat them the same as men. I draw on gender as a category of analysis to understand the complexity of the relationships and identities created and reshaped at the intersection of this moment in time with the people in this study who encountered particular historical, political, and legal forces.[4]

Law was central to the lives of people in Marinid Morocco, regardless of gender, and women approached the law as a framework and a tool for securing (and at times, expanding) their rights, and protecting their interests. Principles fundamental to understandings of Islamic law whose origins were traced to divine sources, granted men authority over women in the family, and influenced every area of social and political life.[5] Yet women did not approach Islamic law as a hostile system, with the goal of subverting it or challenging its jurisdiction over them, or as a sacred structure in which the interpretations of male jurists could not be challenged. Rather, they engaged with it dynamically and extensively, using legal tools and strategies in a variety of contexts, even when seeking to alter the balance of power between themselves and the men in their lives. As Tucker remarks more generally, Muslim women "have not embraced, by and large, an adversarial form of agency but rather have participated in the legal system in a variety of ways, both asserting rights and accepting to fulfill duties and obligations."[6] Moreover, after transgressing social or legal boundaries, women resorted to the legal system to return their lives to a shape that was meaningful to their communities (for example, to facilitate a legally recognized marriage after a premarital sex scandal, as in the case of the young woman from Taza and other cases discussed in chapter 8). In Marinid Morocco, the women who showed up in the sources did not view law as the enemy. Rather, it was an instrument available to them to secure their interests and challenge the misdeeds or oppressive actions of those around them, from family to neighbors to business partners.

These arguments are not unique to the women who navigated premodern Islamic law. Studies from across premodern Europe and Korea show that assumptions made about women's legal agency are often not substantiated upon closer observation of local conditions and legal practices. In the case of Europe, the existence of laws of coverture in particular seemed to translate into a lack of rights for women in financial and legal matters, as coverture subsumed a married woman under her husband's legal and financial identity. Likewise, religious and legal regulation of women's sexuality seemed to be severe and uncompromising. However, recent studies using a range of diverse sources and methods have challenged the notion that married women could not access courts, make contracts, or manage their own or even the family finances. These changing narratives highlight the diversity and overlap of legal systems and jurisdictions as well as the role of the community in supporting women who engaged in both religious and legal transgressions.

In *Married Women and the Law in Premodern Northwest Europe,* Cordelia Beattie and Matthew Frank Stevens bring together a collection of chapters that show how "there has been a tendency to overplay the extent to which *coverture* applied."[7] Archives from across Northwest Europe reveal competing legal systems and the uneven application of laws, showing how "lawmakers, jurists and courts constantly renegotiated these same very elaborate—but sometimes impractical or simply ignored—systems of law with respect to married women."[8] Attention to the details of local practice showed women at times exercising more rights with regard to property ownership, legal access, and financial transactions, although at other times and places these rights were restricted.

Teresa Phipps and Deborah Youngs find similar results through focusing on women's engagement with legal courts in premodern Europe. The collected essays in their volume, *Litigating Women: Gender and Justice in Europe, c.1300–c.1800,* "demonstrate that women were regularly present in the courts, and some were able to tell their own stories in their own right."[9] This research challenges what they deem "overly pessimistic analyses" of women's ability to utilize the law, based largely on earlier studies of legal codes and doctrine.[10] Through investigating a variety of legal sources across space and time, this collection shows that there existed a "plurality of legal systems operating across Europe in this period, a reminder that there was no single legal discourse governing women's legal status or rights."[11] Other relevant findings include disrupting the notion that gender was the only category relevant to a woman's relationship with the law, as well as the importance of women's knowledge of the law, similar to conclusions found in the current study of women in Marinid Morocco.

Studies from premodern Europe also show the interplay between legal, social, and religious norms, particularly when it comes to premarital sex and pregnancy outside of marriage. In *Sex in an Old Regime City,* Julie Hardwick finds that workers in premodern France engaged in premarital intimacies with little formal legal or religious intervention.[12] Rather, it was the community that urged couples to marry and supported women who gave birth out of wedlock. Nevertheless, if legal engagement was required, such as in the case of paternity claims, women did make use of the legal resources available to them. This contrasts with assumptions about how women navigated premarital sex, "because our primary access points have been through the archive of the legal regulation of sexuality in terms of criminality or illegitimacy, a viewpoint that highlights the problematic rather than the ordinary."[13] While gender relations were not equal, women were able to find both community and legal support to help repair their lives. Anne L. McClanan and Karen Rosoff Encarnación note in *The Material Culture of Sex, Procreation, and Marriage in Premodern Europe* that it is "important to keep in mind the broader social and cultural conditions that shape and define the social embeddedness of sex and sexuality, for example: family/kinship systems, sexual regulations and definitions of communities, and national and world systems."[14] This similarly highlights the importance of studying sex and sexuality in relation to local communities and society.

Jisoo Kim's study of women's engagement with the law in Chosŏn Korea (late fourteenth to early twentieth century) challenges similar misconceptions about women's legal subjectivity in premodern Korea. Kim argues that while this state "is often portrayed as a rigid society due to its hereditary status system, which included a slave status, and its gender division based on Confucian concepts," this social stratification did not prevent women from accessing courts, expecting justice, or even challenging elites.[15] She explains how social status differed from legal status, and how "women, irrespective of their status, were recognized as legal subjects equal to their male counterparts and able to air grievances to the state on their behalf."[16] Similar to Marinid Morocco, women and other marginalized groups in premodern Korea could also petition the ruler directly.[17]

These studies from premodern Europe and Korea on women's interaction with the law and their navigation of sex and sexuality within a web of social, legal, and religious norms, highlight points of comparison to the current investigation into women's engagement with Islamic law and its related institutions in Marinid Morocco. Central in providing the groundwork to revise existing historiographies is the use of a variety of historical and legal sources, rather than relying on theoretical legal sources to make assumptions about social history. This in turn allows for the examination of local variations and inconsistencies across space and time and of how different legal expectations and systems overlapped and interacted. As in the case of Marinid Morocco, this type of source makes visible community support for legal systems in areas such as mediation, while also highlighting how legal and social norms governing sex were more complicated, and often more flexible when examined in practice. These studies do not make an argument for legal equality between men and women, or the uniform upholding of women's rights, but instead show that there was more flexibility, room for negotiation, opportunities for strategic engagement, and support from the community than would be assumed from legal codes. In the case of Islamic legal studies, this type of approach makes it possible to address misconceptions formed not just from the study of doctrine and other theoretical texts, but also those built on stereotypes about Muslim women's inability to act and Islamic law's inherent oppression.

This study of Muslim women's interaction with Islamic law in Marinid Morocco reorients attention to this important area of the Islamic world, advancing our knowledge of both the complexity and vibrancy of Islamic law, and of women's lives in this period. Interdisciplinary in nature, it engages theories of history, law, and gender, exploring the range of possibilities for understanding the discourse on gender within a legal system based on religious law. More significantly, it offers a potent challenge to modern debates (including those outside of academia) that take the figure of the invisible, silent, and secluded Muslim woman as their starting point and casts Islamic law and legal scholars in the role of oppressor.

Conceptualizing Islamic Law

This study conceptualizes "Islamic law" not as a fixed category discoverable only in books of legal doctrine, but rather as a historically constructed category contingent on local contexts and conditions. Sharia refers to God's divine law, which jurists tried to categorize and reflect in concrete rules through the process of *fiqh,* or jurisprudence, leading to an expansive corpus of legal doctrine. Here, I use Islamic law to encompass both the legal doctrine elaborated by the jurists, as well as its implementation in a particular context in a collaboration between legal officials, the state, and the community. Legal doctrine itself was a living process interpreted by (male) scholars influenced by their historical moment, as Kecia Ali has shown in multiple contexts.[18] Jurists were intimately connected to their communities, and while their interpretation of law influenced the societies in which they lived, likewise their law making was inflected by the needs, concerns, and local customs of their society, leading Khaled Abou El Fadl to describe Islamic law as "negotiated through the prism of local cultures."[19]

This broad conceptualization of Islamic law provides a framework for engaging with a number of points that are fundamental to understanding law, gender, and history. A key question, which may at first seem overly simplistic, is, where and how do scholars locate the law?[20] The obvious answer would be that law can be found in legal doctrine. However, following my conceptualization of Islamic law, I argue that law can be located at the intersection of doctrine and practice, and is discoverable using sources that show how doctrine is implemented in a particular context. Abou El Fadl broadly defines the "Islamic legal system" as "legal institutions, determinations, and practices that span a period of over fourteen hundred years, arising from a wide variety of cultural and geographic contexts."[21] I would extend this definition to represent not just the Islamic legal system but Islamic law itself, drawing attention to the emphasis on structures that supported the law, such as community institutions.

A related question is, how can we write about Islamic law in history, and how can we write history from Islamic legal sources? Even scholars with sophisticated approaches to historicizing legal doctrine fall into the trap of making assumptions about how these doctrinal rules shaped social norms and practices. For example, if Maliki law says a father can force his daughter to marry, some would assume that was standard throughout time and space in the Islamic past, and would imagine father-daughter relationships characterized by oppression and coercion, an assumption that is not supported by the sources for this study. A similar assumption would be that because Islamic legal doctrine does not recognize a concept of consent to sex within marriage, marital relationships would necessarily be marked by violence and rape, feeding an Islamophobic idea about violent Muslim men and victimized Muslim women and how they relate to each other, regardless of time, place, or specific local norms and conditions.[22] The notion that doctrine alone can serve as a source for writing social history in particular ends up reflecting more about modern concerns than premodern realities.

One other aspect that gets erased by trying to write history from legal doctrine or even fatwas as a standalone source is the support structures that helped the legal system function in a way that was beneficial to society, such as dispute resolution mechanisms, community mediation, social safety networks, and formal and informal structures that met people's welfare needs, particularly those of poor people and women. Law did not stand on its own and was not expected to. Anthropologists in particular have provided a methodology to approach the study of Islamic law and its implementation as tightly connected to society. Lawrence Rosen, in his study of the court of Sefrou, a large town in central Morocco, argues that "it appears more fruitful to view law as part of the larger culture, a system which, for all its distinctive institutional history and forms, partakes of concepts that extend across many domains of social life."[23] This view of the law as intimately connected with society is an essential approach for writing history too. Law, like everything else, has a history and was historically produced.

This book argues that as a historically constructed overarching system of doctrine, people, and institutions, some of the gendered Islamic legal doctrine established the baseline for relations between women and men but was not viewed as a divine ideal. Doctrine defined the starting point for the family rather than laying out a sacrosanct blueprint. As Islamic law evolved, jurists developed methods for deriving law from sources such as the Quran and the sunna (the example of the Prophet Muhammad, understood through hadith),[24] but not every aspect of these sources was incorporated in the same way or valued equally. Larger ethical norms may have been significantly less prioritized as jurists steeped in their own social world elaborated detailed rules to address new situations. amina wadud argues that the Quran's "principles of social justice and human equality, and its objective of guidance" have not all been implemented, and if they had, Islamic jurisprudence would reflect much more equality for women.[25] Fatema Mernissi focuses on hadiths that give insights into the example of the Prophet Muhammad, and argues that the Prophet had an egalitarian vision that elevated the position of women, but that social and political realities in the new Muslim state and later Islamic empires overpowered that vision.[26] Leila Ahmed contends that the Quran itself contains competing strands that envision women's equality while at the same time containing the groundwork for hierarchical marriage.[27] Therefore, while the ranked version of the family was implemented in the early Islamic community, Ahmed maintains that the "Islamic ethical vision . . . is stubbornly egalitarian."[28] An example of this is a hadith that seems to give women the right to consent to their marriages; however, in practice, jurists elaborated complex rules that severely limited when a woman (or girl) needed to consent, with the Maliki school in particular articulating a framework where a father largely controlled his daughter's marriage.[29] The competing discourses that feminist scholars have identified in the Islamic tradition envisage a more egalitarian version of marital rights that Muslim women could aspire to in order to build a marriage and family.

As implemented, the law set out the minimum rights possible for women and the maximum rights available to men, and from there women could negotiate to expand their rights, while men could concede certain privileges. The terms negotiated were not limitless and stayed within certain socially and religiously sanctioned norms, such as those restricting a husband to monogamy, a precedent founded by the women in the

Prophet's own family.[30] A woman might also have to relinquish another right or benefit she was entitled to, such as financial support from her ex-husband, in order to achieve an important objective, like retaining custody of children after divorce and remarriage. Premodern women managed such negotiation through their knowledge of the law, along with support from family and legal officials. As a result, implementations of Islamic law accommodated many of the needs and interests of women and had the full support of jurists as they translated theory to practice, even when these women pushed the boundaries of what was legally or socially acceptable. Some features of the law that facilitated these compromises in Marinid Morocco included informal legal spaces where women could seek out expert advice to construct their cases and navigate areas of Maliki law where multiple valid opinions existed on one point.

Envisioning Islamic law as a historically constructed category that can be found where doctrine meets practice also allows us to rethink the role typically assigned to women in its production, which, on the theoretical side, is an overwhelmingly male domain.[31] Through their sustained engagement with the law, women participated in the coproduction of Islamic law, driving the legal interpretation and defining the content of legal texts that preserved the jurisprudential legacy of this time and place, similar to something that Leslie Peirce noted in the context of sixteenth-century Anatolian court records.[32] The dynamic nature of law and the specific ways in which it was historically produced is visible in sources that detail how people lived the law, and particularly in those sources that capture what happened outside of the courtroom, like the lengthy narratives of disputes included in some fatwas. These decrees help us to write a social history where women, conjugality, and the household become the center of the story.[33]

While Islamic law is central to this study, the concern here is not with minute legal details or tracing every opinion back to the Quran or hadith, or trying to prove that particular jurists were right or wrong in their interpretation of the law. Rather, this work sees law as dynamic, contingent, and fundamentally tied to the people who engaged with it, as jurists or litigants, while seeing no contradiction in its clear grounding in and connection to the early Islamic sources. This is likewise not an argument to revive the idea of a gap between theory and practice as posited by Orientalists and which (some) anthropologists embraced, but rather to argue that law as understood here includes both legal theory and its implementation, and that to understand Islamic law is to understand how both worked together.

Women, Gender, and Law

This work draws on theories of women and gender to analyze how the latter was constructed in Marinid Morocco in the context of people's encounters with the law. I do not use "gender" here as a more scientific or neutral-sounding word to denote women; rather, I employ Joan Scott's definition of gender as "a constitutive element of social relationships based on perceived differences between the sexes, and gender is a primary way of signifying relationships of power."[34]

The first part of this definition is the more commonly referenced understanding of gender and has been used by a number of historians writing women's history in the Middle East, particularly to help disentangle constructed roles and relationships in the context of law. In *Morality Tales*, Peirce uses gender to analyze how both man and woman were not monolithic categories in the eyes of the law, although each had a default construction that stood in for the category, and those who fell outside were distinguished against this default.[35] In the case of women, lifecycle and social status both played a role in how they interacted with the law, along with other factors such as religion and residence in urban or rural areas. Peirce uses the example of the crime of rape, which Ottoman legal discourse assumed was a man breaking into the home of a properly secluded woman in order to assault her, whereas in reality, many assaults occurred in the streets where women of lower social status were required to move about for a variety of reasons.[36] Peirce also analyzes how gendered voices appeared in the court records, particularly in areas concerning morality (for example, an accusation of *zina*, or fornication) where a woman might feel the urgent need to clear her name and relied on specific gendered strategies to accomplish that goal.[37]

Judith E. Tucker also uses gender as a category of analysis in her studies of Ottoman law, showing how muftis, through their fatwas, constructed what she designates "a definable 'Islamic' vision of a gendered social order in that time and place."[38] Tucker primarily uses gender as a descriptive way to identify where laws and relationships break down along gendered lines, rather than using gender to analyze the relationships, and she sees the category as a fixed male/female binary.[39] In her analysis of the jurists' discourse on women's mosque usage, Marion Katz sees more of an interplay in the construction of gender, with gendered rules and discourse "subject to ongoing negotiation," and that "if the evidence suggests that legal doctrine influenced or constrained women's mosque-going behavior, it also suggests that women's behavior had an impact on the thinking of legal scholars."[40] Katz considers not only how women's actions influenced legal discussion, but how discourse did (or did not) impact women's behavior.

These scholars show how gender analysis can be used in the context of Middle Eastern women's history and particularly how Islamic law was gendered, and how the jurists' discourse constructed gendered roles; however, these studies do not take up the second part of Joan Scott's definition of gender, which highlights how it can be used to analyze power relationships that are not necessarily concerned with women, but are nevertheless built on a symbolic gendered discourse. Scott explains that "gender, then, provides a way to decode meaning and to understand the complex connections among various forms of human interaction. When historians look for the ways in which the concept of gender legitimizes and constructs social relationships, they develop insight into the reciprocal nature of gender and society and into the particular and contextually specific ways in which politics constructs gender and gender constructs politics."[41] This part of the definition of gender allows for the application of gender as a category of analysis to relations of power beyond the typical scope of women's history, for example, to help understand the relationship between the sultan and the jurists, or between jurists from different regions. My analysis will also draw on Scott's definition of gender as a category, analyzing both the ways in which the law and people's relationships were gendered, while also using gender to understand the power relations between distinct actors in society.

Afsaneh Najmabadi asks us to contemplate how categories of analysis can travel in space (particularly outside of the United States or Europe) and also outside of the modern contexts in which they were developed. In particular, she asks how Scott's approach to gender as a category of analysis can apply to the premodern Middle East. I take Najmabadi's cautionary note about the contingency and constructedness of the category and the need to historicize binaries and categories that seem "normal." Therefore, I do not assume woman as a fixed category with the same meaning as a woman today (which of course is also not a fixed, but assumed, category), a warning Scott also sounds in her contribution to a 2008 retrospective on her original article.[42] I also pay attention to the ways in which an assumed male/female binary obscures rather than elucidates gendered norms.

The category of woman on its own had very little meaning in a premodern Islamic legal context. To those who wonder about the existence of "lesbians (or lesbian-like women) in medieval Europe," Najmabadi asks, "were there any *women* in medieval Europe?" because one category can be assumed as constructed or historically contingent while the basic category of woman is assumed to be fixed and natural: "there have always been women."[43] Rather, what we recognize as woman is created when biological sex intersects with other categories of meaning. Islamic legal theory makes it glaringly obvious that it contains no fixed category of woman, or perhaps that there is a default category of woman about which many assumptions can be made, but that many biological women fall outside of this category. In Katz's examination of Islamic legal theory, and especially rules pertaining to women's mosque attendance, she determines that "early jurists universally presumed that women of different ages or statuses were subject to significantly different standards of behavior."[44] Peirce notes that in Ottoman court records, women were not referred to by gender alone, but also by their place in a culturally constructed lifecycle that was relevant to local society, for example, child/unmarried, newly married, and anywhere past early marriage, including divorced or widowed.[45]

The easiest way to see the implosion of a uniform category of woman is when it intersects with slavery, as very few Islamic legal rulings on "women" hold in relation to enslaved women. The law distinguishes free and enslaved women in areas from marriage to dress, to expectations and roles. For example, in modern times, Muslim women have become associated with particular forms of dress, including covering their hair and at times their face and hands. However, while most jurists agreed that a free woman should cover her hair (and for some, her face also), this rule did not apply to enslaved women, even in prayer, and some jurists only required them to cover the same parts of their body that a man was required to cover—the space between their navel and knees.[46] As Omar Anchassi argues, the intention behind this rule was to "enforce[] the free/slave binary."[47] Fatema Mernissi describes how the directive about covering and hijab was mandated in a specific historical context amid political tensions to protect and distinguish free Muslim women, the key word here being "free."[48] This means that according to some interpretations, an enslaved woman did not even need to cover her breasts around unrelated males. This does not compute with the seemingly monolithic modern category of "Muslim woman" who is required to cover, although in practice, considerations of social status still fracture this category to a certain extent, as women who perform paid domestic labor in households are not expected to fully cover. This is a sensitive area of the Islamic heritage, as in theory slavery is no longer a relevant category in modern life, but considering these rulings demonstrates how drastically rules could vary for different categories of women within the Islamic tradition.

There is very little we can actually say about a "woman" legally. However, in the sources for this study, most of the women are free, Muslim, of medium or lower social status, not formally educated, and from large or small cities. Information about their race, ethnicity, or tribal affiliation is provided infrequently. For the most part, their legal status changes with their different life stages, from minor/virgin to married/non-virgin (and often to divorced/widowed) and finally to senior citizen/elder. When I use the term "woman" here, it will typically refer to this construction of woman unless otherwise specified, while still not envisioning it as a monolithic category.

In general, this work assumes that terms, concepts, and categories are historically constructed, that each have their own particular history, and that a concept that applies here might not look the same in another area of the Muslim world at the same time, or in modern Morocco. Even a seemingly basic concept like "justice," which I will use occasionally when discussing the goals of women as they interact with the legal system, in this context, means protecting the rights women expected and felt entitled to, rather than some notion of full equality with men or in front of the law. Lila Abu-Lughod argues that even for modern women, justice does not necessarily mean the same thing, and that "there might be different ideas about justice and that different women might want, or choose, different futures from what we envision as best."[49] While my questions and concerns are intimately tied to the preoccupations of modern Western academic studies and the particular package of assumptions that goes along with them, this study acknowledges the lack of universality of these assumptions and meanings. Using gender as a category of analysis allows us to destabilize the binary of male/female and man/woman and helps us get beyond entrenched ideas about what a man or woman means in Islamic law. A gendered analysis of these sources shows how identities were constructed yet remained unstable, and contingent on, particular historical conditions and actors. It will also allow us to see how gender was used in the production and deployment of power relations.

The Marinids in History

This study is concerned with law in Morocco under the Marinids, an Amazigh dynasty whose boundaries, at times, stretched beyond modern Morocco into present-day Spain, Algeria, and Tunisia. The Marinids began their conquest of the Almohad Empire in the early thirteenth century, taking control of Fez in 1250, and remained in power until the mid-fifteenth century.[50] As their state stabilized in the early fourteenth century, the Marinid sultans turned their attention to the patronage of learning and culture, building mosques, madrasas, and hospitals and supporting scholarship through endowments of teaching positions and libraries.[51] As a result, intellectual life in North Africa flourished, with the city of Fez at its center. At a time when other traditional centers of Islamic learning were destabilized, with the Mongol sack of Baghdad in 1258 and the reduction of al-Andalus to the small Nasrid kingdom, the Marinids contributed to the physical preservation of books, and more generally to the continued transmission of knowledge.[52] The Marinid sultans not only supported scholars, students, and at times, poets and scientists financially, but they also attended the classes of the most respected teachers of their era.[53] The second half of the Marinid period was marked by political decline and disintegration, as the Spanish and Portuguese took over port cities, and the Ottomans encroached from the east. Marinid power waned and the sultans became mere figureheads for their powerful viziers, yet the cultivation and transmission of scholarship continued despite the social and political turmoil.

In this book, I use the designation "Morocco" as shorthand for the area being studied, even though some of the legal opinions examined here were articulated in cities beyond the borders of the modern Moroccan state. Indeed, at times, the Marinids extended their reach as far as what is today Tunisia, and for a short time they tried to regain control of al-Andalus. Boundaries were especially fluid for legal and intellectual activity and scholarly networks transmitted ideas and opinions throughout the Islamic West and the rest of the Muslim world. Ideas and debates circulated across political boundaries, both showing the unity of Maliki thought in the Islamic West and revealing local specificities in the reasoning of jurists. This study takes the imperial capital of Fez and surrounding areas as its focus but draws comparisons to the margins of the Marinid realm, in addition to competing regional capitals such as Tunis under the Hafsid dynasty (1229–1574).

Both the current ruling Alawi dynasty, which has been in power since the seventeenth century, and their predecessors, the Saadis, who held power in the sixteenth and seventeenth centuries, claimed legitimacy based on their status as descendants of the Prophet Muhammad (sharif), as did the Idrisid dynasty, who founded the Moroccan state in the eighth century. The two Amazigh dynasties that ruled Morocco and large adjacent territories prior to Marinid rule, namely the Almoravids and the Almohads, seized power fueled by programs of religious reform.[54] The Marinids are distinct in the genealogy of dynasties as they did not hold Sharifian status and did not come to power on a program of religious reform. For the most part, political histories of Morocco focus on the ruling sultans and how they legitimized their power.[55]

Fatwas and Women's History

There are no court records extant for Marinid Morocco (or premodern North Africa more broadly), making fatwa literature the most important source for examining both legal practice and the lives of ordinary people. A fatwa record consists of two parts: a question asked to a mufti (*istifta*) and the mufti's response.[56] A mufti's opinion (the fatwa itself) was advisory, not binding; people could choose to follow it or not, and a judge who requested an opinion could choose whether to incorporate it into his ruling. However, muftis were scholars and members of the community, at times connected to the sultan, and their opinions held weight and were respected. A fatwa was only intended to respond to one specific case, based on the facts presented to the mufti, who was not involved in any kind of fact finding or verification. The mufti had the role of responding to situations that arose in the society around him and searching for an appropriate solution within the vast Islamic legal tradition.

Previous studies on fatwas in the Islamic West (North Africa and Muslim Spain) have been concerned primarily with legal history and have analyzed fatwas for what they reveal about legal practice, rather than the societal spaces that the law inhabited. One method of study favored particularly by French scholars was to translate, summarize, and present the fatwas without extensive historical contextualization.[57] These studies are interested in social practice as read through legal sources, but have often assumed a straightforward translation of a particular norm or practice across time and space, without taking into account local context. Other studies have taken a take a broader view of legal practice, particularly when it comes to women and the family, but without tying the analysis to one particular historical context. Amalia Zomeño's *Dote y Matrimonio en al-Andalus y el Norte de África* (Dower and Marriage in al-Andalus and North Africa) draws on fatwa sources to investigate the different types of financial transactions that surrounded a marriage throughout the Islamic West, based on fatwas from the *Mi'yar*, a compilation of fatwas that also serves as a source for the current study.[58] Zomeño documents the ways in which a woman could accumulate wealth and the study is concerned with the laws surrounding these exchanges of gifts, using sources that cover the full range of the *Mi'yar*'s fatwas from across North Africa and al-Andalus over five centuries. A recent study of fatwas from the *Mi'yar* related to women is *Awda' al-Mar'a bi al-Gharb al-Islami* (The Circumstances of Women in the Islamic West), by Zuhur Arbuh, which similarly keeps the focus on the law itself.[59] Arbuh incorporates a large amount of data and conducts a quantitative analysis of the *Mi'yar*'s fatwas on women (for example, thirty-one fatwas contain information about conditions in marriage contracts), with an emphasis on the doctrinal context of the rulings discussed. The primary concern of studies such as these is the information that the fatwas reveal about jurisprudence and what they presume this in turn reveals about women's lives and social practices.

My study does not make such assumptions about jurisprudence alone providing insights into social history, heeding Marion Katz's caution that "legal texts do not allow us to predict the nature of the concrete activities that women chose to pursue; juxtaposition of legal and nonlegal sources suggests that jurists did not succeed in setting the ritual agenda for most women."[60] Katz uses a variety of sources, such as observations of travelers and complaints of contemporaries, to understand how legal theory and prescriptive discourse impacted women's use of the mosque and was in turn impacted by it, not assuming a simplistic one-way relationship. My study of fatwa sources follows this model by incorporating additional types of sources to provide context about how legal practice is reflected in a geographically and temporally bounded space.

A number of studies have taken into account additional sources to contextualize fatwas and better interpret both the jurisprudence and the social and legal context. David S. Powers, in his important work on the *Mi'yar* fatwa collection, *Law, Society, and Culture in the Maghrib, 1300–1500,* closely analyzes a small number of fatwas from Marinid Morocco to understand how the legal system of that time functioned, arguing that "the most important actor within the system was the mufti."[61] He demonstrates the mufti's creativity in resolving disputes and making law, claiming that "the fatwa was part of an ongoing conversation between muftis and the Muslim community in which adherence to the principles of Islam was ensured."[62] In his book and related articles, Powers is interested in the implementation of the law and the various legal actors, and how the law in practice compared to the doctrine. Jocelyn Hendrickson's study of the life and afterlife of a fatwa by *Mi'yar* compiler Ahmad al-Wansharisi (d. 1508) provides a model for how to contextualize a legal opinion in its historical circumstances, demonstrating how external considerations can distort how generations of scholars view this legal interpretation.[63] This study shows how historicizing a fatwa can help improve understandings of legal practice. Maya Shatzmiller's economic history of Granada, *Her Day in Court*, establishes additional context for fatwas through the use of court records and family archives from fifteenth-century Granada, a type of legal source not available in this period for North Africa.[64] Shatzmiller demonstrates that in fifteenth-century Granada, women's rights to own and inherit property were upheld by the jurists. Even though a woman might be entitled to inherit only half as much as a male relative, Shatzmiller shows that a woman's ownership of that share was legally protected, and she did not hesitate to seek judicial recourse when her rights were infringed.

Several studies by Moroccan historians provide a model for utilizing fatwas as a source for the social history of medieval Morocco. Muhammad Fatha employs a methodology that supplements fatwas with other sources, such as manuals on public behavior (*hisba*), Sufi texts, books of attributes of saints (*manaqib*), in addition to chronicles, geographies, and travel literature, a similar methodology to that proposed by Omar Benmira.[65] Fatha also emphasizes the importance of knowing the biography of the mufti to locate the fatwa in space and time and provide additional context.[66] While these two studies are concerned with the law itself, other Moroccan social histories use fatwas as one among numerous types of sources to explore the lives of ordinary people. Another characteristic that sets Moroccan scholarship apart is the use of a wide range of fatwa literature, available in Moroccan archives in manuscript form, to supplement published works such as the widely studied *Mi'yar*. Due to this combination of sources, Moroccan historians have been able to take into account factors such as regional differences in social and legal practices, conditions specific to urban and rural contexts, change over time, and politics and social structures below the level of the ruling dynasties.

My work benefits both from the legal groundwork laid by scholars such as David S. Powers, Jocelyn Hendrickson, and Maya Shatzmiller, and from the wide range of fatwas related to women and marriage detailed by scholars such as Amalia Zomeño and Zuhur Arbuh, and tries to take this further by focusing on the points where law, women's interests, and society interact, and what this interaction tells us about women and gender in this particular time and place. I also draw on the methods elaborated by Moroccan scholars and diligently consider source material from multiple fatwa collections while thoroughly grounding the fatwas in the social and historical context of the litigants and the muftis.

Fatwas serve a dual purpose in the current research. The question that prompted the fatwa provides important information about the lives of women and men, including the reasons for their encounter with the legal system, and the role the law played in their lives. The answer gives further insight into societal relationships, in addition to helping us understand how the law was implemented, and how jurists thought about the law and its relationship to society and their own relationship to society. Fatwas offer a window into how the law functioned through both formal institutions such as the courts and informal social structures.

When approaching fatwas as a source for social history, Judith E. Tucker cautions that a particular fatwa "was not a mirror of reality, certainly not a photograph of events in the lives of a seventeenth-century peasant family, but rather a distillation of these events with legal resonances in mind."[67] In her in-depth study of women and gender in law in Ottoman Syria and Palestine in the seventeenth and eighteenth centuries, Tucker reads fatwas and court records alongside other historical sources, contextualizing the fatwas issued by three muftis according to their specific city, educational background, political connections, and historical and legal context more broadly. In analyzing the fatwas of these muftis, Tucker is able to draw comparisons between their jurisprudence based on each one's specific context and argues that "their ability to respond with flexibility, creativity, and even compassion to concrete legal problems in their communities remains a hallmark of their approach to the practice of law,"[68] a theme similar to the results of other studies from the Ottoman Empire, and a conclusion that the sources of the current study also support.

Tucker sees fatwas as providing insight into the intellectual world of the jurists and how their thinking interacted with the social context, and how jurists constructed gender in their discourse to give insight into women's history through these discussions. Yet, her sources are unable to provide much information about the daily lives and activities of women and what they were seeking in their encounters with the law. Whereas fatwas from the Ottoman Empire and central Middle East usually only contained a short question stripped of identifying details, at times clearly hypothetical in nature, North African fatwas frequently retained substantial details narrating the events leading up to the dispute that prompted the fatwa request. The question in North African fatwas could include names, locations, and dates relating to the case, and the compiler of the fatwa collection sometimes included associated documents or contracts pertinent to the case. The rich narratives of the questions and other features of these collections, such as including responses from multiple jurists, constructs a robust archive of the North African environment that enables further investigation into the lives and social relationships of the people involved in the dispute, beyond simply their interaction with the law, and allows for a different kind of women's history than it is possible to construct from Ottoman legal sources.

This research relies on a corpus of exceptional cases that were selectively preserved for reasons that do not necessarily align with the goals of a historian. These sources were largely conserved for what they said about the law and for the guidance they could provide for other jurists. In *Silencing the Past,* Michel-Rolph Trouillot argues that "the presences and absences embodied in sources (artifacts and bodies that turn an event into fact) or archives (facts collected, thematized, and processed as documents and monuments) are neither neutral or natural."[69] It is natural that silences would be created around women in these sources and this archive. In some instances, it is possible, even from within the sources themselves, to detect silences created in the construction and editing process. Questions to muftis were posed with the intention of seeking legal advice on a particular point of law and even when the question included a more detailed narrative of events surrounding a case, a mufti confined his response to what he considered legally pertinent. An example of this is cases that mention a woman running away with a man. An opinion was often sought on a technicality in the case, such as how to contract a legally valid marriage between the couple. In two cases discussed here, multiple versions of fatwas were preserved, with the key detail of the elopement omitted in some versions due to either the inquirer or a later compiler considering it a legally irrelevant detail.[70] These examples serve as a cautionary tale for the researcher, indicating both the good fortune of having these descriptions of women's activities preserved in some cases, while also providing a hint of just how much has been lost in the compilation and editing of these legal manuscripts, and just how easy it was to erase any evidence of women's independent actions and desires from the sources. Comparison to similar contemporary fatwas alongside other types of sources help to fill in some of the silences that are naturally produced in the creation of this archive.

To analyze and interpret these texts, I draw on methods and analyses from history, anthropology, legal studies, and women's and gender studies. On a most basic level, I approach the sources as a historian, limiting the sources to fatwas issued by a known mufti who can be placed in the Marinid period in or around Fez. This allows for contextualization and framing the sources in relation to the historical and political background, as well as biographical information about the mufti to help read and interpret the fatwa sources. Periodically, I also bring in related cases from other times and places in the premodern Muslim world as points of comparison.

In addition, I draw inspiration from the work of anthropologists on modern implementations of Islamic law. In her comparison of women's use of the courts in Iran and Morocco at the end of the twentieth century, Ziba Mir-Hosseini turns the focus from the law to the women themselves as they navigate the system, an approach I also adopt in this study. As she investigates how women interacted with the law and the strategies they used, particularly in divorce cases, Mir-Hosseini shows how this in turn reveals "not only power relations in the family but how these relations are sustained or modified by the legal order."[71] This approach tries to understand how ordinary women approached and understood the law and the meaning it held in their lives. I apply this framework as I read the fatwas in this study, analyzing what was written and what was omitted to try and situate women's actions and intentions as they navigated familial and legal disputes.

Feminist histories of women's interaction with law from other areas of the Islamic world provide additional methodological insight into writing women's and gender history from legal sources. Historical scholarship from across the Muslim world has shown that women had access to Islamic legal courts.[72] Women used the courts to register contracts of all types, many related to their personal finances, and also to bring complaints in domestic, financial, and other areas.[73] Women also established charitable endowments, such as mosques, schools, and hospitals, and in some cases administered them.[74] In addition to women's clear legal access to the courts, some studies show that even within family law, where women had gendered roles and were often at a distinct disadvantage to men in terms of rights, the actual practice of the law was more balanced.

Recent studies have used a sophisticated gender analysis in combination with diverse legal sources, such as court records, fatwas, and state law books, to further understand both women's and legal history. This contextualization in local historical and social frameworks makes it possible to see women as part of the fabric of the community and to begin to understand their interactions and relations within the family. Leslie Peirce, in *Morality Tales*, analyzed one year of records from a court in a town in Ottoman Anatolia in the sixteenth century, finding that women were able to use various strategies to pursue a favorable judgment, and that in practice judges were more flexible when it came to gendered rules than the stricter Ottoman legal theory would seem to allow.[75] In Peirce's study, however, the court records were only the starting point and her analysis embedded them deeply in the local social, historical, and political context, observing both the household level and the imperial level in one frame. With this method and wide range of sources, Peirce is able to historicize women in their social and legal environments, while also interpreting what women's participation meant for the law made in the court. She argues that the participation of women and the community more broadly in the court helped shape the nature of jurisprudence and legal interpretation there.[76]

The current study takes inspiration from Peirce's method, including her careful attention to the construction of the gendered voices of the court, while adopting an approach that fits the nature of the available sources. The questions I can ask, and answer, are both limited and enhanced by my archive: I do not have court records, I do not have large amounts of data on the workings of the courts, and I do not know how the cases ended. But what my sources have that distinguishes them from Ottoman sources is the details about what happened before people formally encountered the legal system, including background about the family and relationship drama that adds texture to women's lives outside of court and shows the role of law in people's lives and interactions. Most scholars researching Islamic legal courts have focused on the central Islamic lands, particularly the Ottoman Empire, whose extensive yet centralized bureaucracy mandated record keeping, with the result that documents of great interest to historians, including court transcripts, have been preserved. As a result, there is a tendency to universalize the Hanafi law of the Ottoman Empire as "Islamic law," erasing the diversity that existed within and among the different legal schools, and introducing and perpetuating misconceptions about Islamic law due to this overgeneralization.[77] One of the aims of this book is to expand our knowledge of law in areas outside of Ottoman control in order to challenge these oversimplifications and misrepresentations of legal theory and practice, family relationships, and many other aspects of life in the Muslim world.

The fatwa records do not describe a complete picture of women's lives or aspirations in Marinid Morocco and rarely help us to understand what gave their lives meaning. In most cases, we do not even know the women's names. This book instead puts together the fragments and draws on the rich methods of history and its neighboring disciplines to help understand women's relationships, legal power relations, and constructions of gender.[78] Despite the limitations, these sources can show us something about women's lives and relationships as they navigated conflicts within a legal framework. Fatwas read alongside other sources fill in some of these sources' gaps and allow for comparison to legal implementation in other areas of the premodern Muslim world. Despite different bureaucracies, political situations, and schools of law, this comparison can provide insight into continuities in practice in different areas (as well as local distinctions). For example, studies from across the premodern Muslim world have consistently found that Islamic law in practice was more accommodating of, and flexible for, women than doctrine would seem to allow.

Sources of the Study

The most important archive of this study is fatwa records from Marinid Morocco related to cases of women's relationships and disputes within the family. While abstract theoretical questions could be posed to muftis, the fatwa collections from North Africa more frequently contain responses to actual cases and thus offer a reflection of real problems encountered by real individuals. Muftis were consulted on questions ranging from belief and religious practice to human relationships and crime. There is evidence in the legal records themselves of people, including women, seeking out the advice of muftis within their communities; however, these oral questions and answers were not preserved unless they were mentioned in the context of more complex ongoing litigation.[79] Fatwa collections from North Africa compiled more formal questions for prominent jurists, often based in Fez or other important cities, that were frequently asked as part of a court case, either by a judge or one of the parties to a dispute.

One of the most important sources of fatwa literature for premodern North Africa (and Muslim Spain) is the *Mi'yar* of Ahmad al-Wansharisi (d. 1508).[80] This thirteen-volume collection contains an estimated six thousand opinions from all parts of the Islamic West, from the tenth century until the late fifteenth century, with a focus on the fatwas of later jurists.[81] Unlike other fatwa collections, in which the texts were edited to remove identifying details and make them more generic and thus more broadly relevant, al-Wansharisi often retained legally extraneous yet historically significant information, and included documents related to ongoing litigation.[82] For a period from which there are no extant archival records, the documents associated with legal cases preserved by al-Wansharisi provide an invaluable, richly detailed historical source, particularly about the lives of ordinary people. The composition of the *Mi'yar* highlights the importance of the Marinid period for Moroccan Maliki legal thought, as it includes a large number of opinions from jurists of that time.

This study also draws on fatwas from several other collections devoted to preserving the opinions of individual Marinid jurists. The earliest collection is that of Abu al-Hassan al-Sughayyir (d. 1320–1), *al-Durr al-Nathir,* which was compiled and commented on by a contemporary of al-Wansharisi, Ibn Hilal al-Sijilmasi (d. 1497–8).[83] Abu al-Hassan al-Sughayyir became chief judge of Fez after serving as judge of Taza and people from all over the Islamic West sent him their questions, including many questions originating in Taza. This study also focuses on the opinions of Abdullah al-Abdusi (d. 1445), a subsequent Marinid jurist, whose fatwas can be found across several manuscript collections.[84] Abdullah al-Abdusi was one of the most prominent jurists of his age and came from a scholarly family famous for both its male and female scholars. The fatwas of both al-Sughayyir and al-Abdusi feature prominently in the *Mi'yar*. The lives and intellectual world of these and other Marinid jurists will be explored in chapters 3 and 4.

The mufti was a key figure in the legal system of Marinid Morocco, playing a role in informal legal spaces, in court cases, and advising the sultan on legal issues and appeals to overturn judicial rulings. The roles of jurists were not static and they often held multiple positions throughout their careers. This included offering opinions as respected legal scholars, political appointments as judges or imams, advisory roles to judges or the ruler, and teaching positions in mosques and madrasas. Jurists also served the state in diplomatic roles, being sent as emissaries for a range of issues, such as negotiating a strategic marriage on behalf of a Marinid sultan with a Hafsid princess, as was the case with two Marinid sultans.[85]

Relationships with political powers changed over time, with jurists falling in or out of favor and some rulers keeping their legal scholars closer than others. The Marinid sultans appointed judges, selected particular jurists to serve as their advisors, and helped shape the educational curriculum through the construction of madrasas. However, there is little evidence that they tried to control the process of lawmaking more directly or attempted to influence opinions or rulings. Likewise, the scholars did not hesitate to criticize the actions of the sultans if they believed they were inconsistent with legal principles. The sources consulted here include opinions that held sultans accountable to the law in cases of inheritance, charitable endowments for their family members, land sales, and use of state land, among other issues.

Cases examined in this book also shed light on both the advantages and shortcomings of using fatwa collections as a source for social history. A distinctive characteristic of many fatwa collections from the premodern Islamic West is that they preserved details of disputes leading up to court cases that reveal much about people's relationships with each other and to legal authorities, in addition to the interactions and disputes between the jurists themselves. The frequency of a particular type of case indicates only that it was contentious, or that an aspect of it illustrated a point that the compiler believed could serve as guidance for other legal practitioners. In a number of instances, al-Wansharisi's *Mi'yar* cataloged debates that took place between the jurists of one city, or debates that drew in opinions from all over the Islamic West, and this type of engagement would not be visible in a collection that cataloged the opinions of one particular scholar.

Additionally, fatwas given by respected scholars started to be preserved in compendia from the tenth century, and Wael Hallaq sees the increase of fatwa preservation from this period onward as "a telling example of the importance of fatwas as legal decisions and precedents."[86] Omer Awass likewise designates fatwas as "indicators of social change" because they responded to the current needs of society.[87] Hallaq argues that the muftis were central figures in elaborating Islamic substantive law.[88] It was mostly their decisions that were collected and preserved, to be reviewed by later generations of jurists, and in some cases incorporated into the doctrine of Islamic law, which very directly inserts women into the production and evolution of Islamic legal doctrine. This mechanism enabled Islamic law to evolve and adapt to new situations faced by societies at different times and places.

Book Structure

Women featured prominently throughout the fatwa literature, though in some areas more than others. Women owned and managed businesses and property, served as guardians, and managed the money of their charges, had business partnerships and frequently challenged their own family members over financial disputes related to inheritance, gifts, dower, or the right to manage their own property. One conclusion from these records is that women's rights, as defined by the law, were largely upheld when they sought redress through legal avenues. In cases where laws were not gendered and the same rules applied to men and women, the legal system enforced the claim of the party understood to be on the most solid legal footing, whether male or female. This cursory assessment will not be surprising to specialists in Islamic law.

The most interesting negotiations and jurisprudence took place in areas of the law where men and women were assigned distinct and gendered roles, and at times assumed claims that belonged to the other—such as women being assigned the right of divorce that normally belonged to the husband. In order to investigate these spaces of contradiction, this research is particularly attentive to a number of issues that arose in the context of family relationships, following the Taza case as a guide. In areas such as marriage, divorce, and premarital sex, the distinct legal roles and gendered identities assigned to women and men were contested and debated. In the cases examined here, women worked within the Islamic legal system, using the strategies available to them to expand their rights in marriage by limiting the options awarded to men by the jurists, by having aspects of men's rights transferred to them, or by forcing the legal system to accommodate them when there appeared to be no legitimate way to secure their demands. Many of these cases revolved around men fighting to retain the rights to which they were legally entitled, whether in the context of fathers marrying off virgin daughters, or husbands fighting to take advantage of their right to marry additional women and retain control over when to end a marriage. At times, men were unhappy when their authority was challenged or limited, even through legal means, and fought vigorously to preserve their entitlements. While the rules surrounding Islamic marriage and divorce gave men more rights and more control over when to begin and end a marriage, this study investigates the spaces that women carved out for themselves within this system to enhance their positions in relation to their husbands and families. These disputes provide unique insight into aspects of the legal process and the workings of law at the level of individuals, family, community, the legal system, and in some cases, the Marinid state.

Chapter 2, "'I Refuse Anyone but Him': Contesting Paternal Authority," introduces the reader to a single legal dispute from premodern Morocco, the story of the young woman from Taza, detailing claims and counter claims, the local disputes, and regional power struggles. It highlights some of the key issues in premodern Islamic law and society explored in the rest of the book. Chapter 3, "Judicial Authority, Community, and Lawmaking," provides an overview of the intellectual and legal worlds of the jurists who made the law, and their relationships with society and argues for the importance of viewing law as produced by the interaction between people within the confines of a particular historical context.

It also describes the relationship between scholars and political powers, between Fez and regional centers such as Taza, and the role of law in upholding the legitimacy of the Marinid dynasty. Chapter 4, "Women, Men, and Legal Knowledge" turns its attention to women's education and intellectual activities and shows that even below the level of the elite, women had access to information about law that allowed them to construct sophisticated strategies to help protect their interests and realize their ideal family configurations.

The remaining chapters take different strands of law drawn from the Taza case and explore aspects of women's relationships with the men in their lives through a legal framework. These chapters rely primarily on fatwa sources from the Marinid period, opinions issued by the jurists dealing with cases that arose in the society around them. Chapter 5, "Negotiating Marital Life," explores the process of making a marriage, with a particular emphasis on contracting the alliance. I argue that women used the tools available to them within the legal tradition, such as contract stipulations, to renegotiate the terms of marriage, to expand their rights, and to build a partnership that met their expectations. The fluidity and ease with which male rights, such as the right to divorce, were transferred to females complicates rigid notions of laws and rights that are inherently male and reveals their contingent and flexible nature.

Chapter 6, "Divorce and Re-envisioning the Family," examines the disparate and highly gendered options available to both spouses to dissolve a marriage. In particular, female-initiated divorce (*khul*) showed that what many women wanted was to keep custody of their children, regardless of what legal doctrine said, and not only could the law adapt to this need, but jurists came to expect it. Chapter 7, "Divorce Oaths and Legal Flexibility," examines conditional divorce by oath, a form of divorce which would seem to place women and marriage on a very precarious footing but resulted in an outlet for women to leave a marriage with their financial rights intact. These conflicts demonstrate that although the legal system in Marinid Morocco was exclusively Maliki and did not therefore feature the pluralism derived from the availability of multiple legal schools (*madhdhahib*), as has been demonstrated for the Islamic East, the presence of multiple opinions within the Maliki school provided space for jurists to use their discretion in a particular case, and in cases of divorce oaths this often benefited the women involved.

Chapter 8, "Transgressions and Legal Accommodation," returns to a key theme of the case of the young woman from Taza to investigate women who ran away (often with men) and related transgressions, such as *zina* (fornication). Even in the case of legal transgressions, the law remained a defining feature of women's lives, something that they approached not as a hostile system, but as one through which to seek justice and as a tool to restore harmony to a family or community.

2

"I Refuse Anyone but Him"

Contesting Paternal Authority

Taza Anecdote

The young woman at the center of our story had one local legal official on her side, the qadi of Taza, Iysa al-Turjali, who died around 1339 while the case was still unresolved. According to al-Turjali, the young woman, whose name is never mentioned in the sources, ran away from her father, claiming he had abused her.[1] Al-Turjali presented the woman's side of the story sympathetically, describing allegations that she raised in his court after she left her home for the second time:

> Her father beat her because she had been accused of fornication [*zina*], so he whipped her from noon on Friday until nearly evening with her private parts exposed, and he put saddle bags on her, and he cut her hair and dressed her in a sack and he began to spit in her face whenever he saw her and he threw her and he began to starve her and give her food that she wasn't accustomed to, and he sent for midwives to look at her genitals [i.e., to verify her virginity] and he began to look in her vulva with them, and he threatened her and menaced her with killing. This got to the point that she found an opportunity and she ran away by herself.[2]

Al-Turjali's account of the young woman's humiliation and abuse at the hands of her father is graphic and jarring. Although these details are not the most legally relevant to the case, al-Turjali frames his narrative in this way to sway the opinion of his audience (i.e., the jurists of Fez) and set up the young woman's father as a man of poor character. The qadi's support for the young woman remained steadfast, despite the strong opposition he faced from the jurists of Fez that made up the sultan's council. Ibrahim al-Anbaki's daughter was able to break free of her father and create a new life because of the support she received from the local legal community.

Introduction

The case of the young woman from Taza ties this book together and introduces the themes and arguments of the chapters that follow. This case was highly exceptional in a number of ways, including the lengths both the father and daughter went to in order to get what they wanted. It likely owes its preservation in the sources to the controversy it provoked among regional legal scholars, even drawing in the sultan. Yet, despite its exceptional nature, this case underscores the centrality of marriage as a cultural and religious institution and was a preoccupation for most young women and their families. This case demonstrates how families approached marriage and what women in particular wanted from it. Ending a marriage was also a common feature of life in the premodern Islamic world. Through this case, we see how men had nearly complete control over ending a marriage and how their advantage in initiating a divorce strained marriages on a regular basis. Few women would have encountered the legal system because of sexual transgressions, such as fornication or adultery. Nevertheless, cases that pushed the boundaries of the law give remarkable insight into how women reacted when they could not find a way to work within these boundaries.

In addition to highlighting a number of features of the lives of women in premodern Fez and its surroundings, the case also allows for an analysis of the coproduction of Islamic law, primarily through ordinary women's interpretation and engagement with it in their everyday lives and disputes. Altercations show how ordinary women engaged with complex legal principles, repositioning them as active participants in law-making, rather than helpless victims subject to edicts that had been elaborated and implemented by men. Narratives of disputes also hint at spaces in which educated elite women participated in the interpretation of Islamic law.

The case of the young woman from Taza provides the backdrop for understanding law, society, and women's lives in Marinid Morocco. This chapter presents a detailed overview of the conflicting narratives presented to the muftis of Fez, the one from Qadi al-Turjali clearly taking the side of the daughter, and the repeated appeals from the father as no action was taken. It also examines the responses of the jurists as they attempted to make sense of the legal principles, becoming increasingly frustrated when their advice was ignored. Their responses show how they grappled with their own personal biases despite their obligation to remain neutral. They relied on gossip and attacked the judge not only from a legal perspective, but also on a personal level.

This case also highlights some of the fragile gendered identities and power shifts between these identities, with specific insight into the category of virginity. In legal theory, virginity was a key category that determined the rights a woman had in consenting to marriage. In the Maliki school of jurisprudence, a virgin daughter of any age could be compelled into marriage, while in the Hanafi school, this compulsion declined when a woman reached majority even if she had never married.[3] The Maliki school was the only school that did not recommend even consulting a virgin daughter about a marriage (her consent was not required either way).[4] The category of virginity in the context of marriage was not significant for all women, but was specific to a woman whose father was alive and present and could oversee her marriage. It was irrelevant for an enslaved woman, whose consent to a marriage was never required, and was also not legally relevant to an orphaned woman, whose consent was always needed; likewise, virginity had no impact on the legal status of boys or men.[5] This case shows that while in theory virginity was an important and seemingly stable legal category, the actions of the young woman from Taza turned it on its head, showing the precarity of virginity as a category and simultaneously threatening the authority of her father, which was anchored in her virginity. It also hints at the different meanings of virginity in legal theory and as a social category. As the young woman moved from virgin to non-virgin, and possibly back to virgin again before definitively remaining in non-virgin territory after her marriage, she demonstrated the inherent instability of this category and the fissures in the power her father held over her. Far from being powerless in the face of her father's seemingly unshakable legal position, the young woman deployed a creative (albeit unorthodox) method for circumventing his control. The father himself took advantage of shifting gender identities by portraying himself as weak and a victim and drawing attention to his feminized role as a single father just trying to care for his children and look out for their best interests.

The Young Woman's Perspective

Taza qadi Iysa al-Turjali began his summary of the young woman's case with the above quote describing the abuse she had endured at the hands of her father. While not legally pertinent, it was clearly important to him to foreground this treatment before discussing the legal aspects of the case. Neither al-Turjali nor the responding jurists explicitly condemned the father's treatment of his daughter and the jurists from Fez summarily dismissed the allegations of abuse as unsupported and legally irrelevant. However, al-Turjali's narrative implicitly condemns the violence through his presentation of the case and through sympathetic quotes from witnesses concerned by her father's abuse.[6] Furthermore, al-Turjali, the second judge Ibn Atiyya, and all the jurists of Taza consistently supported removing the young woman from her father's home and legal authority, clearly showing their stance through their actions.

Although part of this case hinged on the young woman's status as non-virgin, the judge's description of events also sheds light on the social meanings of virginity. First, the father's informal investigation of his daughter's virginity was not legally pertinent, although the results of such an investigation could change her status within the family or community.[7] Second, the father's actions demonstrate a social conceptualization of virginity that was not tied to honor in the same way it was in the central Middle East. Despite his violence toward his daughter, the father's behavior was not seen as a threat to his daughter's life, or as a potential "honor crime." Historically, honor crimes did not exist as a legal or social category in North Africa. Additionally, her father "talked with all the people he saw and met and gossiped about her fornication, and that she was born from fornication . . . and he covered her with slander to the men of the village families and their wives."[8] It is evident that her alleged status as non-virgin due to fornication was not something he tried to conceal. And, according to his narrative, he continued to try and arrange her marriage, although she disputed this point.

The two relevant legal points of the case were that the daughter accused her father of preventing her from marrying at least four potential suitors and the fact she confessed that she was not a virgin because she had fornicated. The most important claim for her case, however, was her father's refusal to allow her to marry. In the Maliki school, a father had complete authority over his daughter's marriage, including the power to coerce (*ijbar*) his virgin daughter into marriage even if she was no longer a minor.[9] If she was a non-virgin (which typically meant previously married), she had the right to consent to a marriage. A father's refusal to allow his daughter to marry was one of the few reasons a judge could remove him as his daughter's marriage guardian and oversee the marriage himself.[10] Certain procedures had to be followed, however, such as first ordering him to allow her marriage and giving him the opportunity to comply, and the judge could only begin these procedures after the father had refused a number of suitors.[11] The daughter claimed that more than four suitors had asked for her hand and her father refused them and that when Ibn al-Turjuman proposed she had agreed, but her father would not allow the marriage.[12]

At some point, the daughter confessed to the judge that she had committed *zina* (fornication) and was therefore no longer a virgin, a revelation that according to Maliki law could remove her father's right to compel her to marry.[13] While an accusation of fornication without solid proof (i.e., four male witnesses to the act of penetration) did not change her legal status, so her father's allegations were meaningless and in fact put him at risk of punishment, her own confession did change her legal status from virgin to non-virgin. Technically, a non-virgin from fornication was a different legal category than a non-virgin from a previous marriage, and Maliki jurists were not in agreement about whether a non-virgin from fornication was no longer subject to her father's compulsion about marriage. The judge acknowledged this in making his case, citing an opinion that supported removing a father's right to coerce his daughter who was not a virgin due to fornication, one of the valid assessments in the Maliki school. And, while this change in status did not allow the judge to take control of the young woman's marriage on its own, it did undermine her father's authority over her.

The young woman's allegation that her father refused to allow her marriage and her confession of *zina* demonstrate a remarkable understanding of the law, which was likely gained from talking to other women or from an informal consultation with a legal scholar, as either the allegation or the confession would destabilize her father's domination. She stated to the judge, al-Turjali: "It is my desire to get married and I am asking to do so. There is no husband for me except the one who asked for my hand now, and I refuse anyone but him."[14] Although it is the young woman's actions that drive the case, this quote is the only time we hear from her directly, albeit through mediated legal language. The man she refers to in her statement was Ibn al-Turjuman, a neighbor of the family, and the man her father had accused of corrupting her. The daughter produced witnesses who testified to the judge about both her father's abuse and Ibn al-Turjuman's suitability (*kafa'a*) as a prospective husband, a requirement for a valid marriage. They also attested that the marriage would be the right course of action to "rescue her from his torment," referring to the daughter's horrible treatment by her father.[15]

The judge concluded that it was his "duty to see to her marriage" and sent his deputies to bring the father, Ibrahim al-Anbaki, to defend himself against the allegations.[16] He gave al-Anbaki a certain amount of time to mount his defense, but he also imprisoned him (and beat him, according to the father's narrative). Ibrahim al-Anbaki informed the judge that he had sworn a divorce oath not to marry his daughter to that particular suitor, which meant that if he did allow his daughter to marry Ibn al-Turjuman, his own wife would be divorced.[17] This seemingly strange proclamation was actually the most common reason for divorce cases to appear in Marinid legal sources, as men used divorce oaths to emphasize how serious they were about something, even if it was completely unrelated to their marriage. This type of divorce will be explored further in chapter 7.

The father missed the deadlines given to him by the judge to produce his own witnesses and declared, "I am incapable of defense so I will do as you see fit."[18] The judge sought and received confirmation from a local mufti that he was within his rights to nullify the father's legal guardianship over his daughter in marriage and the judge married her to Ibn al-Turjuman.[19]

After the marriage was consummated, the father complained to Sultan Abu al-Hassan (r. 1331–48) in the nearby Marinid capital of Fez. This powerful Marinid sultan, who ruled for around twenty years, was a great patron of scholars and religious and educational institutions. He surrounded himself with jurists who served as his consultative body on legal matters. In the council (majlis) while the sultan himself was present, jurists including Ibrahim al-Yaznasni (d. after 1339–40) and Abu Abdullah al-Satti (d. 1350) reviewed al-Turjali's summary of the case. The jurists agreed that the ruling was sound based on the facts presented and al-Yaznasni responded to al-Turjali in writing confirming the ruling's validity.[20] The jurists of Taza also reviewed the ruling and found it sound. The judge claimed that at this point the father, Ibrahim al-Anbaki, accepted al-Yaznasni's opinion. The young couple remained married.

Three years later, however, Ibrahim al-Anbaki resumed his protest against the ruling by again appealing his case to the sultan and petitioning the jurists of Fez directly. The jurists responded sympathetically to the father's petition, reversing their earlier support for al-Turjali's ruling, and advising that the marriage be annulled. They criticized al-Turjali's handling of the case and his decision to marry the daughter to Ibn al-Turjuman, and their responses also contained personal attacks on the judge. It was at this point that al-Turjali composed his comprehensive summary that included his legal reasoning and his justification for ruling in favor of the marriage. He sent it to the jurists of Fez, attempting to balance the father's contradictory account. Al-Turjali's counterclaim alleged that Ibrahim al-Anbaki was lying and asked the jurists to re-evaluate the status of the marriage. He also asked them how the father should be punished for submitting a false claim to them, which projects a certain level of confidence in his ability to sway the muftis.

Ibrahim al-Anbaki Protests

When Ibrahim al-Anbaki protested the qadi's ruling that allowed his daughter to marry Ibn al-Turjuman, he presented one petition directly to the sultan, and another to the jurists of the sultan's council. The language of the petition to the sultan was flowery and praised him extensively, while the language of the petition to the jurists was straightforward and narrated the events and relevant legal information. This indicates that the father received help in crafting each narrative, as there is no indication he was educated, or even literate. The father's chronicle recounted a completely different version of events from that of al-Turjali. In Ibrahim al-Anbaki's version of events, the neighbor, Ibn al-Turjuman, had corrupted his innocent young daughter with the help of the judge, Iysa al-Turjali, who then punished the father for trying to protect his daughter's best interests.[21] More importantly, this version accused the judge of violating the father's fundamental right to oversee the marriage of his daughter:

> Your servant, Ibrahim bin Abdullah al-Anbaki,[22] brings a suit to you seeking refuge in your justice and he kisses your noble carpet, and he takes refuge in what is explained your proper and pure investigation (*nadhr*). A great matter happened to him that ripped his sanctuary to pieces, and it weakened his honor, and it changed a lot. "And the command of God is certain destiny [Quran 33:38]." That is that the servant has small children who do not have a mother to look after them, nor grandmother to raise them. They are in his house and under his charge and protection, and he does not leave them except to seek a living or to improve their situation, securing them from the accidents, not suspecting the neighbors. And a man from the neighbors sent to his small daughter among his indicated children with a hint [of marriage] and other things, and he scared her and he could not convince her. Then he sought help from his mother and his sister and he sent them to her with a deceptive plot, trying to convince her time after time, and he did not take into account the right of the neighbor and the closeness of the neighbor, and he didn't fear the rulers, and he didn't fear God and he didn't fear what He had in revenge. And the servant in spite of all of that did not know what was happening, and he did not have knowledge of what was involved, until the matter ended in what God wanted and judged. And the servant found out and he was not able to keep it secret and could not swallow his heartbreak. He raised his matter to the one who was judging in the city [i.e., the qadi], and he did not find help from him. Then the Corruptor [Ibn al-Turjuman] asked for help [i.e., from qadi] and he transgressed. And the servant did not find any way out other than coming to you, the highly esteemed, who God made his correct sight above any other sight, and his orders are reflected in

> everything that he rules, and especially in preventing corrupted people and changing the reprehensible (*taghayyir al-mankir*), and taking the specified right on what was evident [protecting rights of people against oppression], and healing the heart from the corruption that broke it.[23]

Ibrahim al-Anbaki describes himself plaintively as the sole caregiver for his children. He appeals to the sultan's power, his lineage, his religious responsibilities, and his duty to help the weak and oppressed, a group to which al-Anbaki is trying to claim membership. Al-Anbaki assigns to himself language typically associated with femininity, including his powerlessness, his inability to determine he was being tricked, and his status as primary caregiver for his children, a role that would rarely fall to a father thanks to the more typical support of extended family networks. The father does not directly mention *zina* or the virginity of his daughter in this petition, although he alludes to it.

The scandal exploded one night when Ibrahim al-Anbaki caught Ibn al-Turjuman in his house, allegedly with the intention of having sex with his daughter. The events of that evening are described in the petition submitted to the jurists of Fez on behalf of Ibrahim al-Anbaki:

> Your answer in the case: A man has a virgin daughter in his guardianship, and under guardianship (*hijr*) and supervision (*wilayat nadhr*). It was likely that his daughter was being deceived, and he had sex with her in his [her father's] house, and the man was not aware of that. So that was unbearable to him when he found out about it and could not find a way to get a ruling against him. Then the boy that corrupted the girl came to the house of her father one night to have sex with her, and the father of the girl noticed. So he went out to look for him and he caught him so he grabbed his clothes and he left them in his hand and fled from him. Then the father of the young girl returned to his house but he did not find her, so he called for just witnesses and mentioned the issue to them. The witnesses went to the house of the corrupter of the girl, and they called him and asked him about this issue and where his clothes were. He mentioned to them that the father of the girl called him and he went out [of his own house] to him and he took his clothes. And they denied this to him because the father of the girl was not someone who would do this. They wanted to leave him, but he asked them to return

> and wanted them to try and resolve the issue with the father of the mentioned girl for him. So they returned to him and said to him that her father swore not to marry her to you. Then they said to him, where is the girl, return her to her father. He said to them, "Look for her in my room," so they entered his room but they didn't find her. Then they returned to him, and he said to them, "Look in the house of the qadi," so they entered the house of the qadi and they did not find her so they left. After it was the morning of that night the girl was found in the house of the qadi. The girl was returned to the house of her father, and she stayed with him around two years.[24]

This version of events raises several important points. First, it highlights the key role of witnesses who tried to help resolve the dispute and negotiate a marriage between the young woman and Ibn al-Turjuman.[25] The group of concerned neighbors shuttled between the two homes in the dark, dusty streets of Taza in an effort to restore harmony to the neighborhood. Second, it shows how the father limited his options by swearing an oath not to allow this marriage, which later made it impossible for him to cooperate with the judge without breaking his oath, even if he had wanted to. Third, it is significant that Ibn al-Turjuman assumed the young woman would seek refuge with the judge, as this shows that al-Turjali was someone she trusted to provide her with a safe space, and perhaps they had had a previous connection. However, the judge did not intervene directly at this point (and he did not mention this earlier incident in his narrative), and the daughter returned to her father's house, where she stayed for two years before her situation became unbearable and she decided to take more direct action.

The conflict reignited two years after the initial incident when Ibrahim al-Anbaki contracted his daughter in marriage to a local religious scholar. If in fact the father believed his daughter had committed *zina* with Ibn al-Turjuman and was no longer a virgin, as he claimed in his petition to the jurists of Fez, he technically no longer possessed the power to coerce his daughter into marriage, but clearly he did not respect this legal rule, or, as one jurist suggested, he did not actually believe that his daughter had committed *zina*.[26] Yet, one day after the marriage was contracted (but before it was consummated), the groom returned to the father and said that he was afraid of Ibn al-Turjuman, whom this section of the documents referred to as "the Corruptor." The groom wanted out of the marriage contract.[27] The father then tried to marry his daughter to a man from Fez, but when he returned from the city after making the arrangements, he found she had taken matters into her own hands and brought a case against him alleging that he had abused her and prevented her from marrying. The father mentioned that the daughter was now twenty years old, describing her as a "non-virgin old maid" (*thayb mu'anisa*).[28] The judge demanded that the father consent to a marriage between his daughter and Ibn al-Turjuman "since he is the corruptor of the girl," but the father refused, so the judge whipped him and threw him into prison.[29] Jurists of the time often preferred to marry a couple who had already committed *zina* to each other, although they required that they first observe a waiting period (*istibra*) to ensure that the woman was not pregnant as a result of *zina*. After he was released from prison, the father went to Fez to present his case to the sultan. When he returned, he found that the judge had already issued the ruling and carried out the marriage.

Although the young woman from Taza is the protagonist of this book, whose actions were the catalyst for a chain of events that ensnared local legal and political officials, and captured the attention of the modern researcher, the documents reveal very little about her life and don't even mention her name. Assuming there is some truth in both sides of the story, we can piece together a few details about her situation.[30] She was born in Taza in the early fourteenth century, sometime around 1316. She had siblings but her mother had likely died at some earlier date, so she lived in a household under the control of her father, who she portrays as a violent tyrant. At some point, she became romantically interested in her neighbor, Ibn al-Turjuman, perhaps with the facilitation of his mother and sister. This interest may or may not have resulted in a sexual relationship, but she likely spent unsupervised time with him in a manner that was not socially appropriate. After her father uncovered this relationship and refused to allow their marriage, the young woman fled her father's house, and sought refuge with the local judge, Iysa al-Turjali. She then returned to her father's home for the subsequent two years, likely suffering from his abuse and not being able to escape the situation. Although her father tried to contract her marriages to other men, she refused, and she and Ibn al-Turjuman maintained an interest in getting married, although they were likely unable to continue a relationship during this time due to the increased surveillance by her father. Finally, when she feared she would be married off without her consent, she ran away again and appealed to the judge for help. She convinced the judge of the merits of the case, including by providing witnesses to her father's abuse, and was finally able to get out from under her father's authority and marry Ibn al-Turjuman, the man she had been waiting for. All the evidence points to the fact that the marriage remained intact and produced children, perhaps giving her a happy ending after the trauma she had endured. Al-Turjali largely shielded her from the subsequent legal battle, taking the heat from the jurists of Fez himself, but the uncertainty surrounding her father's efforts to annul her marriage and regain control over her must have contributed to a sense of instability in her life and marriage.

Ibn al-Turjuman is even more difficult to get to know from the sources. The father's narrative accused this neighbor of first trying to seduce his naïve young daughter and when that did not work, getting his mother and sister to help win her over. He then likely carried on some kind of relationship with his neighbor, although his later statements seem to clear him of fornication. It is possible that he also saw no path to marriage due to the father's character and animosity, because more typically, his mother and sister would have been enlisted to help facilitate a marriage, not an illicit relationship. He did ask the neighbors who intervened on the night of the scandal to help negotiate his marriage, confirming both his desire to marry the young woman, and his inability to negotiate the union on his own. Al-Turjuman's father is never mentioned, and his absence could explain why he did not have someone to negotiate more effectively on his behalf. Although never mentioned, it is likely that he aided the young woman as she gathered the information to construct the case that would remove her father's authority over her marriage arrangements and allow the judge to marry her.

Ibn al-Turjuman remained a presence in the young woman's life, even if from afar, during the two-year confinement to her father's home after she initially ran away. The father's narrative complains that he was unable to marry his daughter to someone locally because he was afraid of Ibn al-Turjuman. An alternative account of Ibn al-Turjuman is that he was rich and powerful and abused his position to sway a local judge and possibly bribe him.[31] However, there is little evidence for this interpretation, aside from reference to witnesses testifying that Ibn al-Turjuman was suitable "in status and money" to marry the young woman, which does not imply great wealth, but rather social equality.[32] His final recorded act was to go to the judge after his wedding night and state that he had found his wife a virgin. This strange statement, mentioned in a response by one of the muftis from Fez who clearly had other avenues for gathering information about the case, was perhaps an effort to restore his wife's honor if she had felt forced to confess to *zina* as the only way by which to escape her father's home. The narrative of al-Turjali and most of the responses from the jurists of Fez largely ignore Ibn al-Turjuman's role. Only one mufti suggests in retrospect that he should have been consulted as a witness to Ibrahim al-Anbaki's refusal to allow his daughter's marriage. Both the young woman and Ibn al-Turjuman faded from the picture as the legal battle continued.

When the jurists of Fez responded to the father's petition, they agreed that based on the events described, the marriage should not have taken place. This seeming reversal of their earlier positions is understandable in the context of the role of a mufti, which was to respond to the question he was asked, assuming the facts were as stated, without further investigation or calling witnesses. The complaint submitted to the jurists was based on the father's version of events, which made no mention of abuse and denied that he had prevented his daughter from marrying. He accused the judge of usurping his right to marry off his daughter and of marrying her to the man with whom she had committed *zina*.

Perhaps it was Qadi al-Turjali's familiarity with the case and the parties involved that explains his refusal to annul the marriage, despite forceful demands from the Fasi jurists that he should do so. He had participated in the events of two years earlier, when the daughter ran away and sought refuge in his house. At that time, he allowed her to be returned to her father's house, perhaps expecting that the two families could resolve the issue and facilitate the marriage. However, this resolution did not happen, and when she returned to the judge with new allegations of her suffering, he intervened more directly on her behalf and may even have taken some legal shortcuts to allow her marriage to proceed, such as not following proper procedures for verifying her accusations or requiring her to observe a waiting period after she confessed to *zina* to ensure she was not pregnant. In further support of the daughter's case, the judge who was appointed after al-Turjali's death did not overrule the verdict, despite renewed efforts from the father to have the marriage annulled, and so, when the documentary trail ends, the young woman from Taza was still married.[33]

Response to Taza Case

The case of the young woman from Taza occurred at the height of the Marinid reign, when the state was well established but still trying to push its boundaries into North Africa. The jurists from Fez who became involved in the case were among the most prominent of their age. Many of them were students of Abu al-Hassan al-Sughayyir (d. 1320–21), a prominent scholar in the early Marinid period, who was appointed qadi of Taza in the time of al-Turjali's father, and later promoted to chief judge of Fez.[34] Al-Sughayyir's life was entwined with the Marinid royal family, who attended his classes and appointed him to official positions, including Ambassador to al-Andalus.[35] As a respected mufti, many of the questions al-Sughayyir received came from Taza, which shows he was still held in high regard there after his promotion to Fez.[36] His fatwas form one of the sources for this book. Many of the jurists in the Taza case served as advisors to Sultan Abu al-Hassan (r. 1331–48).[37] This powerful Marinid sultan, like his father before him, ruled for around twenty years, and the jurists served as his consultative body on legal matters. Although there were learned women in this generation, including women within the palace, they were absent from these gatherings, except in the case of female petitioners, as Ibn Battuta describes.[38] One member of the sultan's council, Ibn Marzuq al-Khatib (d. 1379), mentioned one tense meeting in which the sultan summoned the leading jurists and notables of Fez to discuss irregularities in tax collection; five of those jurists of Fez who were present at the meeting, as part of the sultan's council, were also involved in the case from Taza.[39]

Taza qadi Iysa al-Turjali's initial ruling was confirmed by Ibrahim bin Abdullah al-Yaznasni (d. after 1339–40) after he conferred with other jurists in the sultan's council. Ibrahim al-Yaznasni was the grand mufti of Fez and his grandson and great-grandson both later served as chief judge of Fez.[40] The most prominent jurist in this group was Abu Abdullah al-Satti (d. 1350), who had begun his career in Taza, and was perhaps most famous for being counted among Ibn Khaldun's teachers.[41] Ibn Marzuq referred to him as a "treasure of the Maliki school."[42] Although al-Satti did not respond in writing to the Taza case, he was among the jurists on the sultan's council who verified al-Turjali's initial ruling, although only al-Yaznasni responded in writing. Among the jurists who responded at various points in the ongoing case were: Abu Diya Misbah al-Yalsuti (d. 1349–50), originally from Taza, a prominent jurist, and the namesake and first teacher at the Misbahiyya madrasa in Fez, built by Sultan Abu al-Hassan;[43] Abu Abdullah Muhammad bin Abd al-Karim al-Aghsawi, a member of the sultan's council, and al-Wansharisi included many of his fatwas in *al-Mi'yar*;[44] Abd al-Aziz al-Qayrawani (d. 1349–50), a student of Abu al-Hassan al-Sughayyir and a teacher of Musa al-Abdusi, who was close to the sultan but also at times in conflict with him;[45] and Abu al-Rabii Sulayman al-Sarifi (d. 1349), who we know little about beyond a handful of fatwas compiled in *al-Mi'yar*, including one fatwa that mentions a session in which al-Sarifi and Ibn Abd al-Karim answered questions jointly, pointing to their history of working together.[46]

When these same jurists were presented with the father's side of the story three years later, the shift in the Fasi muftis' opinion was dramatic. The issue at hand was whether the judge was at fault in removing the father's right to conduct the daughter's marriage as her legal guardian (*wali*). Qadi Iysa al-Turjali had not followed the correct process for verifying the father's refusal to allow her to marry, nor had he handled the *zina* confession in a proper way. According to Malik ibn Anas (d. 795), the eponym of the Maliki school of Islamic law, if the father had refused to marry his daughter to a number of suitors, the judge should have ordered him to allow his daughter to marry, and if he still refused, the judge could remove his right as marriage guardian to his daughter.[47] Likewise, the daughter had confessed to *zina* in order to remove her father's coercive capacity, even though this was not a confirmed principle in the Maliki school; al-Yaznasni alone maintained that a non-virgin (*thayb*) from fornication (as opposed to marriage) still fell under the guardianship of her father. He stated that his view was "according to the *madhhab*," that is, the Maliki school.[48] And, some jurists note, even if the father could not force her into a marriage, he still remained the preferred marriage guardian in this situation. The jurists argued that despite the fact she later retracted her confession, the judge should have ensured that she observed a waiting period (*istibra*) as a precaution. This waiting period of three menstrual cycles was required after *zina* to ensure there was no pregnancy.[49] In Maliki books of doctrine, this term is typically discussed in the context of the sale of an enslaved woman to ensure that she was not carrying her previous enslaver's child, and it only lasted one month or one menstrual period.[50] The waiting period in the context of a legal marriage, which occurred after divorce or a husband's death, was called *idda*. A less common application of this concept in the context of *zina* reframed the *istibra* as the three menstrual periods that matched the *idda* of free divorced women, a pragmatic approach that will be discussed further in chapter 8.[51] Furthermore, the witnesses to harm had allegedly retracted their testimony. From a strictly legal perspective, it appeared that the judge's ruling did not hold up, and the marriage should not have been allowed and should now be annulled.[52]

The answers from the Fasi muftis seemed to contain an element of personal attack. While perhaps this simply owed to the judicial errors they saw in the case, it is also likely that due to Taza's proximity to Fez, and Fez's role as a center of learning, they would have had a more personal knowledge of al-Turjali. The muftis belonged to a community of jurists as well as the larger community and the events of the neighboring town would have been big news, generating gossip, and the circulation of information, as is evidenced by the muftis constantly including details about the case not contained in the original petitions.[53] Some of the muftis were originally from Taza or had family connections there, which also would have facilitated the circulation of informal news about the case and the people involved, or meant that previous relationships existed. Several of the jurists had previously had positive interactions with al-Turjali in other documented cases (and likely numerous other cases that were not preserved).

Table 2.1
Father's Petitions and Responses

Doc #	*Author*	*Type of Document*	*Responding to Other Doc*	*Content Summary*
#1	Ibrahim al-Anbaki	Summary and petition to Sultan[1]		Petition to Sultan from father presenting self as victim of judge. Does not explicitly mention virginity.
#2	On behalf of Ibrahim al-Anbaki	Fatwa request to jurists of Fez[2]		Detailed summary of case from father's perspective.
#3	Ibrahim al-Yaznasni	Fatwa[3]	Response to al-Anbaki	Response focused on prevention of marriage aspect of case.
#4	Abu Diya Misbah	Fatwa[4]	Response to al-Anbaki	Dated Tuesday May 18, 1339. Response focused on prevention of marriage aspect of case.
#5	Ibn Abd al-Karim	Fatwa[5]	Response to al-Anbaki	Marriage should be annulled. No prevention of marriage in this case. Husband unsuitable because sinner (i.e., due to *zina*). Implies al-Turjali was either ignorant or biased and might even have taken a bribe.
#6	Unknown	Fatwa[6]		Critiques response of muftis to case. Argues that father's refusal to allow his daughter to marry was the only legally relevant aspect of the case. States that witnesses should have been consulted to verify claims. Marriage should be annulled if contracted without father's approval, no matter how much time has passed. Only fatwa to extensively cite Maliki doctrine.

[1] Al-Wansharisi, *al-Mi'yar*, 3:74–76.
[2] Al-Wansharisi, *al-Mi'yar*, 3:76–78.
[3] Al-Wansharisi, *al-Mi'yar*, 3:78.
[4] Al-Wansharisi, *al-Mi'yar*, 3:78–80.
[5] Al-Wansharisi, *al-Mi'yar*, 3:80–82.
[6] Al-Wansharisi, *al-Mi'yar*, 3:69–74.

Table 2.2
Al-Turjali's Petition and Responses

Doc #	*Author*	*Type of Document*	*Responding to Other Doc*	*Content Summary*
#7	Iysa al-Turjali	Summary and petition (*Istiraa*)[1]		Summary of case of young woman from Taza; details, events, and legal reasoning behind decision; mentions original ruling from three years earlier that was confirmed by al-Yaznasni. Compiler notes that document was written in al-Turjali's own hand.
#8	Abu Diya Misbah	Fatwa[2]	Response to al-Turjali	Summarizes objections to ruling. Says daughter's non-virginity not verified.
#9	Muhammad al-Qayrawani	Fatwa[3]	Response to al-Turjali	Objects to all aspects of ruling. Notes that witnesses to the harm had come forward and said they had never testified. Uses very harsh language about case and judge.
#10	Ibn Abd al-Karim	Fatwa[4]	Response to al-Turjali	Only addresses *zina* aspect of case. Virginity not verified; alleges young woman only confessed to remove father's compulsion. Mentioned here that after the wedding night, the daughter's husband had confessed to the judge that he had found her a virgin, confirming her false confession, a detail not included in the judge's summary.
#11	Ibrahim al-Yaznasni	Fatwa[5]	Response to al-Turjali	Only responds to issue of non-virginity from fornication, says irrelevant, and doesn't remove compulsion. Harsh language about judge.

[1] Al-Wansharisi, *al-Mi'yar*, 3:59–62.
[2] Al-Wansharisi, *al-Mi'yar*, 3:62–63.
[3] Al-Wansharisi, *al-Mi'yar*, 3:63–64.
[4] Al-Wansharisi, *al-Mi'yar*, 3:64–65.
[5] Al-Wansharisi, *al-Mi'yar*, 3:65.

The main focus of attention here was on the judge; the daughter and her new husband were marginal considerations. In the documents included in the *Mi'yar* that related to this case, the jurists were almost unanimous that the marriage between the daughter and Ibn al-Turjuman should be annulled. However, the language they used was very cautious, as their responses were supposed to rely solely on the facts given in the questions put to them. Therefore, they usually began their fatwas with phrases like: "If the information provided here is true" or "If the girl was indeed a virgin [as stated in a question posed to them]." They ended their responses with "and God knows best," a standard formulation in legal texts that left room for the possibility of human error in interpretation.

The documents preserved for this case in the *Mi'yar* take up twenty-three pages in the modern edition of the text and present various perspectives on the case. They do not appear in order; I have organized them in the accompanying charts based on clear indicators of chronology, such as references to the first judge's death and other events. There are eighteen documents in total, including a petition to the sultan from the father, four separate questions put to the muftis of Fez, and twelve fatwas issued by muftis in response to these questions. One of the fatwas evaluates the case in general without responding to a particular request for an answer. There is also the letter al-Yaznasni wrote to the second judge after al-Turjali's death. The letter was unsolicited and no response to it is recorded. In total, six muftis issued fatwas, with three of them responding multiple times. The timeline, key points, and authors of the texts are summarized in the charts.

New Petitions after Death of Qadi al-Turjali

No further action would have been taken on this case, as the judge refused to overturn his ruling, the official appointed by the sultan to review the case did not recommend annulment, and the sultan refused to overturn al-Turjali's ruling. Al-Anbaki's daughter was eighteen when the scandal broke and twenty when she finally received the judge's permission to marry Ibn al-Turjuman. She was twenty-three when her father began his quest to have her marriage annulled; the couple had been married for three years and most likely had children.[54] However, sometime after the initial flurry of legal opinions, Qadi al-Turjali died, and the jurist asked by the sultan to examine the case was appointed the new judge of Taza. The sultan maintained his aversion to direct intervention in the workings of the legal system and did not order the judge to rule in any particular way.

The new judge, Abu Abdullah Muhammad Ibn Atiyya, was one of the jurists of Taza whom al-Turjali had originally consulted on the case. Little is known about this judge, aside from a handful of mentions as part of cases in al-Wansharisi's *Mi'yar*, and none of his own fatwas are preserved.[55] Ibn Atiyya was written into history when Abu Abdullah Muhammad bin Muhammad al-Maqqari (d. 1357), the ancestor of the Ahmad al-Maqqari (d. 1632), the author of *Nafh al-Tib*, passed through Taza and mentioned meeting three jurists there, identifying one as Ibn Atiyya.[56] Ibn Atiyya lived in the same community in which the events had taken place and was presumably familiar with the issues and people involved. This, along with the fact that the couple had already created a stable family, may have contributed to his hesitance about intervening. The father, Ibrahim al-Anbaki, approached al-Yaznasni and asked him to write to the new judge about the case, which he did in a short letter urging Ibn Atiyya to rule appropriately.[57]

At this time, a new petition was presented to the jurists of Fez that summarized the case and included some new details.[58] This petition was written on behalf of al-Anbaki, based on information he provided, and al-Turjali was no longer alive to dispute the facts. The daughter's side of the story was marginalized, although at this point the burden of proof fell on her father. After all this time, al-Anbaki now said he had proof that there was no abuse or refusal to allow his daughter to marry. He also said he had proof that the judge was wrong to remove his right to marry his daughter on the grounds of her confession of *zina*: when his daughter's marriage to Ibn al-Turjuman was consummated, the groom found her to be a virgin, a revelation he had allegedly confessed to the judge after his wedding night. The muftis who responded to this petition agreed that if Ibrahim al-Anbaki could prove his allegations, the new judge was obligated to overturn al-Turjali's ruling and annul the daughter's marriage.

The new judge did not, however, annul the marriage, as evidenced by an additional question that recounted the story in detail, and also stated that the second judge did not annul the marriage despite the father's

Table 2.3
Activity after Death of Qadi al-Turjali

Doc #	*Author*	*Type of Document*	*Responding to Other Doc*	*Content Summary*
#12	Ibrahim al-Yaznasni	Letter to newly appointed judge[1]		Short letter on behalf of Ibrahim al-Anbaki that urges new judge to rule according to law (implying overturning al-Turjali's ruling).
#13	Request for fatwa after death of al-Turjali	Request for fatwa[2]		After death of al-Turjali; likely on behalf of father. Al-Anbaki claimed proof that there was no abuse or refusal to allow his daughter to marry. Groom found her a virgin on wedding night.
#14	Ibrahim al-Yaznasni	Fatwa[3]	New fatwa request after death of al-Turjali	Short response stating that if a judge has committed an injustice the ruling needs to be overturned.
#15	Abu al-Rabii al-Sarifi	Fatwa[4]	New fatwa request after death of al-Turjali	If father can confirm injustice of judge, ruling should be overturned and marriage annulled.
#16	Ibn Abd al-Karim	Fatwa[5]	New fatwa request after death of al-Turjali	If father can confirm injustice of judge, ruling should be overturned and marriage annulled.
#17	Request for fatwa after second judge refuses to annul	Request for fatwa[6]		Likely on behalf of father. Mentions that new judge refused to overturn al-Turjali's ruling. One final attempt to overturn ruling and annul marriage.
#18	Abu Diya Misbah	Fatwa[7]	Response to above request	Urges second judge, Ibn Atiyya, to look into the ruling or says the sultan should appoint someone new.

[1] Al-Wansharisi, *al-Mi'yar*, 3:66.
[2] Al-Wansharisi, *al-Mi'yar*, 3:66.
[3] Al-Wansharisi, *al-Mi'yar*, 3:66–67.
[4] Al-Wansharisi, *al-Mi'yar*, 3:67.
[5] Al-Wansharisi, *al-Mi'yar*, 3:67.
[6] Al-Wansharisi, *al-Mi'yar*, 3:67–68. This may be one document, or it is possibly two fragments.
[7] Al-Wansharisi, *al-Mi'yar*, 3:68–69.

claims of new evidence.[59] Here, Misbah responded for the third time in this case, urging the second judge, Ibn Atiyya, to overturn the ruling; if he did not, the sultan should appoint someone who was not afraid to do so. This response is the final document preserved in the case of the young woman from Taza, and while there were clearly forces still trying to overturn her marriage, it seems as though the momentum had perhaps died down, as only Misbah answered the final query. Although we don't know for sure what happened after the documentary trail ends, we can assume there was not enough evidence or political will to change the status quo, and the young woman remained married. Or perhaps the jurists became distracted by other concerns, because their ties to the sultan and other contemporary catastrophes would soon lead to many of their deaths.

Gender and Virginity in Law and Society

One aspect of this case that reveals the instability of gendered identities is the young woman's confession to having committed *zina* and therefore no longer being a virgin. Virginity was an important legal category, as it determined whether or not a father could coerce his daughter into marriage. As a social category, the sources hint at a greater yet more ambiguous meaning for virginity. The young woman's vacillation between these identities emphasizes their lack of fixity and susceptibility to competing demands. Lama Abu-Odeh describes how historically, in the Arab Middle East, an entire family's honor was tied to a woman's virginity.[60] If a woman did not bleed on her wedding night, she would be returned to her family, and killed by them.[61] In this system legal and social categories overlapped, as this crime was not subject to punishment, and the virginity of a woman was central to the gender identity of both male and female family members.[62] Constructions of virginity in North Africa were stripped of honor and any associated violent component, leaving a very different type of category which was mainly associated with consent to marriage, and social fears of unmarriageability or a lower dower.

In Maliki North Africa, a father's absolute power over his daughter's marriage was tied to her virginity; without this, his power was significantly reduced to a more advisory role, and her consent to marriage was now required. From the legal theory, we would understand the father's authority as unshakable, and the daughter as completely without options in the face of her father's opposition to her marriage choice. Only a marriage would change her status to non-virgin and allow her more of a voice in a subsequent marriage. Except somehow, the daughter in the case from Taza became aware of a legal loophole that was not itself a guarantee to remove her father's power to coerce her into a marriage, due to disagreement on this point by the jurists, and successfully navigated a path from virgin to non-virgin and thus out of her father's control. Fornication was a crime, so this approach to changing her status from virgin to non-virgin was not without risk, but in this case and in others we will see in chapter 8, this potential risk must have been worth the benefit.

The muftis of Fez do not linger on the issue of virginity beyond its legal relevance. There is no moralizing or reproachment on the topic; this, they reserve for the qadi. Some voiced their suspicion that the young woman's initial confession was simply a ploy to remove her father's power of coercion over her. They acknowledged the uncertainty of the category in practice, with the unknown mufti pointing out that the father likely did not believe the accusations, or he would not have tried to force her into marriage after that.[63] Others mentioned the claim that Ibn al-Turjuman came to Qadi al-Turjali after the wedding night and stated that he had found his wife a virgin, ultimately highlighting the unknowability of this category. In al-Yaznasni's response to al-Turjali, he dismissed the matter of virginity entirely, as he takes the position that fornication does not remove a father's compulsion to marry his daughter.[64]

Only one mufti gestures to the morality of the matter, which may have been such an obvious point that it did not need to be stated explicitly. However, in this case, mufti Ibn Abd al-Karim is not highlighting the immorality of the young woman; rather, he states that Ibn al-Turjuman had sinned by committing *zina*, and therefore was not of adequate moral status to marry the young woman.[65] This appears to be a rare occurrence where a man's status of non-virgin could possibly impact his legal status in a marriage, although Ibn Abd al-Karim could simply be trying to get his point across by bringing this up.

The ambiguity of the category of virginity is further complicated by the legal mechanism of *istibra*, the waiting period required after fornication, which has the effect of softening the edges of the category by absorbing any suspicion of fornication. The mufti who engaged most thoroughly with the issue of virginity was Ibn Abd al-Karim. He noted that a retracted confession was enough to avoid punishment, but did not remove the necessity of observing the *istibra*.[66] He argued that "she is not believed when she withdraws the confession of fornication except in the dropping of the *hadd* punishment."[67] Observing the *istibra* would restore the young woman's legal status and ability to marry and remove the possibility of punishment, but it would not restore the assumption of virginity. In practice, this points to a possible third category between virginity and non-virginity of assumed but unprovable non-virginity, which would follow the legal rules of non-virginity to be on the safe side. However, just as quickly, Ibn Abd al-Karim returns the young woman to the previous status of virgin when he mentions that Ibn al-Turjuman found her a virgin on their wedding night, essentially negating his earlier stipulation that she was of ambiguous virgin status, and should have observed a waiting period; with Ibn al-Turjuman's statement, the mufti sees the coercive capacity of her father restored. The seemingly clear boundaries of virgin/non-virgin in legal theory quickly unravel when faced with rebellious women and their confounding maneuvers. And, with this unraveling, the authority of the father falls and is undermined and minimized, reducing him to a victim of the judge's much greater power.

Virginity as a social category is much less clearly defined, and it is inherently more ambiguous than the seemingly stable legal equivalent. Outside of a court, an unsupported accusation would be enough to damage a reputation. The young woman herself claimed that no one wanted to marry her because her father had been telling everyone she had committed *zina*.[68] And yet, virginity was still to a certain extent unknowable. Ibrahim al-Anbaki had midwives examine his daughter without the sources mentioning a conclusive determination. He continued to accuse her of not being a virgin, but simultaneously tried to force her into marriage, which means that he was either unaware of the ruling on this matter or did not believe his own accusations.

The muftis' discourse reflects a consideration of the consequences of an ambiguous virginity status. The clearest concern is that a woman of this status would not be able to marry. For example, the unknown mufti criticized the possibility of al-Turjali not annulling the young woman's marriage "because in her marriage contract there is a disgrace on her and no one could be found to marry her."[69] The mufti acknowledged the possibility that al-Turjali had preserved the daughter's marriage because it would have been difficult for her to remarry after the scandal, but dismissed this as setting a dangerous precedent. Al-Yaznasni accused his fellow jurists of being reluctant to recommend annulment as "they see that it would lead to the annulment of a lot of marriages."[70] This is intriguing because it suggests there are other marriages of this nature in the community, perhaps of couples that married after some kind of relationship. Nevertheless, at the same time it also points to the fact that after this kind of transgression women could get married despite any social stigma. These comments reflect the complex social construction of virginity and the variability of any associated consequences.

History Intervenes

The jurists in the Taza case and others of their generation were swept up in historical upheavals that cut short their lives and legacies, disrupting what should have been prestigious careers, and preventing a more significant written record of their jurisprudence. Pursuing the Marinid goal to reunite North Africa, in 1347, Sultan Abu al-Hassan led a campaign to capture territory that had been ruled by the Hafsid dynasty since the fall of the Almohads. The Hafsids, who ruled the area known as Ifriqiya (encompassing today's Tunisia and beyond) from 1207 to 1573, claimed continuity with the Almohad Empire.[71] Less than a decade after the Taza case, Sultan Abu al-Hassan had conquered much of North Africa, establishing himself in Tunis in 1347 and reportedly bringing hundreds of jurists with him, including al-Satti and at least four others with roots in Taza.[72] In Tunis, al-Satti continued to teach and give lectures, and his students included Ibn Khaldun (d. 1406), who praised his knowledge, and mufti Ibn Arafa (d. 1400).[73] The great Moroccan traveler Ibn Battuta (d. 1369) also passed through Tunis on his return from his lengthy travels, while Abu al-Hassan had his court set up there, and frequently visited with the sultan to share stories of his adventures throughout the Muslim world and beyond.[74] Ibn Battuta noted how the sultan surrounded himself with his jurists, including al-Satti, in addition to the prominent jurists of Tunis.[75]

However, as the sultan's hold on the surrounding areas weakened, his son, Abu Inan Faris (r. 1348–58), took advantage of his father's absence and pre-emptively seized power in Fez.[76] Abu al-Hassan never re-established control of his state and died in 1351. Ibn Battuta continued traveling from Tunis to Fez, stopping in Taza in late 1349, just a decade after the events of our case, when most of the participants were likely still living. It was in Taza that he heard the news of his mother's death.[77] Upon Ibn Battuta's arrival in Fez, he entered the service of the new Marinid sultan, Abu Inan, who had taken over the empire from his father. Ibn Khaldun also traveled from Tunis to Fez several years later and remained at the court of Abu Inan for six years, from 1354 to 1362.

Unlike Ibn Battuta and Ibn Khaldun, most of the jurists who accompanied Sultan Abu al-Hassan to Tunis never made it back to Fez. Proximity to the sultan obviously came with a degree of risk and uncertainty as political fortunes changed. In this case, disaster struck as the embattled sultan's scholarly entourage returned from Tunis by ship, and al-Satti was among a group of jurists who drowned when their ship sank off the coast of Bougie.[78] These scholars met their death as a result of their close relations with the sultan, not because they got caught up in political intrigue. Sources record the same year of death for many other scholars; some were victims of the plague that raced across North Africa from the east at this time, while others died accompanying the Marinid sultans on other campaigns.[79] These events wiped out a generation of jurists and left a void in the record where their scholarly legacy should stand.

Conclusion

The case of the young woman from Taza will serve as a guide through the complex social and legal world of Marinid Morocco, highlighting women's agency and engagement at every step of the way. Although this case might be read as an example of oppression of a man whose right to choose his daughter's husband was appropriated by a corrupt judge, this argument is plausible only if the daughter's perspective is minimized, and only the petitions of the father are taken into account.[80] Based on the compelling evidence presented on the daughter's behalf, I argue that the case instead represents the perseverance of a young woman who contested her father's authority and married the man of her choosing, with help from the local judge and legal officials, despite the enormous odds stacked against her, including the weight of opinion from many of the scholars of Fez.

Law, like life, is complicated and messy. It does not exist only in books of theory or doctrine but comes alive as ordinary people and jurists navigate its translation to real-life situations. Jurists are not objective, distant observers interpreting the law for laypeople; they belong to local communities and become involved in local turmoil and can get dragged into interpersonal relationships and speculation like anyone else. Outside of legal texts, law becomes a web that binds families, neighbors, local legal officials and scholars, regional jurists, and regional political powers. Like the woman from Taza, women participated in the coproduction of law through their engagement in legal disputes, demonstrating their knowledge of legal principles and strategies. A smaller number of elite women participated in legal interpretation through advanced scholarship, forming part of the intellectual world of male scholars. The marriage in the Taza case was not typical, but it points to what the expectations were for a typical marriage. The divorce oath pronounced by the father, Ibrahim al-Anbaki, on an action unrelated to his own marriage, was a surprisingly common way of destabilizing or ending a marriage, but it was not the only option for divorce. The daughter's confession of sexual transgressions (which may in fact have been a false confession) illustrates how the jurists responded to legal infractions and how communities and legal structures worked together in such cases to restore participants to a legally valid framework, which in this context meant marriage. The changes to both society and legal structures that came with colonialism and independence jeopardized these mechanisms and forced women into more vulnerable positions with less family and community support to resolve transgressions. The chapters that follow are mapped onto this case, each bringing in the stories of additional women and their disputes to show how they deployed Islamic law to safeguard their interests, expand their rights, and express a vision for their families that transcended the starting point set by law. Each chapter also considers the different gender identities constructed, negotiated, and traded as women navigated different life and legal stages.

3

Judicial Authority, Community, and Lawmaking

Taza Anecdote

When Taza qadi Iysa al-Turjali initially submitted his ruling to the jurists of Fez for review, they agreed that the ruling was sound. However, when Ibrahim al-Anbaki submitted his own petition to the jurists of Fez and the sultan three years later, the jurists' favor shifted dramatically. The jurists who responded were unanimous in taking the father's side against the qadi and advocated overturning the judge's ruling and annulling the marriage between the young woman and Ibn al-Turjuman. The jurists of Fez were the most respected in the region and closely connected to the Marinid ruler, some of them sat on his advisory council, and their opinions carried weight. Some of those involved in the case had family roots in Taza and the personal connections may have contributed to the intensity of their responses. And yet in their capacity as muftis they could only issue advisory opinions, but they lacked the power to overturn a ruling made by a regional judge. They harshly criticized the legal reasoning behind al-Turjali's ruling from a number of different angles, they critiqued al-Turjali personally, and they brought in additional information about the case that must have flowed through gossipy local grapevines. They urged the sultan to overturn the ruling or appoint a judge who could do so. Although the sultan refused to overturn the ruling himself, he did appoint another judge to look into the case. This judge, however, did not overturn the ruling that had originally allowed the marriage. And thus, despite strong opposition from authoritative regional legal figures, al-Turjali's ruling stood, and the young woman's marriage to Ibn al-Turjuman was preserved.

Introduction

This chapter examines the local and regional workings of the legal system more closely. Law took shape in Morocco from the mid-thirteenth to the mid-fifteenth century at the intersection of political concerns, legal exigencies, and societal realities, in a vibrant intellectual and complex political atmosphere. Law as implemented in Marinid Morocco was grounded in the lives, culture, and intellectual traditions of the jurists who produced that law. Law was elaborated by (male) jurists who lived in a particular environment and society, with specific influences and needs, and who brought the concerns of their time and place into their interpretation and practice of law. This chapter will explore the workings of the different components of the legal system and its social and political connections through the jurists' response to the case from Taza. A key argument of this book is that context mattered in the interpretation of Islamic law. Likewise, the individuals who interpreted and implemented the law in a given period were influential intermediaries between ordinary people and legal theory, bridging abstract legal situations and real-life experiences and disputes with their legal interpretations. Although it is male jurists who take center stage here, their actions, reactions, and relationships to each other and to the Marinid sultan are expanded through a case centered on a woman's needs.

The response to the marriage of the young woman from Taza illustrates how the different components of the legal system worked together. Power was dispersed between three sites: the sultan, the jurists of Fez, and the jurists of Taza. While a judge's verdict could be appealed, the ruler chose not to intervene and reverse his decision. The renowned muftis of medieval Fez, whose opinions are respected even today and who enjoyed close relations with the ruler, only had advisory legal powers and could not force their opinions on a judge or anyone else. This was an unusual case: in a typical case a judge would respect and apply the opinion of a mufti, whose knowledge of the legal tradition was usually more profound than his own. This case, however, demonstrates that a judge was not obligated to do so and could use his own discretion to make an independent ruling.

The Taza case provides insight into the role of the Marinid sultan in the regional balance of legal power. I argue here that while the sultan did have the power to intervene in the legal process, particularly when appeals were brought directly to him, he did not overreach or abuse this power. He closely observed the unfolding of this case and intervened at a few points to ensure the process was running smoothly and in the interest of justice. The sultan, like all other parties in the case, would have had his own networks for gathering information and learning more about the background to the case, and at some point, he summoned al-Turjali and other local parties involved to meet with him. While the sultan agreed to appoint a new judge to investigate the case, he did not directly intervene, even when that second judge chose not to overturn al-Turjali's ruling. And, while he consulted and listened to his respected legal advisors, he ultimately let the case from Taza play out at the local level, acting as an arbiter between the parties.[1]

Scholars have highlighted the Marinids' construction of legitimacy through their support for Maliki Sunnism, a commitment to orthodoxy that set them apart from their predecessors.[2] They built and supported religious institutions, especially the madrasas that trained jurists, and surrounded themselves with the prominent jurists of their age. However, this case highlights the cracks in this understanding of the Marinids as upholders of orthodoxy. Rather, their priority was to uphold the stability of state and society. In this instance, the sultan was not afraid to minimize the strong urgings of his jurists. His main concern was not to protect the father's authority over his daughter, or to regulate the sexuality of the young women in his realm. This example signals how stable the Marinid state was at the height of its power; no longer so dependent on legal scholars to legitimize its rule that the sultan would prioritize the opinions of the jurists above the social realities or needs of his community.

The Marinids and History

Western historians of premodern Morocco have been preoccupied with sultans and sharifs, Sufis and saints, a convergence driven by the concerns of French colonial scholarship.[3] However, even in political histories, the Marinids are often treated as an afterthought, or footnote, due to their anomalous nature in the genealogy of Moroccan rulers.[4] Their reign has no connection to the dynasty that rules today, through either bloodline or sharifian status, and is therefore of less significance to historians of the current monarchy. Nor did the Marinids base their legitimacy on either a program of religious reform or sharifian status, two other concerns of Western scholars.[5] The aspirations for a greater Moroccan empire ended for the most part with Marinid rule and the boundaries of the Marinid state remained the approximate parameters of today's Moroccan state. The lack of territorial expansion and absence of strong claims for religious legitimacy are precisely what make the Marinid period a meaningful site of historical inquiry in the present study. These hallmarks of Marinid rule are what led them to focus on building religious institutions and sponsoring the production of knowledge in the religious sciences and beyond.

While still concerned with power and dynasties, Moroccan historians have highlighted the intense intellectual and cultural production of this time. They view the Marinid dynasty as overseeing an important period in the development of the modern Moroccan state. Mohamed al-Manouni argues that at this point, a number of aspects of Moroccan identity became solidified, marked by unity in language, Maliki law, religious identity, and a unified defense of borders.[6] Scholars trained in the new madrasas began writing histories of their region, one of the many factors leading to a new sense of unity under the Marinids.[7] Moroccan historians also recognize the Marinid period as one of intense activity in the areas of religion, intellectual production, art and architecture, and cultural advancement, with royal patronage supporting these initiatives. Some of the most promising historical scholarship on the Marinid period and Morocco comes from a new generation of Moroccan social historians, whose interest in the lives and activities of people serves as a foundation for new inquiries into areas such as histories of women and the family.[8]

Taza in History

The case of the young woman who ran away from her father began in the town of Taza, a city approximately seventy miles east of Fez. Taza is located in a strategic mountain pass where the Rif and Atlas Mountains meet. Historically, it served as the connecting point between Fez and the rest of North Africa and the Arab East via Tlemcen. Abdelhadi Tazi, a Moroccan scholar with ancestral roots in the city, described Taza as a respected center that held together the north and south, the east and west of the country.[9] Under the ruling Marinid dynasty, Taza was one of the most important cities in the region, and not just for its strategic value to the rulers. It was a hub of learning that valued its institutions and nourished distinguished scholars. As they passed through on their way to Fez, travelers remarked on the scholars they met and the city's other attributes.

Today, far from the seaports and modern economic centers, Taza has lost its geographical centrality and historic importance, and has been reduced to just a stop along the route traversed by train or highway from Fez to Oujda. The Great Mosque has been stripped to its bones and is undergoing renovation, awaiting restoration to its previous splendor.[10] Today, residents and travel guides focus more on the natural beauty around the city, including the panoramic vistas into the valley as well as the nearby mountains that contain a national park and extensive cave system. Writer Nassima Chahboun confirms the depreciation of modern Taza, noting that "the genius locus of the medina of Taza is not found in the physical space, but rather in narratives and poetry."[11] Some residents share this negative view of the city as it stands today and reduce its rich history as an important political and cultural center in premodern Morocco.

The medina of Taza, the old part of the city where the case involving the young woman unfolded, is built on a hillside above the Ouad al-Abiyad River, with the Great Mosque at its center. Following their typical colonial strategy, the French colonizers built a new city on a plain below the old city, separating themselves from the local population; today, the new part has grown far beyond its colonial boundaries and sprawls in all directions, at times crossing the river below. The Great Mosque was built by the Almohads, an Amazigh dynasty that ruled Morocco before the Marinids, from the mid-twelfth to the mid-thirteenth century. The Almohads established the attached library (*khizana*) to store the works of the twelfth-century scholar Qadi Iyad (d. 1149) and elevated Taza to a seasonal capital.[12] Marinid sultans solidified Taza's status as a city of learning, expanding the mosque and its library, building three madrasas, and maintaining close connections with the city's scholars. The Marinid sultan Abu al-Hassan, who became embroiled in the current case from Taza, built a madrasa attached to the Great Mosque there, likely while he was still Crown Prince during his father's reign in the early fourteenth century.[13] The houses in the old city of Taza cluster around the Great Mosque, and the house of Qadi al-Turjali, where the young woman sought refuge from the violence of her father, was likely close to the mosque.

Although not as well known as some of the larger cities, Taza was nevertheless considered a center of learning in the premodern Islamic West, and was particularly famous for its scholarship on Arabic grammar.[14] Most premodern travelers who passed through mentioned the scholars they had met there on the way to Fez, highlighting the city's cultural importance. Al-Hassan al-Wazzan (Leo Africanus, d. ca. 1554), a Moroccan trader and traveler originally from Granada, visited Taza almost two hundred years after our case took place and left a more substantial description. Al-Wazzan passed through the city during the reign of the Wattasids (1472–1554), the dynasty that succeeded the Marinids. In his *Description of Africa*, written after his capture by Catholic pirates and enslavement in Rome by Pope Leo X (d. 1521), he describes Taza as the third most important city under the Marinids, after Fez and Meknes, with "three colleges (madrasas) with diverse bath houses (hammams), and a great number of hospitals."[15] Like the Marinids, the Wattasid sultans still sent their princes to govern this provincial center. The populous city was known for its riches in both wealth and scholarship and al-Wazzan notes that it was home to five hundred Jewish families. He describes fertile plains and flourishing agriculture, which attracted Arab tribes to the town on a yearly basis to stock up on provisions. He also mentions that the Marinids passed the summer in Taza, and other sources note that they also spent holidays there.[16] Al-Wazzan's description shows that under the Wattasids, Taza still occupied an important political and economic role. Today, the city is surrounded by hills covered with olive trees; in premodern times, it was known for its agricultural production in addition to its industries producing soap, copper, paper, and glass.[17]

Ibn Battuta reached Taza in 1349 on his return to Morocco after nearly twenty-five years of traveling, just a decade after the events of the Taza case. He wrote only that he was met there by news of his mother's death from the plague, which he had witnessed as it spread west.[18] Perhaps due to these circumstances, he did not mention anything else about the city or the scholars he may have met. Abdelhadi Tazi, however, reads more into this one sentence about Taza, noting that Ibn Battuta's choice of route through this city shows its importance as a destination and pivotal axis for trade and travel, while people there having received news of the death of Ibn Battuta's mother shows its significance in the exchange of information.

One scholar who passed through Taza on his way to Fez from Tlemcen was Ahmad al-Wansharisi (d. 1508), the compiler of the fatwa collection, *al-Mi'yar,* which contains the documents related to the case of the young woman from Taza. While in Taza, al-Wansharisi collected many fatwas from the scholars of Taza which he included in *al-Mi'yar.*[19]

Law and Learning in Taza

The jurists of Taza were shielded from the pressure of the Marinid court by their distance from it and few reached the prominence of the Fasi jurists unless they relocated and established their careers in Fez or another large city, or traveled to the central Middle East.[20] Abu al-Hassan al-Sughayyir exemplifies this trajectory, beginning his career as judge of Taza and later attaining higher positions in Fez, and maintaining close ties to the Marinid sultans. The jurists who stayed in Taza rarely made their way into the biographical dictionaries that honored the scholars of the age, as they remained less connected to networks of power. Little is known about their lives and training, although sources occasionally mention one of their teachers or students. Travelers who passed through Taza sometimes highlighted a meeting with a particular scholar, ensuring their place in the historical record. For example, Abu Abdullah Muhammad al-Abdari al-Abili (d. 1356), a teacher of Ibn Khaldun, mentions meeting Iysa al-Turjali's father when he passed through Taza, and Abu Abdullah Muhammad al-Maqqari the Elder (d. 1357) mentions his encounter with the second judge in the Taza case, Ibn Atiyya, when he visited the city.

Fatwa records offer more clues about the activities of the jurists of Taza and their connections to regional networks, and specifically the jurists of

Fez, as well as to their own community. The jurists of Taza formed a tight-knit group and were deeply engaged with the local community. The case of the young woman from Taza makes it clear how accessible the jurists were to the local population, in both formal and informal venues. For example, when the young woman ran away from her father's house, she sought refuge in the house of the judge, Iysa al-Turjali, which she only would have done if she trusted him. In another example, after the young woman's father appeared in court, al-Turjali sent him, along with a group of legal scholars, to the house of the mufti of Taza, Abu Muhammad Abdullah al-Batu'i, who was at home sick that day.[21] Although al-Batu'i was absent from the court, al-Turjali still sought his opinion on the case and felt comfortable sending people to his home to consult him. From these examples and others, we see that lawmaking took place in official venues, such as the mosque and the court, and also in informal venues, like the homes of legal officials. This made the latter more accessible and responsive to the needs of every level of the population.

As the example of al-Turjali's consultation with al-Batu'i proves, Taza had a strong legal culture, with legal experts who served the court. After al-Turjali issued his judgment against the father, removing his right to compel his daughter to marry, the father protested, and only at that point did al-Turjali consult the jurists of Fez, in addition to three jurists of Taza, whom he names, and others he does not name: "And the fuqaha of Taza, the *faqih* Abu Abdullah bin Atiyya with the mufti Abdullah bin Omar, and Abd al-Wahid bin Abi Zayd al-Wadi and others, also read that judgment, and they did not find an opening for annulment."[22] There was no need to consult the jurists of Fez in ordinary cases, but only in extraordinary cases that became especially contentious or politically sensitive.

Taza produced its own scholars, many of whom went on to achieve senior positions and prominence in Fez. The city was closely connected to the Marinid rulers and benefited from their patronage. Learning took place in the mosques and madrasas. A unique feature of learning in Taza was that in pleasant weather, classes were moved outside to parks and gardens, particularly in the spring.[23] The Great Mosque itself had an outdoor area that was larger than the indoor area. The sources do not mention women's scholarly activities or specific learned women, but it is likely that they participated in the intellectual environment of Taza to a limited extent, like the women of Fez.

A jurist could undergo complete formation in Taza, studying with local legal scholars without needing to study in Fez. He would receive a solid legal education that was not at all inferior, but that did not provide connections to the superstar scholars of the age or to political power. Biographers from larger cities, such as Fez and Meknes, mention how elite women from families of jurists also obtained high levels of education, a topic that will be discussed in chapter 4. A similar historical description of women's activities is not available for Taza, although it likely followed regional trends in the education of elite women. In the case of Taza, we know more about the experience of lower-status women who became involved in legal disputes and had access to local jurists to educate themselves about the technicalities of Islamic law that were needed to navigate their cases. The young woman from Taza is one such example, as she constructed a highly sophisticated case against her father that expressed a clear understanding of the intricacies of Maliki law.

Unlike the jurists from Fez who participated in the case of the young woman from Taza, biographers never honored Taza qadi Iysa al-Turjali with his own entry in their volumes, and little is known about his life outside his work as a judge and mufti in the city. His full name was Abu Mahdi Iysa Ibn Muhammad al-Turjali, and he was sometimes also referred to as Abu Asbagh.[24] He was appointed qadi of Taza by Marinid sultan Abu Said Uthman (r. 1310–31) sometime before 1324 and served in this position for at least sixteen years until he died in or after the year 1339, while the Taza case was still unresolved.[25]

Iysa's father, Abu Abdullah Muhammad bin Fatah al-Qaysi al-Turjali al-Tazi (d. 1321), also served as qadi of Taza, and his death was noted by al-Wansharisi in his *Wafayat*.[26] The attribute *al-Qaysi* indicates affiliation to the Qaysi Arab tribe, while the family name *Turjali* comes from the Arabic name for Trujillo, a city in western Spain that was under Muslim rule until 1232. Iysa's father Abu Abdullah Muhammad had strong connections to the local scholarly networks. He taught grammar and theology to Muhammad bin al-Baqal al-Tazi (d. 1325), a scholar who later achieved prominence in Fez.[27] He was also a contemporary of a scholar of Quranic recitations, Abu al-Hassan Ibn al-Bari (d. 1331). Ahmad al-Maqqari records an anecdote that shows the lively intellectual culture of Taza in which Muhammad al-Turjali participated. When al-Abili, teacher of Ibn Khaldun, passed through Taza, he was hosted by Ibn al-Bari along with Muhammad al-Turjali, and the traveler became tired as they talked into the night.[28] Al-Maqqari's story brings to life the vibrant local culture of Taza, where a guest would be welcomed and drawn into the world of local scholars.

Iysa al-Turjali's first teacher would have been his father or other close relatives, and his most prominent teacher was his father's friend Ibn al-Bari. He likely completed his intellectual formation in Taza before his appointment to the judgeship. An incident from early in Iysa al-Turjali's career as judge of Taza suggests how seriously he took his job. His teacher, Ibn al-Bari, served as a notary for the court, and al-Turjali felt it would be a conflict of interest for his teacher to appear before him as a witness or carry out other court functions. Ibn al-Bari was therefore transferred to Fez in 1324 to act as a secretary and scholar for Sultan Abu Said Uthman, where he achieved scholarly recognition.[29]

A document from approximately one hundred years after Iysa al-Turjali's death suggests that the Turjali family still produced distinguished scholars who were appointed by Marinid sultans to important local positions. Fasi mufti Abdullah al-Abdusi sent a question regarding one case to Abu Ali al-Hassan al-Turjali, the current qadi of Taza.[30] No biographical information exists for this judge, but his connection to Abdullah al-Abdusi tells us that he was active in the first half of the fifteenth century. While this information does not mean that the Turjali family held the position of qadi of Taza continuously for a century, it does show that the family was still recognized for its legal scholarship.[31]

Al-Wansharisi's *al-Mi'yar* shows that Iysa al-Turjali's status rose above that of most regional judges. Iysa al-Turjali participated in four distinct cases preserved in the *Mi'yar*, none of which were typical. All four cases involved women and were in areas such as marriage, divorce, and inheritance. Remarkably, in two of the cases al-Turjali actually assumed the role of mufti, not judge, as the questions had been submitted to him for advice and he issued a fatwa in response.[32] In a third case, in which he was acting as a judge, he is referred to as qadi but also as *faqih*, or legal scholar, a term of honor that not all judges received.[33] This is significant as it puts him at the level of a mufti, a position that required a higher level of legal knowledge than a qadi as well as recognition of this learning. Moreover, while people consulted local muftis in relation to ongoing cases or disputes, these consultations were often oral and would have been preserved in the sources only as part of a larger case, such as when the muftis of Taza were consulted in the case of the young woman who wanted to get married. Yet, not only were the two questions that earned al-Turjali the role of mufti written, but al-Wansharisi saw them as significant enough to include in *al-Mi'yar* alongside the most famous muftis of the Maliki school in North Africa.

The two cases of al-Turjali's that appear in the *Mi'yar* occurred as part of his work as qadi of Taza, and one of them was the case of the young woman from that city.[34] The cases share a number of similarities in that they were highly complex and contentious cases involving regional players, including the jurists of Fez and the sultan. In both cases, al-Turjali showed himself to be in complete control as he made law in Taza, and he demonstrated confidence in his legal reasoning. Both cases highlight the interaction and power dynamics between the legal community of Taza and the jurists of Fez who surrounded the sultan, although the case of the young woman from Taza shows this in more vivid detail.

In a case from *al-Mi'yar* analyzed by David S. Powers, a man claimed paternity and thus a share in the inheritance of his deceased father.[35] The case was complicated by the fact that the man's mother had been enslaved in the household of the deceased father, but was technically owned by the latter's daughter, meaning the father did not have the right to sexual access to this woman. Powers argues that in this case, which came before al-Turjali, "the qadi ignored the letter of the law in order to legitimize a *de facto* familial relationship."[36] In the end, with the advice of Ibrahim al-Yaznasni and Misbah, and with the sultan's refusal to intervene (in this case, Sultan Abu Said Uthman, father of the sultan who reigned during the case of the young woman from Taza), al-Turjali ruled in favor of establishing paternity and thus restoring the financial rights of the young man born to the woman enslaved in the deceased father's household. Powers notes that a takeaway from this case could be that al-Turjali was working on the side of justice, helping someone from a marginalized group obtain his legal rights in the face of more powerful interests.[37] This pattern certainly seems to hold true for the case of the young woman from Taza, in which al-Turjali also partially manipulated legal principles and procedures in an effort to protect the right of the young woman to marry the man of her choosing and free herself from a toxic and abusive family situation.

Iysa al-Turjali is mentioned in one other fatwa in the *Mi'yar* as part of a situation narrated by a mufti from Taza, Abu Abdullah Muhammad bin Abd al-Mu'min.[38] This mufti describes how a group of people who followed the doctrine of the Almohad leader Ibn Tumart (d. 1130) repented at the hand of Ibn Atiyya (the judge appointed after al-Turjali's death), thus avoiding the death penalty, after Sultan Abu al-Hassan ordered the investigation of the group.[39] The mufti describing the case, who was present at the time (although he must have been young as he belonged to the subsequent generation of scholars), specifies the time period in which this took place as "the time of al-Turjali," which pins it down to sometime before al-Turjali's death around 1339. That he used al-Turjali's tenure as Judge as a point of reference to locate the events in time highlights al-Turjali's significance in the local legal scene.[40]

Law, Society, and Power

The case of the young woman from Taza offers a revealing study not only of how women engaged with the legal system in Marinid Morocco, but also of how the system itself functioned in conjunction with different elements of society. It specifically makes visible the role of the sultan in overseeing the functioning of the legal system and the relationship between the sultan and the jurists, and between the jurists of Fez and the jurists of Taza.

At this stage of the dynasty, the role of the Marinid sultan was to oversee the legal system with a close eye but a light hand. Ultimately, however, he was in complete control and delegated his authority through his appointments of judges and other religious and legal officials.[41] The sultan appointed judges, heard petitions, sought advice from a group of legal experts, and ordered additional investigations, such as in the case of the group that followed Ibn Tumart that Ibn Atiyya investigated. Sultan Abu al-Hassan was himself well educated and knowledgeable about legal matters. His official court historian, Ibn Marzuq, describes an atmosphere in which issues were raised and debated in the court. The sultan solicited opinions from the members of his council and tried to reconcile differing points of view. Ibn Marzuq notes that he was "present on some occasions in which differences of opinions were produced among the people, and the debate continued until a solution was reached."[42]

Ibn Marzuq also mentions a tense meeting between Sultan Abu al-Hassan and the leading jurists of Fez, many of whom issued opinions in the case of the young woman from Taza, in which they argued openly with the sultan. The meeting ended in disagreement, with the sultan furious, but the following day the sultan accepted the apologies of the jurists and peace was restored to the court.[43] This incident illustrates the dynamics of the court and the openness with which issues could be discussed.[44] Although the sultan had the ultimate authority, he did not necessarily impose his opinion on the jurists.

Ibn Battuta provides a description of the court of Sultan Abu Inan Faris, the son and successor of Abu al-Hassan, who took over from his father a few years after the dispute from Taza. In Ibn Battuta's travel narrative known as the *Rihla*, commissioned in 1356 by Abu Inan,[45] he describes the daily activities of the Marinid court in Fez, including the process by which subjects could bring complaints to the sultan:

> His justice is more renowned than can be recorded in a book. An instance is that he has sessions to hear complaints from his subjects; he devotes Fridays to the poor, dividing the day between men and women, giving women priority because of their weakness. Their petitions are read from after the Friday prayer until the afternoon prayer. Each one whose turn has come is summoned by name. She stands in his precious presence and he speaks to her without an intermediary. If she has been the victim of oppression, it is quickly rectified; if she requests a favour, relief is at hand. When the afternoon prayer has been prayed, the men's

> petitions are read and are dealt with in the same way. The jurists and qadis are present at the audience and decisions connected with the religious law are referred to them. I have not seen any other king act so impeccably and display such justice.[46]

Ibn Battuta also describes other daily meetings that the sultan held with the jurists and scholars to discuss religious knowledge and he portrays the sultan as on an equal intellectual level to his jurists.[47] Ibn Battuta's scribe, Ibn Juzayy, writes about the sultan that "if a difficulty arises in any branch of knowledge in his noble assembly, he clarifies its obscurity, discusses its subtleties, elucidates its enigmas, and enables the scholars in the assembly to comprehend abstruse points which had eluded them."[48] Despite the bias inherent in a work commissioned by the sultan, these passages nevertheless highlight the high level of the sultans' learning at this stage in the Marinid dynasty, including their familiarity with religious and legal knowledge. This makes it easier to understand why Sultan Abu al-Hassan would have the legitimacy (beyond his obvious political power) to make his own decision about how to handle the case from Taza. The sultan, with his wider frame of reference, must have seen something in the case that the Fasi jurists did not. His role was to look out for the greater good of society and thus he proceeded delicately in the case.

The case of the young woman from Taza quickly reached the sultan's council, as al-Turjali sent a summary to al-Yaznasni for review after the father protested his ruling. Al-Yaznasni assessed the case in the sultan's council along with other jurists while the sultan was present. At that time, the jurists saw no issue. Yet, when some time had passed, the father again sought to get the ruling overturned and sent a petition to the sultan. One narrative says that the sultan issued a decree ordering his council of scholars to investigate the situation from a legal (sharia) perspective.[49] At that point, the sultan also summoned al-Turjali and the legal scholars involved in the case. In this instance, al-Turjali was advocating on behalf of his own ruling (and the young woman), and the young woman herself never appeared before the sultan. Al-Turjali does not describe what happened in his meeting with Sultan Abu al-Hassan, but presumably the sultan heard al-Turjali's side of the story and chose to proceed cautiously, instead of ordering the verdict to be overturned like the jurists of his council recommended. And, as with al-Turjali, the sultan did not pressure the second judge, Ibn al-Atiyya, to make a particular ruling in the case.

As these actions show, Sultan Abu al-Hassan followed the case of the young woman from Taza at every step. He heard petitions involving the case and provided a forum for its discussion; he asked the jurists of his council to review the case; he summoned the judge and other legal parties involved to hear their account; and he appointed Ibn Atiyya first to look into the case and then as judge of Taza when al-Turjali died. The sultan provided an accessible venue for appeals that allowed people to bring their grievances, including against legal officials appointed by the sultan himself (or in the case of al-Turjali, appointed by his father, the previous sultan). Ibn Battuta mentions that in the case of Sultan Abu al-Hassan's son, Sultan Abu Inan, this forum for appeals was also open to women, so presumably Abu al-Hassan's court welcomed grievances from women. The sultan consulted his council of jurists or asked them to look into particular claims. Despite his close oversight and his actions to ensure that cases moved smoothly, he chose not to exercise his power to directly intervene and overturn a judge's ruling. He certainly possessed this power, as each mufti reminded him in urgent tones, but he nevertheless let the case play out and let the jurists perform the roles they had been appointed to, either as advisory muftis or as judges.

Superficially, the relationship between the jurists of Taza and Fez was straightforward. The jurists of Fez, and particularly those who made up the sultan's council, were acknowledged as legal experts and their advice was sought in cases throughout the region. On these occasions, they always played a strictly advisory role—a judge in a case would typically rule according to their opinion, or if he received conflicting viewpoints, he could choose which one to rely on to implement his decision. Less common was the kind of pressure that Ibrahim al-Yaznasni put on the new Taza judge, Ibn Atiyya, when he wrote him a letter urging him to rule in the case of the young woman.[50] In general, muftis had a more sophisticated understanding of law than judges and they served an important role advising on complex cases.

As described earlier, a similar system was in place at the local level, with muftis from Taza advising the judge on his cases. Local muftis were knowledgeable and respected, but at times an opinion from a more prominent jurist whose opinion carried additional weight was required, in which case the muftis of Fez were consulted. Al-Turjali consulted the Fasi jurists when Ibrahim al-Anbaki challenged his ruling the first time by going directly to the sultan, and the second time presented his complete version of events and legal reasoning after the father again renewed his objections to the ruling. In most cases, a judge would request an opinion from a mufti before making his ruling (as al-Turjali did with Taza mufti al-Batu'i). By the time the jurists of Fez became involved, however, al-Turjali was mainly seeking confirmation of the ruling he had already made. He made it clear that he was not willing to overturn his ruling, despite the unanimous opinions from the Fasi jurists urging him to do so. His question was not really even about the soundness of his ruling; after summarizing the case, he ends by asking if the father should be punished for all the lies he has told in relation to it.[51] Al-Turjali makes an interesting legal move to deflect any anticipated pressure by claiming that he is only a *muqallid* (i.e., that he has only attained a level of legal understanding that allows him to follow the opinion of another jurist) and is thus unable to carry out his own *ijtihad*, or independent legal reasoning. Citing the opinion of Abu Walid Ibn Rushd the Elder (d. 1126) in his *Bayan*, al-Turjali states that in matters of the Maliki school where there existed multiple opinions and he selected one, and because he is only able to do *taqlid*, "[the opinion] is not overruled to follow the opinion (*taqlid*) of someone else, and he should not revert back from one *taqlid* to another *taqlid*."[52] What seems to be a self-deprecating comment about his legal knowledge is actually a strategic move to argue that his ruling should not be overturned. He is clearly very knowledgeable about Islamic jurisprudence and seems to be making this argument from a place of confidence arising from his mastery of the situation. Judges relied on differences of opinion in the Maliki school in order to administer justice in their courts, but their decisions were based on the evidence presented to them, in addition to their personal knowledge of the litigants and their situations. A judge who saw a young woman suffering from abuse at the hands of her father and provided a place of refuge for her would have had a different perspective on the situation than a jurist who was further removed. The judge, on the other hand, would be able to make use of the ambiguities in the doctrine to secure a favorable outcome for the daughter. The case shows that the regional jurists deferred to, and had respect for, the jurists of Fez, but certainly did not feel a sense of inferiority, and regardless, the boundaries were clear: law was implemented by judges at a local level, and even the most brilliant legal minds of Fez could not overturn their rulings.

The stakes were also different for the regional judges and the Fasi muftis. Al-Turjali took a personal interest in safeguarding the young woman from Taza and protecting her marriage. Ibn Atiyya, the second judge appointed after the death of al-Turjali, was also from Taza and had been involved in the case almost from the beginning, when al-Turjali consulted him and other local muftis after the father challenged the ruling. Both judges stood firm against pressure from the Fasi jurists and because the sultan did not order them to rule in a particular way, they refused to overturn the ruling and continued to protect the interests of the young woman. Al-Turjali in particular withstood sustained personal and professional attacks because of his ruling, which would deal a blow to his reputation, and he died in the midst of this pressure. In the end, it was the local process of lawmaking that mattered: the personal, community-engaged verdict, and the upholding of that verdict that protected a vulnerable member of the community.

Conclusion

The case of the young woman from Taza was highly contentious and drew in the leading jurists of the area in addition to demanding the attention of the sultan. While I have described the situation as the story of a young woman and the risky actions she took to marry the man of her choosing, it was not this aspect of the story that engaged the attention of the jurists of Fez. Rather, from the perspective of these jurists, it seemed like an obvious example of judicial misconduct and an abuse of power on the part of the judge in removing the father's authority over his daughter, and this is what prompted their angry responses. The legal significance of this case lay in the conflict between a local judge and the legal advisors attached to the sultan's court, and this heated debate is the reason the case was preserved by al-Wansharisi in *al-Mi'yar.* What was at stake was a father's near-unshakable right to control his virgin daughter's marriage, a gendered right of male authority in the family that was strongly supported by legal doctrine. From the sultan's perspective, the most pressing concern was not protecting a father's authority over his daughter, or regulating a young woman's sexuality; rather, his comprehensive perspective encompassed competing factors on which social, legal, and political stability depended.

For the historian, an additional benefit of these documents is that they show how the different components of the legal system worked together and how ordinary people interacted with that system. Through this dispute we can see the power struggles at a community and regional level, and the complicated nature of legal authority. In this case, the local judge disregarded the exhortations of the muftis, who had close connections to the Marinid sultan, and a legal ruling that prioritized the needs of a young couple remained in place, despite the legal battle that ensued. However, al-Wansharisi preserved the muftis' numerous arguments against the judge's actions as a cautionary tale for later generations.

The case of the contentious marriage from Taza provides a window into the relationship between law and society. When his neighbors were unable to pressure Ibrahim al-Anbaki into marrying his daughter to Ibn al-Turjuman, the daughter ran away to the local judge's house, looking to al-Turjali to shelter her and perhaps advocate on her behalf. Two years later, after no sign of resolution, the daughter once again sought out al-Turjali, armed with multiple allegations that could help her escape from her father's control. This time, the judge intervened and forced her father to accept her marriage.

This incident also illustrates the important role of the judge in the lives of ordinary people. While the muftis who gave opinions here were generally more influential than the judges, and more closely connected to political power, if a case entered a judge's court the final ruling was in his hands. This appears to be an important point in cases involving women, as a judge would ultimately decide based on the information he received from his investigation and his personal knowledge of the parties involved, which could allow for a certain amount of flexibility in his rulings. In this case, these complex dynamics worked in favor of the daughter, as the local judge familiar with her circumstances served as her advocate. We also know that women had direct access to the sultan, as Ibn Battuta described how the current sultan's son and successor, Abu Inan Faris, set aside a part of every Friday to hear petitions from poor women.[53] If things had not gone in her favor, perhaps the daughter from Taza could have presented her own case to the sultan in Fez.

At this point, however, the daughter faded out of the picture, secure in her new marriage as long as the judge's ruling was not overturned. The lens of the story then widened, capturing a picture of legal interactions between the center and the periphery. Ibrahim al-Anbaki, an ordinary man, was able to appeal a perceived injustice at the local level by petitioning the sultan and his leading jurists directly. The muftis of Fez saw in the judge's removal of the father's authority over his daughter a violation of his position that threatened the integrity of the legal system. Nevertheless, the sultan maintained a hands-off approach to the case and engaged with it only to the extent necessary to preserve harmony among the jurists. He instructed his scholars to examine the allegations and later appointed a new judge with a mandate to revisit it; however, he refused to pressure the parties into a specific solution. And thus, the ruling of a relatively unimportant provincial judge was kept in place, despite fierce protest from some of the most powerful and respected muftis of the time. This demonstrates the confidence the Marinid sultan had in his own authority to disregard the alarm of the jurists at the perceived destabilization of a gendered right enshrined in Maliki law. The dynasty's legitimacy was not in jeopardy and the sultan remained in firm control of the judiciary and the implementation of Maliki law. The orthodoxy represented by the Marinids was likewise not destabilized; what was destabilized was only the power of one man over his daughter. The gender anxiety of the Fez jurists remained compartmentalized as the competing points in this constellation of power, the sultan and the jurists of Taza, held firm.[54] Ahmed Khaneboubi argues that even though there is a perceived division of power between the sultan's political might and the jurists' religious authority, in reality, the sultan retained absolute dominance.[55]

This exploration of the world of the jurists who interpreted the law in Marinid Morocco sets the stage for the following chapters, where the concerns and disputes of ordinary women are brought into focus through their engagement with the law. While legal principles, understood as derived from divine sources, did not change, the ways in which the law was interpreted and applied evolved to reflect the concerns and needs of the time and place. The comprehensive legal system in Marinid Morocco was supported by political patronage and served as a source of the dynasty's legitimacy and stability. The appreciation of legal knowledge and its diffusion among laypeople can be seen in the skilled legal maneuvering of people in their daily disputes. The disagreements examined here, which brought people into contact with the legal system, often challenged male authority and at times propelled the legal system into a state of crisis, requiring the intervention of political powers. While the cases that drew the attention of the ruler and the anger of the jurists involved women and their relationships with men, the point of crisis was not anxiety surrounding women's sexuality; rather, it was challenges to male authority from women or even the law itself that precipitated the threat of social and legal breakdown. The Marinid rulers worked to ensure legal stability, which depended on social harmony, and this brought women's disputes with the men in their lives to the forefront of the legal agenda.

The legal records analyzed here show the extent to which law permeated society during this period. The legal system affected interpersonal relationships and business relationships, creating a web that held people together. Mechanisms outside of the formal justice system provided a way for communities to resolve disputes, influenced by both local customs and legal norms, and made the law easily accessible to all levels of society, including women. The following chapters examine the relationship of ordinary people to the legal system, sometimes, but not always, mediated by the muftis discussed here, and the relationships (also structured by legal principles) between society and rulers.

4

Women, Men, and Legal Knowledge

Taza Anecdote

A few years before 1339, the young woman from Taza presented the judge with a seemingly airtight case for removing her father's marital guardianship over her and allowing her to marry her neighbor, Ibn al-Turjuman. The judge, Iysa al-Turjali, subsequently presented this case to the jurists of Fez, framed in Islamic legal doctrine. Maliki law allowed a father to compel his virgin daughter into marriage, even if she had reached the age of majority. The young woman from Taza constructed her case in a way that addressed the only two loopholes in Maliki law that would allow her to circumvent her father's authority. First, she stated that her father had refused to allow her to marry "more than four suitors," which Maliki school eponym Malik ibn Anas said was a reason to allow a judge to control her marriage, after giving the father one more chance to arrange the match.[1] And second, she confessed to fornication, which meant she was no longer a virgin and therefore not subject to her father's ability to force her marriage (*ijbar*).[2] To her case, she added allegations of abuse against her father, which were less legally relevant but perhaps increased sympathy at the local level. Indeed, al-Turjali centered these allegations in his description of the case and made a significant effort to gather witnesses to verify the claims of abuse.

How had an uneducated young woman with no legal training acquired enough sophisticated knowledge of the technical aspects of Maliki law to know that these two claims would allow her to circumvent her father's seemingly absolute authority and achieve her goal of marrying the man of her choosing? This and other cases provide evidence of the sheer ordinariness of women's legal knowledge, and that of laypeople more broadly. Women obtained information through their personal networks and through consultations with local legal scholars, and perhaps even through consultation with female legal scholars in their area.

Introduction

This chapter describes knowledge formation in premodern Morocco at both informal and formal levels, within institutions and outside of them. It shows how both women and men acquired knowledge in similar contexts early in life and later followed different paths with different career opportunities. Men with elite legal educations went on to interpret and implement the law, while women with similar levels of education operated in the intellectual environment of their time but without official positions or institutional support. These women left few written traces, aside from mentions as teachers of prominent men. It was the cases brought by ordinary women, self-taught in legal matters and competent in navigating the complexities of Islamic law, that drove and helped shape the explanation and application of law in Marinid Morocco. Along with the male jurists, these women participated in defining content and boundaries, and in making interpretive decisions, leading to the coproduction of law.[3]

The Marinid interest and investment in education, particularly legal education, was intended to bolster the dynasty's new educational and legal institutions. At the same time, it created an intellectual environment in which men of the empire participated, including the sultans themselves, many of whom were noted for their interest in learning. This educational investment also impacted the lives of elite women due to the nature of informal learning and the tradition of learning within the family in the premodern Islamic world. This process is visible at other times and in other places in the medieval Middle East, as Asma Sayeed notes in the case of twelfth-century Baghdad, where the Seljuk patronage of scholars and institutions also elevated women's learning.[4]

The worlds of learning and scholarship that existed for women in the premodern Islamic West are found at the edges of history. Fragmented references to learned women appear in a wide range of sources, such as autobiographical texts, biographical dictionaries, travel literature, Sufi writings, political chronicles, and city histories. Some of these sources were written by family members of female scholars, and in addition to the insight they provide into the lives of the women, they also point to their respected status.

The story of education in the premodern Islamic West is a story of the interplay between formal and informal education, within and outside of institutional structures. While men benefited from all aspects of this system and could pursue their education through multiple means, women took advantage of informal routes and opportunities at the margins of institutional structures. The barriers to women's education included gender norms that discouraged the mixing of men and women who weren't related. These restrictions were tied to life stages; they excluded children and were relaxed for mature women. Biographies of women from the central Middle East, and to a lesser extent the Maghrib, show study as consisting of children accompanying fathers to classes and intensified study in old age, with large gaps in the intervening years, which were presumably occupied by marriage and raising children alongside continued study.[5] While the previous chapter focused on the jurists, this chapter considers education more broadly, and pays particular attention to the education of women.

There are few studies that focus on women in Morocco in the premodern period, or the Marinid period in particular. Latifa Elbouhsini tackles this gap head-on, exploring the roles and changing status of women in the Almoravid, Almohad, and Marinid periods.[6] Hayat Kara's social history of women in the premodern Mediterranean contains content on Morocco, some of which relates to the Marinid period, and includes a discussion of women's access to knowledge.[7] Abdelhadi Tazi's *al-Mar'a fi Tarikh al-Gharb al-Islami* is a compilation of biographical entries for prominent women in North African history and a good starting point for historians searching for primary sources on medieval women's lives and activities.[8] Muhammad Latif's recent book on the family in medieval Morocco details the formation of families and the different stressors they faced.[9] Aside from Elbouhsini's study, the most promising efforts in this area have been made by Mohammed Yassir al-Hilali, who in one article sets out a methodology for examining a diverse range of historical sources from this period that mention women, and in another discusses primary sources that can be utilized to investigate women's history in the medieval period, in addition to compiling a comprehensive bibliography of secondary sources on the topic.[10]

Early Education: The Family and Quranic Schools (*Kuttabs*)

For children from learned families, education began in the home. Both boys and girls studied with their relatives and received a foundation in the Islamic sciences, primarily Quran and hadith. Girls were taught by their fathers, grandfathers, and other relatives and learned alongside their brothers, and boys also learned from their mothers and grandmothers.[11] Some of the most prominent scholars from Marinid Morocco list women as their teachers, including Ibn Rushayd (d. 1321),[12] Ibn Marzuq (d. 1379),[13] Shaykh Ahmad Zarruq (d. 1493),[14] and Ibn Ghazi (d. 1513).[15] Significantly, female teachers listed in the biographies of Maghribi scholars outside of their childhood are largely located in the Mashriq, pointing to the smaller footprint of female teachers in the Maghrib. Other male scholars, such as Abu al-Qasim al-Abdusi (d. 1433) and Abdullah al-Abdusi (d. 1445), are documented as having taught women.

In Sufi shaykh Ahmad Zarruq's *Kunnash,* which comes the closest to autobiographical writing from this period, Zarruq described his early education and the central role that his grandmother, Umm al-Banin (date of death unknown), played in his upbringing. Zarruq was orphaned at a young age and his grandmother was his earliest teacher, instructing him in the basics of Islamic belief and practice.[16] When he was five, she sent him to a Quranic school to continue his education.[17] Zarruq's tribal affiliation of al-Burnusi points to family origins near Taza, although Zarruq was born and raised in Fez.[18] Legal scholar, mathematician, and historian Muhammad Ibn Ghazi, writing in his semi-autobiographical *al-Rawd al-Hatun,* described his mother, scholar Rahma bint al-Janan, as his earliest teacher.[19] She had memorized many traditions from important hadith collections and Ibn Ghazi learned them from her. She also taught him about the Quran through interpretations of its stories.[20] Zarruq and Ibn Ghazi are among the most important sources of information about contemporary women who were trained in Islamic law, the *faqihat.* Their intimate biographical and autobiographical works include information about their own formation as scholars, revealing a world of learning within the family in which women played a key role.

Boys and girls began their formal studies at a young age by memorizing the Quran at dedicated Quranic schools (*kuttab*s) and learning different recitations, in addition to studying the rules of writing the Quran (*rasm al-Qur'an*).[21] This learning occurred throughout neighborhoods in small shops dedicated to this purpose, or in smaller neighborhood mosques in the case of Taza.[22] *Kuttab*s were accessible to children from different economic backgrounds. Leo Africanus writes that in sixteenth-century Fez there were almost two hundred Quranic schools. He described their method of memorization:

> Of schools in Fez for the instruction of children, there are almost 200, every one of which is like a great hall. The schoolmasters teach their children to write and read not out of a book, but out of a certain great tablet. Every day they expound one sentence of the Quran, and having read through they begin it again, repeating it so often until they have most firmly committed it to memory, which they do well in the space of seven years. Then they read unto their students some parts of orthography, although both this and the other parts of grammar are far more precisely taught in the colleges [i.e., madrasas] than in these minor schools . . . None of them pays any tuition for his school, for all their schools were built many years ago, and were freely bestowed for the training of youth.[23]

Muhammad al-Manouni notes that these schools differed from their counterparts outside of Morocco, which taught other subjects alongside Quranic memorization, whereas the Moroccan schools focused more specifically on Quranic memorization and similar topics.[24] In medieval Cairo, primary schools for memorizing the Quran and the basic study of Arabic (or *maktab*s) were often attached to other institutions and were only open to boys.[25] After this initial education in Quranic memorization, either in *kuttab*s or in the home, young men could go on to study at several institutions of higher learning, such as mosques and study circles, to which women also had access, albeit in a more limited way. The newest Marinid development in formal education, the madrasa, was not an option for women, because it was primarily a space for training jurists and other officials intended to serve the state, employment opportunities that excluded women.

Innovations in Education: The Madrasa

Madrasas were both a powerful visual symbol and a key religious institution of the Marinid dynasty. Training jurists in the Maliki tradition increased the legitimacy of rulers who had risen to power with no ready ideological platform and helped ensure the dominance of the Maliki school of law. The buildings themselves were extravagant architectural marvels demonstrating the power of the regime and "may thus be understood as architectural tableaux on which ornate configurations of knowledge and power are inscribed."[26]

The madrasa originated in the Islamic East (Mashriq) in the tenth century as an educational institution focused on producing scholars skilled in the interpretation of Islamic law.[27] Michael Chamberlain argues that earlier studies have overstated the organized nature of learning and the curriculum in the madrasa and that the madrasa remained just one venue for knowledge (and perhaps more importantly, board and a stipend) in medieval Damascus.[28] Madrasas could be founded by rulers but also by elite people close to the ruler, including women.[29] *Consorts of the Caliphs,* a compilation of biographies of concubines and other women attached to the Abbasid Caliphate in Baghdad, mentions two women who endowed madrasas, including a Hanafi madrasa in Isfahan and a Hanbali madrasa in Baghdad.[30] George Makdisi notes that Maliki rules for endowing a madrasa did not allow the endower to administer the institution or name a family member as Administrator, which led to the foundation of fewer Maliki madrasas in the Islamic East.[31] In Mamluk Cairo, sultans founded the largest and most prestigious madrasas, but there were many others of varying sizes founded by elites.[32] The founder usually served as Administrator, followed by his or her descendants who protected assets and income for family members.[33] This differs greatly from the situation in North Africa, where a Maliki madrasa would typically only be founded by a ruler.[34] Nearly all madrasas founded in the Marinid period were endowed by Marinid sultans, leading to a closer association with the state.

The first madrasa in North Africa was built by the Hafsids in Tripoli in 1260–61.[35] Marinid sultan Abu Yusuf (r. 1258–86) began construction of the first madrasa in Fez in 1276–77, and subsequent sultans built madrasas throughout their domain, including in Meknes, Taza, Marrakesh, Salé, and Chellah in Rabat. They ensured Fez's primacy as a center for the formation of legal officials by constructing nine madrasas there.[36] These madrasas had living quarters attached and drew students from the far rural regions of the territory. The appearance of this new institution can be explained in part by a shift in the Maghrib's orientation toward the Islamic East after the fall of al-Andalus, along with a desire to consolidate the move away from Almohad doctrine to the Maliki school.[37] Ibn Marzuq, an eyewitness to this process, noted that the sultans created charitable endowments (a *habs* or *waqf*) to maintain the madrasas and pay staff, as well as donate books to the libraries.[38] The Marinid chroniclers stressed the piety of the rulers and their desire to promote learning as the driving force behind these institutions. Maya Shatzmiller argues that this new institution was a way for the Marinid rulers to ensure the loyalty of the religious elite while simultaneously reducing their autonomy.[39] The sultans controlled the appointment of key religious officials and co-opted others by awarding them salaries.[40] Although the Marinids no doubt worked to implement a system that gave them further control over the education and activities of jurists, ample evidence suggests that numerous sultans placed a high value on learning and scholarship, with the result that this new educational initiative contributed to a culture of learning in Fez and, as Laroui points out, produced a generation of historians who documented this period.[41]

Learning in Mosques and Study Circles

Scholars also taught at mosques, a practice that formed the core of advanced learning before the establishment of madrasas and continued alongside them. The teacher–student relationship was more significant for a student's career than education in any institutional setting.[42] Teaching in mosques included providing preaching and guidance to the public, in addition to instruction on specialized topics such as law.[43] These lectures or study circles continued the parallel personalized system of learning that had defined education from the early Islamic period, as they did in the

Islamic East.[44] Like their counterparts in the central Middle East, Moroccan women were able to take advantage of these educational opportunities outside of formal institutions.

The Marinid sultans also began the practice of appointing chairs to teach in mosques, making the influential teachers government employees.[45] Each Chair was designated to teach in a specific area, or even to teach a specific book, and most of these positions were related to the teaching of jurisprudence.[46] The three most important Maliki legal texts studied and taught in Marinid Fez were *al-Mudawwana al-Kubra* by Sahnun bin Said (d. 854); the *Risala* of Ibn Abi Zayd al-Qayrawani (d. 996), an abridgment of Maliki fiqh; and the *Tahdhib al-Baradhi'i*, an abridgment of the *Mudawwana,* by Abu Said al-Baradhi'i (d. eleventh century), Ibn Abi Zayd's student.[47] An example of this type of learning from the life of one of the muftis discussed here is the chair held by Abu al-Hassan al-Sughayyir at the al-Azda mosque in Fez for teaching *Tahdhib al-Baradhi'i.*[48] Biographies show the rising influence toward the end of this period of the *Mukhtasar* (abridgment) by Khalil Ibn Ishaq al-Jundi (d. 1365), a work that described the dominant Maliki position on each issue, and which would replace the *Mudawwana* as the most important legal text in the Islamic West.[49] Mohammad Fadel argues that the rise of the genre of legal abridgments served as a means to standardize judicial decisions and reduce inconsistencies in legal implementation.[50] The legal disputes surrounding divorce examined in chapter 6, however, show that even at the time the *Mi'yar* was compiled, jurists continued to exercise discretion in their lawmaking and did not necessarily follow the opinions favored in Khalil's *Mukhtasar.* Makdisi argues that law and legal studies were central to defining orthodoxy.[51] The evolution of favored texts shows how orthodoxy itself was reshaped and reinterpreted over generations of scholarship and practice.

A fascinating marginal note in one of the manuscripts of Ibn Ghazi's *Fihris*, which the editor believes was added by the author himself, illustrates the connections between the scholars discussed in this chapter and to previous generations of Maliki jurists.[52] Ibn Ghazi recorded a chain of transmission of the *Mudawwana* that connected him across six centuries to the *Mudawwana's* author, Sahnun. This chain included many of the great jurists of Fez whose lives are discussed here, starting with Abu al-Fadl

Chart 4.1
Chain of Transmission of Sahnun's *Mudawwana* by Marinid Jurists[53]

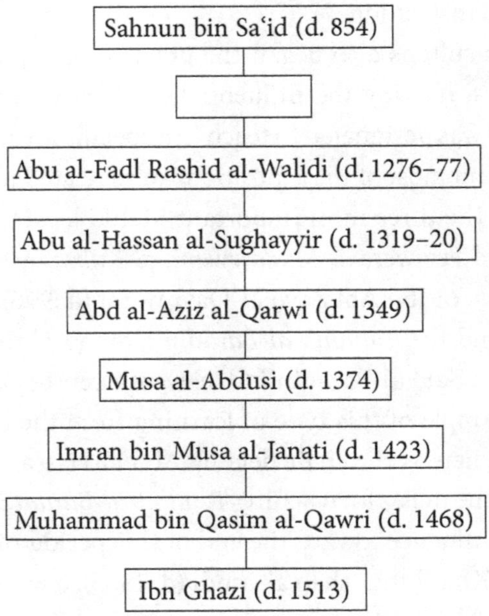

Rashid (d. 1276–77), who taught the *Mudawwana* to Abu al-Hassan al-Sughayyir, who passed it on to his student Abd al-Aziz al-Qarwi (d. 1349), who taught it to his student Musa al-Abdusi. His student Imran al-Janati then compiled these teachings in a multivolume work and passed them on to his student Muhammad al-Qawri (d. 1468), Ibn Ghazi's teacher.[54]

This exemplary chain of transmission shows how knowledge was transmitted from teacher to student, for the most part orally, connecting generations of jurists. This chain confirms the integrity of the transference and enhances the status of students who could trace their knowledge back to great scholars of the past.

Scholars from this period also traveled in search of knowledge, a practice that had a long tradition in Islamic history. They moved easily between the cities of the Maghrib, and between the Maghrib and al-Andalus. In the central Middle East, the pilgrimage to Mecca was also combined with study, and some scholars from the Maghrib spent time in the Arabian Peninsula and Egypt and later returned to their homelands with impressive credentials, while others settled in the Mashriq and continued to study and teach there. Travelers in this period popularized the travelogue (*rihla*), a new literary genre, in which they recounted their journeys and the people and places they encountered. The most famous and widely traveled writer was Ibn Battuta (d. 1369), who recounted his recollections of his travels to Ibn Juzayy (d. 1340), at the request of the Marinid sultan, Abu Inan.[55] Among the Marinid jurists whose fatwas form the basis of this study, however, few actually traveled to the Islamic East for pilgrimage or study. Nonetheless, books and ideas circulated widely throughout the Islamic world and Maliki texts were studied and taught throughout the regions where the school was followed, including in North Africa and al-Andalus, as well as in Egypt, where the Maliki tradition existed alongside the other three schools of Islamic law.

Although travel was less common for women, travel narratives mention women in the caravans that made their way across North Africa toward Egypt, and beyond to Mecca, including as family members of the scholars themselves. Some Marinid royal women also made the pilgrimage to Mecca. One female scholar who will be discussed below, Sara al-Halabiyya, whose name designates her place of origin in Aleppo, Syria, seemed to travel relatively independently, arriving in Hafsid Tunis and later traveling to Granada, Fez, and Sabta.

Women's Learning in the Islamic World

Sources from across the Islamic world show patterns of educational opportunities available to women, especially those raised in elite scholarly families. A core value of Islam encouraged all Muslims to seek knowledge and this included women as well as men, although the sources were somewhat ambiguous on the topic of women's learning.[56] Jonathan Berkey's study of women in Cairo under the Mamluks, a dynasty that ruled at the same time as the Marinids, shows that while women did not participate in institutionalized education as students or teachers, they endowed and managed institutions, and studied and taught outside of institutional contexts.[57]

Women's education often began in the home with family members. Beyond that, they participated in learning in mosques and private homes, in addition to study circles led by other women. They also received instruction in other contexts, such as Sufi lodges, and both royal women and slave women learned in palaces. Educated women distinguished themselves as transmitters and teachers of hadith, as Quran reciters, and as Sufi mystics. Fewer women were recognized in the area of Islamic legal interpretation, which was a traditionally male domain.

The available sources describe a much more robust world of women's learning for the Islamic East than sources for the Maghrib. The earliest women to be considered knowledgeable in the Islamic tradition were the women closest to the Prophet Muhammad, such as his wives. Women like his wife Aisha bint Abi Bakr (d. 678) were immersed in the sources of early jurisprudence as they lived and directly experienced the Quran and the Prophet's sunna. Aisha in particular was recognized for her discernment in legal matters, or *fiqh*,[58] while women in later generations distinguished themselves in the field of hadith transmission. Sayeed shows how women's participation in this field changed over time, with periods of significant contribution followed by periods of near absence from the discipline. She argues that these fluctuations in women's engagement with this area of scholarship was related to shifts in the larger field of hadith transmission, as well as changing political, institutional, and social contexts.[59]

Biographical dictionaries from the central Middle East provided evidence for women's learning on a large scale. Ruth Roded's analysis of these works estimates that women represented anywhere from less than one percent to twenty-three percent of the total number of entries in each work.[60] Some authors interspersed women among the entries, while others included a section for women or even constructed an entire volume devoted to women.[61] Roded gives an overview of the rich biographical material concerning women who knew the Prophet or came soon after him and shows how the availability of biographical information declined in the centuries after this.[62] Women thrived, particularly in the areas of communicating hadiths and Sufism, but were less well represented in the specialty of Islamic law, for reasons related to both gender and the more institutionalized nature of this field and its closer connections to the state.[63] In al-Andalus, women were often noted for their skill in poetry, as well as in religious sciences such as Quranic recitation and hadith studies, and in fewer cases, legal studies.[64]

A number of recent studies explore women's engagement with Islamic law, particularly in the central Middle East in the formative period of Islam.[65] Mona Hassan outlines the studies and career of Amrah bint Abd al-Rahman (d. 724) of Medina, a woman who was known for her legal knowledge, as well as her hadith transmission.[66] Amrah was able to build her knowledge and authority partly because of her family connections, and some of her legal interpretations were incorporated into the Islamic legal tradition.[67]

An additional venue for women's learning in Islamic societies was the palace of the ruler. Ibn al-Sai'i's text about women connected to the Abbasid palace mentions a number of them who gained prominence, particularly for their skills as poets.[68] Ibn al-Sai'i describes a world of highly educated enslaved women who were trained to entertain their owners and guests through poetry, singing, and playing music. Prized for their wit and intellect, these women's interactions with men were unconstrained by the many gender norms that applied only to free women.

Women in the Ottoman harem were broadly educated in skills ranging from music and singing to reading and the finer points of Islamic law, as well as more practical skills such as embroidery.[69] While all the women were initially enslaved, only a small number who were distinguished by both their beauty and intelligence became royal concubines.[70] Others were married to officials or served in administrative roles within the harem. In al-Andalus, enslaved women attached to the ruler's palace were also noted for their skill in poetry, while others served as scribes and secretaries for their owners.[71] Palaces also served as sites of education for princesses and other women connected to the sultan.[72]

Women and Higher Education

As Marinid patronage increased levels of education more broadly and supported a judicial elite, women participated in the informal and personalized venues of knowledge transmission, such as lectures by scholars in mosques or in homes. They also had access to networks of learned women who passed on their knowledge to other women. In his history of the Qarawiyyin Mosque, Abdelhadi Tazi mentions the women's study circles that met throughout Fez, referring to them as "*dar al-faqiha*" (the house of the *faqiha*).[73] Even in rural areas, there is evidence from the sixteenth century to the present day of opportunities for women to teach and engage in more advanced studies, as well as evidence of study sessions accessible to illiterate women through the conversion of religious texts into rhymed verse in local vernaculars.[74] The sources point to a rich social world of elite women and their participation in the vibrant intellectual culture of the medieval Islamic West. Of particular importance in the Marinid period was the documentation of women who reached a level of understanding that authorized them to interpret Islamic law, referred to in the sources as *faqiha* (pl. *faqihat*). This evidence mainly touches on women active in Fez and there is no mention of women's learning in the more limited sources that detail Taza's intellectual world, although we can assume women participated as they did in Fez. Documents establishing charitable foundations do prove that women from Taza financially supported institutions and scholars at the time, including by endowing teaching chairs specifically to teach the key Maliki works, such as Khalil's *Mukhtasar*.[75]

In Abdullah Gannun's (1908–89) early twentieth-century work *al-Nubugh al-Maghribi* (The Moroccan Genius), which celebrates the literary tradition of Morocco, a short section devoted to learned women in the Marinid period provides a tantalizing glimpse into women's education and serves as a map of their activities during this time. The few details about the lives of these women show their connections to each other and to more famous men, as well as the different areas of learning in which they excelled.

> We close this section with a gesture toward the participation of the Moroccan woman in building this imposing structure of scientific renaissance in this age, as they did in other ages, this efficient participation that, even though many historical sources neglect it, reveals itself from behind. To give an example in the field of religious sciences, Sayda Umm Hani bint Muhammad al-Abdusi, the righteous scholar and sister of the Imam and Hafidh Abdullah al-Abdusi. Shaykh Zarruq said in his *Kunnasha*: "She was a religious scholar [*faqiha*] possessing knowledge and piety, she lived until almost one hundred, and died in 860." Ibn Ghazi added: "She was the last of their religious scholars." And her sister Fatima was like her [in learning], and also Sayda Umm al-Banin the righteous

> *faqiha* who was the grandmother of Shaykh Zarruq, and Sayda Rahma bint al-Janan the mother of Ibn Ghazi, and the two Saydas Aisha and Amat Allah the daughters of the Hafidh Ibn Rushayd who received *ijaza*s [a certificate of competency] from scholars, and Sitt al-Arab bint Abd al-Muhaymin al-Hadrami who received an *ijaza* from Ibn Rushayd.[76]

In several paragraphs that follow, Gannun mentions other women known for poetry and literature, and science and medicine, and he includes a biographical entry for one of these female doctors among the biographies of male scholars.[77] I will include one of these women in my discussion of women renowned for their religious knowledge, Sara al-Halabiyya, as in addition to her poetry she awarded an *ijaza* to a fellow scholar.[78] The religious learning of the eight women noted by Gannun spanned the Marinid period, and one woman lived into the Wattasid era. Their lives intersected and overlapped with those of male scholars both within and outside of the family. Four of the women lived at the height of the Marinid period, when the case of the young woman from Taza took place.

Ibn Rushayd (d. 1321) was a prominent hadith scholar who served as a secretary at the court of Marinid sultan Abu Said Uthman (r. 1310–31) and who represents one link connecting the four women mentioned from the first half of the Marinid period.[79] Ibn Rushayd first served the Nasrid vizier Ibn al-Hakim (r. 1303–9) in Granada and moved to Fez after al-Hakim's assassination, where he worked for Marinid sultan Abu Said Uthman.[80] Al-Wansharisi included in *al-Mi'yar* one question Ibn Rushayd was asked regarding the permissibility of describing women's specific features in poetry (cheeks, breasts, figure, etc.). Ibn Rushayd answered by quoting earlier jurists who had said describing women in poetry was permissible.[81] Al-Wansharisi added his own confirmation of Ibn Rushayd's assessment but noted that what was permitted was a general description of women, and not a description of one particular woman.

Most of all, Ibn Rushayd's travel narrative shows that he worked hard to ensure that the women in his family received educational opportunities. As he recounted his travels throughout the Islamic world in private musings, mentioning the scholars he studied with as he traveled, he also noted the parallel intellectual journeys of his daughters and sisters.[82] He writes about how his daughters, Aisha and Amat Allah, received *ijaza*s from a number of scholars they encountered on their travels, and he also discusses the education of other women in his family, including his sister. Ibn Rushayd's hometown, Sabta, was known for its culture of learning, and was particularly distinguished in the areas of literature, linguistics, and jurisprudence.[83]

Ibn Rushayd's presence at the Marinid court shows a link between elite men and unrelated elite women that is rarely visible. For example, he engaged in a poetic exchange with Sara bint Ahmad bin Uthman al-Halabiyya (date of death unknown), who will later be referred to as Sara al-Halabiyya, one of the few women who was recognized for her scholarly achievements without any mention of her family background. A poet originally from Syria who lived in Fez in the thirteenth century, Sara maintained a poetic correspondence with other prominent contemporary poets, including Ibn Rushayd and at least one other woman.[84] Although mostly remembered for her poetry, Sara was also designated as "teacher" by her biographers, and perhaps she taught the women of the palace while she was in Fez. She also recognized a male colleague's scholarly achievement by awarding him an *ijaza* for studying with her.[85] Sara al-Halabiyya's poetry is preserved in a manuscript collection of romantic poetry and biographical entries, and is the only extant piece of writing by any woman mentioned in this study.[86] She traveled from Syria, spending time in the Hafsid court in Tunis, and later in the Nasrid court of Granada.[87] She then settled in Marinid Morocco, receiving patronage from sultans Abu Yusuf (r. 1258–86) and his son Abu Yaqub Yusuf (r. 1286–1307), staying at the court in Fez but also spending time in Sabta.[88] Teresa Garulo suggests that her advanced age when she arrived in Morocco could have made it easier for her to continue scholarly relationships with men of the court and beyond.[89]

Sitt al-Arab, another woman mentioned in Gannun's paragraph, was the daughter of Abd al-Muhaymin al-Hadrami (d. 1348), a celebrated scholar of hadith, language, and history and other areas, who taught Ibn Khaldun and Lisan al-Din Ibn al-Khatib (d. 1374).[90] Al-Hadrami was originally from Sabta and counted Ibn Rushayd among his teachers, but had also learned from a number of women.[91] He also worked for the Marinid court as Chief Secretary, in charge of the secretaries and the royal seal, working first for Sultan Abu Said at the same time as Ibn Rushayd, and then for Sultan Abu al-Hassan.[92] Abd al-Muhaymin was part of Sultan Abu al-Hassan's council at the time of the Taza case and accompanied the sultan on his trip to Tunis, where he died in 1348, a victim of the plague that swept through North Africa.[93] While in Fez, Sitt al-Arab must have had access to the court through her father and obtained an *ijaza* from Ibn Rushayd. Ibn Rushayd participated in court life at the same time that Abu al-Hassan al-Sughayyir was chief judge of Fez. Al-Sughayyir himself thought the women of his time went out too much and tried to ban them from the streets of Fez.[94] One possible scenario is that Sitt al-Arab's father secured an *ijaza* from Ibn Rushayd on her behalf, without the need for her to ever encounter him. Yet, this rigid view of gendered interactions may not reflect the court life of thirteenth-century Fez, where Ibn Rushayd in particular embraced women's learning. Alternatively, we can imagine that Sitt al-Arab perhaps joined other students and learned from Ibn Rushayd directly.

The other four women noted by Gannun for their religious and legal knowledge lived toward the end of the Marinid period, and one into the early Wattasid period. Two sisters noted as *faqihas*, Umm Hani al-Abdusi (d. 1456) and Fatima al-Abdusi (date of death unknown), exemplify patterns of learning within families and the intergenerational prominence of families known for their interpretation of Islamic law.[95] The sources reveal very little about their lives, studies, and activities. Umm Hani al-Abdusi was born sometime after 1356, just a few years after the events of the Taza case were overshadowed by the drowning of so many Marinid jurists, and Abu Inan assumed control of the Marinid state from his father, Sultan Abu al-Hassan. The Abdusis were based in Fez but were originally from Meknes and were known for their knowledge of hadith, *fiqh* (jurisprudence), and teaching.

Three generations of Abdusi men made their mark on the legal landscape of the age: Musa al-Abdusi (d. 1374), his sons Muhammad al-Abdusi (d. after 1388) and Abu al-Qasim (d. 1435), and his grandson Abdullah al-Abdusi (d. 1446), the most famous member of the Abdusi family.[96] Al-Wansharisi's *al-Mi'yar* preserves the Abdusi men's legal record through their fatwas. The family also distinguished itself by its openness to women's learning, and Abdullah is documented as teaching women in Fez, while women attended the lectures of Abu al-Qasim in Hafsid Tunis where he had established himself as a respected jurist. The sources recount Abu al-Qasim's unique teaching methodology, in which he taught through stories and sources that were accessible to people beyond other scholars.[97] Describing the popularity of his teachings, "thus he does in the Qasr Mosque and other places, and the people would race to the places before the early morning prayer (*al subh*), men and women crowding in, and outside of the mosque were more than were inside it, and his voice was loud and everyone could hear."[98] This shows the inclusivity of the mosque lectures, where people who were not scholars, including women, had access to these teachings. In Tunis, Abu al-Qasim al-Abdusi was a contemporary of Abu al-Qasim al-Burzuli (d. 1438), the author of a fatwa collection that served as inspiration for al-Wansharisi's *Mi'yar*, and al-Wansharisi relied on this work as a source of opinions from areas to the east of Fez.[99] Additionally, the Abdusi women were known for their high level of knowledge, particularly in Islamic jurisprudence, although we only know the names of Umm Hani and Fatima, sisters of Abdullah and daughters of Muhammad.[100] Umm Hani was considered the last great scholar of the Abdusi family, marking the end of this learned dynasty.[101]

When Umm Hani and Fatima attended classes taught by their brother Abdullah, they were accompanied by Umm al-Banin (d. ca. 1452), the grandmother of Shaykh Zarruq.[102] This example of female scholarship was preserved in the historical record because Umm al-Banin brought her young grandson along to the classes and Zarruq recorded this in his autobiographical text, *al-Kunnash*, probably to establish his connection to Abdullah al-Abdusi.

Zarruq described how his grandmother, whom he referred to as both a "*faqiha*" and an "*alima*," meaning someone with a high level of religious learning, gained an education as a child by accompanying her father in his studies of the Quran.[103] Zarruq also tells stories about the early education of the Abdusi children, which he must have heard about from his grandmother, or the Abdusi sisters. In his biography of Abdullah al-Abdusi, Zarruq relates how Abdullah's father used to pay him one dirham for every five hadiths he memorized to aid his memorization of al-Qurtubi's abridgment of *Sahih Muslim*.[104] We can envision an Abdusi household that held knowledge in high regard and encouraged both boys and girls to learn. As Abdullah's father Muhammad encouraged his son to memorize hadith, he likely gave the same encouragement to his daughters, Umm Hani and Fatima. These are the two snapshots we have of Umm Hani, Fatima, and Umm al-Banin's education: as children in the home or accompanying parents to classes and attending specialized lectures in old age. While in the intervening years they must have continued their studies, this period likely revolved around marriage and raising a family, leaving less time for scholarly pursuits. It was in old age, with fewer domestic responsibilities, where the elderly women could devote more time to learning, when they were also free of the gender anxiety surrounding younger women's participation in public activities in mixed-gender spaces. Abdullah al-Abdusi's classes were both inclusive and accessible, allowing Zarruq's grandmother to bring him along as an infant and toddler. Like Sara al-Halabiyya, the old age of the Abdusi sisters and Umm al-Banin would have facilitated their movement in spaces that may not have always been welcoming to women.

The final woman mentioned in Gannun's paragraph describing women of the late Marinid period known for their religious knowledge was Rahma bint al-Janan (date of death unknown), the mother of Ibn Ghazi (d. 1513). Rahma's extensive knowledge of hadith came from her study with her first husband, Abu Abdullah Muhammad bin Aziz al-Sanhaji, known as al-Hajj al-Azuz, a jurist and hadith scholar who traveled to the Mashriq and studied with many scholars.[105] Although his date of death is unknown, he was from the same generation as Abdullah al-Abdusi and likely died in the mid-fifteenth century, around the time of the collapse of the Marinid dynasty. After al-Hajj al-Azuz's death while performing his second pilgrimage to Mecca, Rahma married the man who would become Ibn Ghazi's father.[106] She passed on her knowledge of hadith to her son and other children:

> My mother memorized many hadith from him from the sound books of hadith, and she almost completely learned the prayers found in the sound books of hadith. I memorized a lot from her in my younger days and thanks to God I didn't have trouble memorizing them after I grew up. And she was (may God have mercy on her) tenacious in the study of

> the Quran from the physical book, and she had great knowledge of the interpretation of its stories and its information and she benefited us with that when we were young.[107]

A key role for an early teacher was making the material accessible to his or her young charges, for example, by teaching the Quran through stories. These sources provide glimpses into a multilayered world of women's scholarship, particularly in the late Marinid period, during which women served as vital links in scholarly chains and performed important roles in educating the children in their families. Not all jurists approved of women's involvement in higher learning at the time. A fatwa reportedly issued by a fourteenth-century Tunisian mufti, Ibn Arafa (d. 1401), highlighted his discomfort at women's participation. He "forbid them [women] from going to study circles and dhikr and preaching even if they were separated from men."[108] It is important to note that fatwas, while influential, were advisory in nature and not legally binding; women could choose to follow Ibn Arafa's advice or to simply ignore it. For Ibn Arafa, women's observance of gendered boundaries in the physical spaces in which study occurred was not sufficient to allow their participation. Likewise, Ibn Arafa's student, Abu al-Qasim al-Burzuli, expressed his concern over women's attendance of scholarly gatherings, especially in cases where these sessions were *not* guided by a male religious authority.[109] These opinions are significant because the documented disapproval of these scholars shows that women were present in these spaces, including as teachers.

Non-Elite Legal Knowledge

The women discussed above as part of the intellectual culture of Marinid Fez were all members of the elite and were mainly remembered in the sources because of their connections to more famous male family members. Biographical sources do not mention women from lower social strata and these women did not have access to the essential foundation of learning within a scholarly family, although some might have studied the Quran during their childhoods in neighborhood *kuttab*s or attended lectures at mosques. Yet, non-elite women show up in numerous legal cases displaying a strong understanding of Islamic law. Often, we do not even know their names, or if their names are mentioned, we know little about them beyond the specific legal case in which they are mentioned. We have already seen the example of the young woman from Taza utilizing a sophisticated knowledge of the law to get what she wanted, and later chapters will highlight other women who worked the legal system in their favor. These women's cases highlight informal routes of knowledge accessible to people outside of the elite, both women and men.

Knowledge of Islamic law and how it functioned at a local level was widely available throughout the communities in the cities and towns highlighted in the fatwa collections. People learned from discussing cases with others or hearing the results of a particular case. Women also had access to the legal students and jurists who lived in their communities and could consult with them informally before officially bringing a case in front of a judge. This resulted in informal advice and oral fatwas that were typically not recorded, but which sometimes appear in descriptions of ongoing legal conflicts.[110] Although the sources for this period in North Africa do not mention women consulting *faqihat*, it is easy to imagine that at least friends and neighbors would have sought their counsel in religious and legal matters. Biographies of learned women from the Islamic East document this practice, such as the advice given by Medinan scholar Amrah bint al-Rahman (d. 724) to other women.[111] Hussein Ali Agrama argues that a key function of requesting a fatwa and receiving a response was to help guide people toward "an ethical path," a role that supports the idea that fatwas contributed to the education of the general public.[112] We can imagine people sharing the responses they received to their question and others learning from them, whether the fatwa originated with a local scholar or a prominent mufti from Fez. Women acquired legal knowledge from all these different sources and then displayed it as they navigated cases and tried to seek a favorable outcome.

A few instances from cases in the following chapters highlight what women knew, what they were expected to know, how they learned, and how they were able to engage in legal interpretation once they had that knowledge. Chapter 5 describes how marriage contracts included stipulations that allowed a woman to divorce her husband if he took another wife, although this kind of condition was technically deemed invalid by Maliki law. With support from families and knowledge likely gained from other women or local notaries who helped draw up contracts, women could attach a clause to this stipulation that made it enforceable, circumventing the standard Maliki disapproval of preventing a husband from taking another wife. In chapter 6, in a case of a *khul* divorce in which a woman makes financial or other concessions to her husband in return for her release from the marriage, a mufti rebuked a woman for not including the necessary language in the divorce contract to ensure that she would retain custody of her children even if her life circumstances changed. He stated that this was knowledge that women had, and he was unsympathetic to her case because he expected her to have known better. In other words, jurists acknowledged women's understanding of the law and assumed they would use it to protect their own interests. In chapter 7, in the case of divorce oaths, differing opinions within the Maliki school allowed parties to exercise their own interpretive preferences in Islamic law. The muftis educated them about the multiple valid opinions and the parties were allowed to choose the one they wanted to follow. This combination of education and interpretation exemplifies the coproduction of Islamic law where laypeople took part in the process. Chapter 7 also shows how a woman could use her knowledge of divorce oaths to exploit a husband's character flaw of being quick to anger and provoke a divorce, effectively turning the easy male access to divorce against him. In chapter 8, women who ran away with a man or even confessed to *zina* were aware of the prescribed punishment but also knew that it had strict conditions and would not be a serious impediment to their plans. This knowledge must have been common enough that even the threat of running away was sufficient to convince a family to pay attention to a daughter's marriage preferences, as all parties knew that the law and community would facilitate her eventual choice.

Conclusion

In 1447, Umm Hani al-Abdusi came across the young Ahmed Zarruq in Fez with henna on his hands and feet and forbid him from wearing it. Zarruq describes the encounter with his grandmother's friend as follows: "The *faqiha* Umm Hani al-Abdusiyya—the sister of Sidi Abu Abdullah al-Abdusi—saw me when my hand and foot were painted with henna, so she forbid me from it and said, 'If your grandmother says to you, come let's do henna, tell her: no.' And by God I hadn't learned it yet—and I was at that time a boy of five years."[113]

This brief anecdote sheds light on several points related to gender that have been touched on in this chapter. First, Umm Hani would have been around ninety-one years old at this time. Her age and stage of life facilitated her movement around Fez, as gendered norms that restricted the movement and interactions of younger women, both married and unmarried, no longer applied to her. Second, Umm Hani's advice to the young Zarruq was an example of a *faqiha* dispensing specialized legal advice, albeit informally, and to a child. The gendered rules of henna adornment were not common knowledge, as evidenced both by her reference to Zarruq's grandmother (also a *faqiha*) possibly not knowing them, and by a similar question posed to her brother Abdullah al-Abdusi. Abdullah's fatwa in response to the question (that men could only use henna in a limited way) was considered serious legal advice and a compiler preserved it for the guidance of future jurists.[114] We can assume learned women regularly advised other women on relevant points of religion and law, although the sources would not preserve these interactions. Third, the anecdote about the *faqiha* Umm Hani giving legal advice that reinforced gender norms (i.e., henna is only for female decoration) acts as a cautionary reminder to a conscious or unconscious hope of the Western feminist scholar searching for models of proto-feminist or progressive female authority in premodern Islamic history. It would be presumptuous to assume that learned women of that age would reach different conclusions in interpreting Islamic legal sources to men, aside from perhaps taking a more woman-sensitive approach. This projection of modern aspirations erases the accomplishments of women working within an orthodox Islamic legal framework. Finally, this anecdote highlights the instability and fluidity of gender identities. A woman's gendered identity was continually shaped and reshaped as she moved through life and was impacted by additional factors such as social status. The complexity becomes evident in the contradiction of Umm Hani overcoming fairly rigid gender expectations to reach the level of *faqiha*, a rare achievement for a woman, while still trying to reinforce the ambiguously gendered rules of who can wear henna and how.

Modern struggles for women's education, alongside high rates of female illiteracy in today's Morocco, support assumptions that women's access to education is something new that only became available in the postcolonial period.[115] Although literacy and access to education were not widespread in premodern Morocco for women or men, elite women could take advantage of family connections to obtain educations that paralleled that of the men in their families. Some women, such as the Abdusi sisters and Zarruq's grandmother Umm al-Banin, were recognized as *faqihat*, or qualified to interpret Islamic law. These women moved in the same intellectual world as the jurists, serving as their earliest teachers and attending their lectures later in life. Although it is difficult to assess how this impacted the jurisprudence of the times, it is significant simply that these women occupied these spaces in the lives and careers of these male jurists.[116] The culture of learning created by Marinid patronage allowed knowledge, and particularly legal knowledge, to diffuse into the population in a way that made law part of ordinary life and disputes, and allowed people outside of the elite to structure relationships within legal parameters.

While it is rare to find *faqihat* in the sources, it is much more common to find women of a lower social status educating themselves in Islamic law and navigating disputes to their advantage. This legal knowledge was widespread and accessible within communities, and it allowed women to protect their interests, such as retaining custody of their children after divorce. Women shaped the law of the time by the disputes they brought to jurists, by the boundaries they pushed, and by the creative use of legal theory in their own lives. In particular, the young woman from Taza demonstrated a sophisticated understanding of the technicalities of the Maliki school, which allowed her to drive the local legal process and secure the outcome she favored—freeing herself from her father's authority and marrying Ibn al-Turjuman.

5

Negotiating Marital Life

Taza Anecdote

The woman at the center of the Taza case wanted to get married, a common aspiration among young people. She had her eye on a particular groom, her neighbor, Ibn al-Turjuman. In the case she brought to the judge of Taza, she stated that he was the only man she wanted to marry. Typically, at this point, her father or another close family member would arrange the marriage with the prospective groom's family, taking care to ensure that the bride's financial rights were secured in the marriage. Ibrahim al-Anbaki claimed that he tried to arrange other marriages on his daughter's behalf, but she rejected them. As she told the judge: "It is my desire to get married and I am asking to do so. There is no husband for me except the one who asked for my hand now, and I refuse anyone but him."[1] However, because the young woman was a virgin (which was the usual assumption about a woman who had not been previously married), she did not actually have the power to reject a marriage that her father arranged. A typical father might listen to his daughter's desires and take her point of view into account, but al-Anbaki was not a typical father, and technically, the power rested in his hands. The first time al-Anbaki contracted a marriage for his daughter, the young man returned to al-Anbaki before its consummation, claimed he was scared of Ibn al-Turjuman, and asked to be let out of the contract—perhaps the latter had threatened or intimidated him. When the father left town to try and contract another marriage for his daughter farther away from the drama of Taza, perhaps hoping the gossip or Ibn al-Turjuman's threats would not reach a distant groom, the daughter did the only thing in her power—she ran away and sought refuge with the judge.

Because the young woman's father opposed the marriage, she was forced to take creative steps in order to marry Ibn al-Turjuman, including a (possibly false) confession of *zina*. The case the young woman brought to the qadi conveniently contained elements that addressed each possible exception in Maliki law that would help destabilize a father's authority over the marriage of his (virgin) daughter. And so, in the midst of this messy conflict that continued even after the death of the judge, the young woman was able to marry Ibn al-Turjuman.

Introduction

The case of the young woman from Taza presents an extreme example of the lengths a woman would go to in order to achieve her marriage goals, and the lengths a father would go to in order to prevent his daughter's marriage to a man he hated. The behavior of neither father nor daughter was representative of other marriage cases. And yet, the young woman's story allows us to explore more typical aspects of marital relations in legal doctrine and social practice, such as adding stipulations (*shurut*) to a marriage contract that protected or enhanced a bride's rights. Stipulations were often included in marriage contract negotiations and allowed women to secure a better position for themselves within a marriage, by using the legal strategies available to mitigate the impact of marriage laws that seemed to leave them with little decision-making power.

Women had many opportunities to express their desires and advocate for their interests during the process of contracting a marriage. This was not a solitary or independent activity. Negotiations over a marriage, especially in the case of a first marriage, often involved male family members negotiating on behalf of the bride. After agreeing to a particular husband, the overwhelming concerns of women and their families were financial, and the main goal was to secure a wife's long-term material security. Emotional needs were also considered in the process, although this led families into more legally contested territory.

Islamic legal doctrine gave a father extensive rights in contracting a marriage for his daughter. The case of the young woman from Taza appears to prove what one might fear from reading Maliki beliefs: that because a father had the right to force his (virgin) daughter into marriage, he would do so. This case, however, is highly exceptional, and hundreds of other cases do not support this reading. Legal doctrine also gave a husband gendered rights in marriage, such as taking another sexual partner or controlling divorce. But what the doctrine outlined was actually the baseline for what marriage and family arrangements should look like, and not some kind of ideal for the family. Women were able to draw on competing notions of more egalitarian relationships from the Quran and the example of the Prophet's life. The law itself provided the tools for women to adjust these terms to achieve marital configurations that were closer to what they wanted.

In practice, women had multiple opportunities to intervene in the marriage process. This included the chance to express displeasure about a specific suitor before marriage, at times very forcefully; looking for technicalities in the law that would prevent her marriage to a certain man; and designating a particular marriage guardian (*wali*) in the case of orphans and other women without guardians to facilitate a desirable marriage choice. After a groom was agreed upon, a woman had various strategies available to help improve her position in a marriage. Demands for a good dower (*sadaq*), often facilitated by a father or another guardian, helped to ensure her financial stability.

Stipulations inserted in marriage contracts or volunteered after the marriage were one strategy for limiting a husband's rights.[2] These included preventing a husband from taking a second wife or concubine, moving a wife away from her family, or limiting his wife's mobility. At the same time, stipulations served to expand the rights of a woman in a marriage, or to provide a means of enforcing the rights to which she was legally entitled. Stipulations could also signal a vision for combining two families, with the new husband agreeing to take care of his wife's children from a previous marriage, a family configuration that Islamic law did not explicitly condone. Such stipulations were utilized at different times and places throughout the Muslim world and provided a legally valid path for creating a marriage that more closely matched the needs of both parties.[3] The conditions varied depending on the time and place, as did responses from the jurists when these contract clauses were disputed. As a woman entered marriage with fewer rights than her husband, stipulations were always used to expand a wife's rights and reduce those of her husband. The law established the starting point for marital relations and from there a husband and wife could renegotiate to enhance the financial, emotional, and legal security of the wife.

This chapter examines conflicts that arose in Marinid Morocco over contract stipulations that restricted a man's authority in his marriage, specifically those that regulated polygamy and caring for stepchildren. Information about these stipulations, preserved in fatwa records, reveals what was important to women in a marriage, and how women and their families worked to create secure and stable partnerships. Cases show that many women desired a monogamous marriage, despite a husband's fundamental legal right to have other wives and concubines. Financial disputes also suggest more complicated family configurations than those defined in legal theory, with husbands agreeing at the time of marriage to assume responsibilities for their stepchildren, which were not required by law. These cases also provide insight into why men would relinquish some of the rights to which they were entitled. Although Islamic jurisprudence (*fiqh*) put more emphasis on preserving and enforcing men's rights in marriage and the family, the law also had built-in mechanisms that women could exploit to partially level the playing field, one of which was the use of marriage contract stipulations. Marriage contracts provided a mechanism through which a couple could redefine the gendered rights and responsibilities enshrined in Islamic law and these rights were transferred or revoked with a surprising ease.

These cases show that what seem like stable categories that deeply enshrined male privilege were actually open to a certain degree of negotiation. As discussed in the case of the young woman from Taza and seen in discussions about marriage here, a father's absolute right to control his daughter's marriage arrangements was much more fluid in practice. Likewise, a husband's right to have multiple legal sexual partners (up to four wives and unlimited concubines, if he could afford it), a symbol of status and masculinity, was restricted in marriage contracts. And the law's primary concern with lineage as traced only through the father still held, while also allowing a second husband to accept the duties of the father in raising his children, a duty taken on willingly by stepfathers. The power of father over daughter, the sexual license of the husband, and the strict legal view of the father as the only provider for his children; all these gender identities were subject to reconfiguration as couples and their families negotiated marriage arrangements that met the needs of all parties, but particularly the women who gained rights not granted to them by the law and were able to keep their children from a previous marriage and integrate them into a new family unit.

The sources also provide evidence of a legal culture that permeated society. Ordinary people had a basic understanding of law, as is illustrated by the ways in which they wrote their marriage contracts. People could also seek advice or legal strategies from scholars educated in Islamic law, and as we will see in the following chapter, these resources were available to women as well as men.

Marriage in Marinid Morocco

Despite the Maliki school giving women limited bargaining power in the marriage process, legal sources describing the practice in Marinid Morocco show that at every stage, women intervened in ways that enhanced their positions when they entered a marriage. The fatwas considered here show that these interventions were not made by women fighting alone; rather, they received support from male relatives, who often negotiated on their behalf, and their wishes were frequently accommodated by their families and the law. In modern Moroccan discourse on family law, the requirement that a marriage guardian (*wali*) oversee a woman's marriage was a key practice that feminists fought to discard as a symbol of a patriarchal system that allows men to control women, and the 2004 reforms to the Moroccan family code removed this requirement for females over the age of eighteen.[4] In Marinid Morocco, however, the guardian played a critical role in protecting the bride's interests and was often the person advocating on her behalf to include stipulations in the marriage contract.

In cases where a family did not respect a woman's demands, or if she had no close family, she had the option of going to court or seeking resolution through other means, such as mediation by community members or other legal officials. When legal avenues were seemingly closed off, however, such as in the case of a father trying to impose his choice of husband on a virgin daughter under his authority, some women resorted to desperate measures to force their families to negotiate with them, such as running away with a particular man they wanted to marry or taking other extreme measures, like those in the case from Taza and other cases discussed in chapter 8.

The law did not require marriages to be registered, and thus they entered the historical record only when something went wrong and interventions by family and the community failed to resolve the situation, resulting in an encounter with the law. The cases discussed here describe areas of tension where disputes arose in the marriage process, and at the same time provide some insight into what a typical marriage looked like before the relationship deteriorated. Thus, they provide unique glimpses into how ordinary women negotiated family and marital relationships at this time.

Challenges to a father's right to guardianship were rare, which is why the case from Taza is such a spectacular diversion from the norm. More typical guardianship cases involved women who were seeking to marry but had no marriage guardian. Such cases presented to judges or rulers were those in which women without a guardian sought out someone to negotiate and conduct their marriages.[5] At times, women explicitly stated that they were afraid for their chastity, or that they feared poverty.[6] These cases did not mention whether the women were seeking to marry a specific man or they simply had a more general desire to marry. In cases concerning orphan women, the decision of who should act as guardian on their behalf could be disputed, either before the marriage or after the fact. If the bride chose a particular guardian, other relatives might object to that choice. Alternatively, an orphan woman could challenge her marriage by saying she had not authorized a guardian to act on her behalf.

Fatwa records provide glimpses into women's movement between towns in North Africa. Cases arose where a woman was traveling through an area, for example on her way to perform the pilgrimage to Mecca, and requested that the judge arrange her marriage.[7] Several fatwas dealt with women who were living in a town where no one knew them and requested that the judge perform their marriage. Another situation that necessitated this kind of petition arose when a woman fled a prior marriage. Such a case often came to the attention of the law when a woman remarried without divorcing her first husband and the latter tracked her down and challenged the new marriage, a situation which will be discussed further in chapter 6.

The overwhelming concern when negotiating marriage contracts was to ensure the new bride's financial security, which began with the required payment of dower (*sadaq*) from husband to wife.[8] Financial negotiations were a standard part of the marriage process, often involving complicated property exchanges and other financial obligations by both families, but they were also an aspect of a marriage that was frequently and fiercely contested. Women fought for their rights, their families looked out for these rights, and the legal system respected and enforced these rights. In many ways a marriage contract was like other contracts, and was in fact compared to a sales contract by early jurists.[9] Financial agreements in a marriage contract were not complicated by issues of gender and were disputed on very different terms than stipulations, which sought to alter the balance of the explicitly gendered rights within a marriage. A sizable proportion of the fatwas dealt with the intricacies of financial negotiations and arrangements agreed on or contested in the process of making a marriage.

Marriage Contract Stipulations

While the primary concern of a woman and her family in marriage negotiations was financial, other concerns related to quality of life were sometimes included in marriage contracts and served to limit certain rights of a husband while expanding those of his wife. Unlike financial stipulations, these areas of law were highly gendered and involved complicated and sensitive issues related to disrupting and redistributing the rights explicitly assigned to men and women, such as a man's right to have multiple wives and to control divorce. Due to the complex circumstances surrounding these cases, they are an ideal prism through which to examine relationships within families and relationships between women and the law. Likewise, jurists' discussions on the topic of these voluntary stipulations reveal a complicated discourse on gender.

Maliki doctrine did not support stipulations that restricted a husband's rights in a marriage and considered some of them, such as restricting his access to polygamy, invalid.[10] Malik ibn Anas was quoted as allowing men to disregard two types of stipulations, specifically those restricting a husband's right to move his wife to another town, and those limiting his access to legal sexual partnerships, a disapproval which jurists generalized to other situations.[11] Yet, Malik also maintained that if such a stipulation was tied to divorce using the mechanism of a divorce oath (a topic that will be the focus of chapter 7), it became legally binding.[12] An analogous and equally enforceable mechanism was to tie a stipulation to the manumission of a slave, meaning if the terms were met, the slave immediately gained her freedom. These fatwa sources show the complexity of implementing Islamic law, including, in this case, how men were held accountable for contract stipulations the doctrine disliked.

Contract Stipulations across the Muslim World

Few scholarly studies examine how stipulations were used in practice in Islamic marriage contracts in the premodern Muslim world, and many of the existing studies focus on Egypt. Judith E. Tucker notes that some stipulations "underscored the rights to fair treatment that many jurists thought women enjoyed in any case," while also providing the wife with the option of enforcing those rights.[13] Amira El-Azhary Sonbol argues that the ability to include stipulations in marriage contracts represents one area where Egyptian women fared better under premodern Islamic laws than under the modern Egyptian personal status law, which restricts the use of stipulations.[14] Such requirements concerning Egyptian women were similar to those requested by Moroccan women, including restricting a husband's access to polygamy, or preventing him from moving his wife away from her family.[15] Another common stipulation demanded by premodern Egyptian women was for their husbands not to beat them, a demand that did not appear as frequently in the Islamic West, likely because the Maliki school allowed a woman to request a divorce based on harm whereas other schools of Islamic law did not.

Historical studies show that stipulations were common in marriage contracts in Mamluk and Ottoman Egypt, while they were infrequently found in documents from eighteenth-century Syria and Palestine.[16] In seventeenth-century Cairo, the women who put stipulations in their marriage contracts had often been previously married and were from financially stable families.[17] The use of stipulations in Ottoman Egypt shared some similarities with Marinid North Africa, such as a concern with caring for the wife's children from a previous marriage, and restricting the husband from marrying another woman.[18] Other stipulations reflected local circumstances, such as those conditions secured in Egyptian port towns where the contracts showed a greater occurrence of stipulations that limited the time a husband could be absent from his family.[19]

Marriage contracts from al-Andalus show the inclusion of a standard list of five stipulations suggested by notaries, or the absence of any at all, as was the case in fifteenth-century Granada.[20] The absence of stipulations in a marriage contract does not, however, necessarily indicate that they were not employed at all, as some of the fatwas examined in this chapter describe stipulations that were agreed upon after a marriage had already taken place. The Andalusi stipulations addressed concerns about monogamy, a husband's lengthy absence, good treatment, and ensuring decent relations with the wife's family. Amalia Zomeño lists the following five stipulations that were contained in the templates notaries used for guidance in preparing marriage contracts:

1. The husband will not marry a second wife, or take a concubine, without the permission and consent of his first wife.
2. The husband will not absent himself from his wife's side for more than six consecutive months, except to fulfill the obligation of the pilgrimage, in which case he is allowed three years and must make provision for his wife's maintenance (*nafaqa*) during his absence.
3. The husband will not mistreat his wife, either physically or economically.
4. The husband will not oblige his wife to move to a city other than the city where she lived before her marriage.
5. The husband will not forbid his wife to visit her female relatives and male *maharim* (males in non-marriageable relation) or to receive visits from them.[21]

These stipulations were usually followed by the necessary language to enforce them—that is, by linking them to the threat of divorce.[22] They also stated that the husband agreed to the stipulations "voluntarily and willingly, in order to seek her friendship and trying to keep her happiness."[23] This justification for including the stipulations points to the affective dimensions of marriage: a husband would willingly limit his rights in order to please his new bride.

Negotiating Stipulations in Marinid Morocco

By restricting a husband's rights, stipulations typically gave the wife additional rights and benefits that she was not entitled to by law.[24] One stipulation related to the emotional and financial stability of the family that was common in sources from Marinid Morocco involved a husband volunteering to maintain his wife's children from a previous marriage, even if the children did not live with the couple. Less common were stipulations that restricted a husband from taking a second wife or relocating without his wife's permission, ensuring a wife's mobility, limiting a husband's absence, and ensuring family visits. In one case from fourteenth-century Tunis, the wife, a hairdresser, included in her contract that her husband must allow her to continue to work.[25] Occasionally, a wife also included stipulations demanding good behavior, such as not harming her, not drinking alcohol, and not spending her money. Certain stipulations, such as those limiting a husband's absence, appear less frequently in cases from Marinid Morocco; however, we cannot assume that these stipulations were necessarily less frequent or unknown due to the shortcomings of the sources that are available for any kind of quantitative analysis.

Disputes over stipulations related to the well-being of a woman and her family appear much less frequently in the sources from Marinid Morocco than disputes over financial stipulations, which could indicate that their use was not widespread among the population. Social status likely played a role in securing stipulations for women, as it did in Ottoman Egypt, although this is difficult to establish from the existing data.[26] We do, however, see evidence of strong family support, especially from fathers, in imposing stipulations and challenging husbands for their noncompliance. Another party to drawing up these contracts was the notary, who would have advised the family on their different options in a marriage contract. Notaries, however, are less visible in Moroccan sources than in sources from al-Andalus, where manuals contained templates of marriage contracts.[27] One indication that women and their families understood how to correctly word these stipulations, perhaps aided by local notaries, is that in all the disputes from the Marinid era over polygamy stipulations, only one contract failed to include the language required to enforce the provision.[28]

Stipulations included in a marriage contract usually came to the attention of the jurists when a husband attempted to circumvent a condition he had agreed to. In a smaller number of cases, a husband was challenged for breaking the terms of a stipulation but not divorcing his wife—for example, by an heir after her death.[29] Therefore, we have little understanding of how stipulations functioned when they were not disputed, and if they served their intended goals, such as integrating stepchildren into a new family unit or limiting the husband to behavior his wife did not object to. In cases of disputed stipulations, however, we can see the expectations of each party, and how the law interpreted and either enforced or rejected certain stipulations. Here, the discussion focuses on stipulations regulating mobility and limiting polygamy, two types of stipulations that restricted a husband's rights, in addition to a stipulation in which a husband volunteered to accept a responsibility not legally required of him, namely, to provide financial support for his stepchildren.

Enforcing Monogamy and the Reimagination of the Family

A stipulation present in Muslim marriage contracts from the early Islamic period placed restrictions on a husband's right to have up to four wives, in addition to concubines.[30] This was a concept that Muslim jurists struggled with, however, as they understood that the Quran specifically condoned these activities. The life of the Prophet Muhammad and his family provided evidence that the Quranic permission was not necessarily a divine ideal. The Prophet's lengthy first marriage to Khadija bint Khuwaylid (d. 619) was monogamous and hadiths record that he forbade Ali Ibn Abi Talib (d. 661), the husband of the Prophet's daughter Fatima, from taking a second wife. His great-granddaughter, Sukayna, stipulated in her marriage contract that her husband was restricted to monogamy.[31]

Stipulations attempting to enforce monogamy appeared throughout the Marinid period and were equally common in other times and places in the Islamic West. The standard method of attaching consequences to a stipulation requiring monogamy was to transfer the option to initiate a divorce to the wife, much like the enforcement mechanism for other types of stipulations. This clause could be worded so that a divorce took place automatically upon consummation with a second wife or a concubine. Unless challenged, this type of stipulation would serve to redefine the marital relationship, reducing the emotional and financial insecurity that might come with polygamy.

Often, a husband hesitated before breaking a stipulation and first sought informal legal advice on how to circumvent it. A clause added to a stipulation could also allow the wife to decide when the stipulation was violated whether she wanted to remain in the marriage or exercise her right to divorce. Another clause that put the wife in a position to make a decision stated that the stipulation would be enforced unless the wife gave her permission to drop it; without such authorization, she could initiate the divorce herself.

The knowledge that stipulations were imposed could deter a husband wishing to take a second wife, to avoid losing his first wife and the financial consequences that came with that. These consequences included immediate payment of any part of the dower that had been delayed, in addition to spousal support and child maintenance. Yet, while the wife was in a better bargaining position if she had a stipulation limiting her husband's sexual activity, in the event that he followed through with another marriage or took a concubine, her options were to accept the situation or leave the marriage. The divorce mechanism most commonly used to enforce stipulations did not force a husband into monogamy; it simply acted as a deterrent by providing penalties.

A case from Meknes in the mid-fourteenth century illustrates some of these dynamics. Guidance was requested from mufti al-Hassan bin Atiyya al-Wansharisi (d. 1379–80) in the event of ongoing negotiations between a husband and wife.[32] The wife in question had a clause in her marriage contract specifying that if her husband married another woman, took a concubine, or harmed her, she was authorized to divorce herself.

> The Qadi al-Sayd Abu Ali al-Hassan bin Atiyya al-Wansharisi Rahimuhu Allah asked about a man who wanted to marry although his wife had conditions against him in the original marriage contract: that he not marry on her, and not take a concubine, and not harm her, and whenever he did any of those things the matter [i.e., power to divorce] is in her hands. So, she said to him give me everything that is in your hand from money or a portion of it that she named from his property, and I give you permission to marry and I accept to live with you and her partnership. And he was afraid that if he gave her all that she wanted from him and she stayed with the one that he wanted to marry, that she would come against him with the condition of harm and she would be trusted and divorce herself from him.[33]

While the presence of this type of clause technically invalidated a marriage contract, a fact well known to all parties involved in drawing up the agreement, after the marriage was consummated, the contract was considered valid. Despite the existence of this clause, however, the husband later wanted to take a second wife. His first wife agreed to drop the stipulation that confined him to monogamy if, in exchange, he gave her a substantial amount of his money and property. Perhaps from her perspective, financial stability and independence was more important than restricting her husband to monogamy. While this should have been a solution that satisfied both parties, the husband remained suspicious about his wife's intentions due to her solid legal position and perhaps because of stories he had heard from other men. Even if she dropped the stipulation that prevented her husband from marrying, she would still retain the other clause in the contract that permitted her to divorce herself in the case of harm (*darar*). Because of this, her husband feared that she would take the money, wait for the second marriage to take place, and then invoke the condition of harm on account of having to put up with a co-wife. This would allow her to leave the marriage and keep the financial compensation he had given her in return for accepting the second wife.

Even without the deceptive tactics feared by the husband, this contract put the wife in a strong position, giving her the option of divorcing her husband if he took a second wife by alleging harm, or remaining with him after receiving compensation for any hardship that would arise from the new conjugal configuration. The husband proposed a solution: he would make the gift in return for revoking the monogamy stipulation contingent on a new agreement requiring that if she later chose to divorce him, she would return this gift. The question presented here to Ibn Atiyya al-Wansharisi was not about the validity of the wife's contract stipulations or her options in exercising them if she wished. Rather, the reason for consulting the mufti was to determine whether the husband's proposed solution of providing his wife with a financial incentive to remain in the marriage was valid.

Ibn Atiyya's answer suggests why the jurists might interpret taking a second wife as both legal and yet possibly harmful to the first wife.[34] He referred to an opinion that said it was permissible for a woman to take financial compensation in return for accepting a co-wife, because each spouse was giving up something. The husband could pay to remove the stipulation because he had surrendered something that was his God-given right, namely to take up to four wives and as many concubines as he wished. In Ibn Atiyya's explanation, the harm to the wife came from the forbearance she would need in accepting this new family situation, which included tolerating various types of hardship that come with having a co-wife. Likewise, the first wife would have to share her husband's money with the new wife, therefore negatively impacting her financial situation while he was alive and her inheritance after he died. Polygamy also required that she give up some of her rights, including her exclusive right to sexual fulfillment from her husband.[35] The jurists understood that accepting a co-wife was not only an inconvenience but had real consequences for a woman's financial and sexual rights, and therefore they considered it fair for her to be compensated for this concession, provided she had had the foresight to impose such a stipulation in the marriage contract. This acknowledgment by the jurists that having a co-wife could harm a woman in multiple ways coexisted alongside the reality that the law permitted it.

New Family Configurations: Providing for Stepchildren

Under Islamic law, fathers were obligated to financially support their young children, both during marriage and after divorce, and in the event of the father's death, the children should be provided for by an inheritance or by the father's family.[36] In reality, however, support for the children from the ex-husband or his estate was not always available or desired. When a mother remarried, her new husband had no legal obligation to support her children from a previous marriage, and in fact she was expected to give up physical custody of them when she remarried.[37] In practice, however, families were combined and men did support their stepchildren, creating a vision for the new family that went beyond what legal doctrine required of a stepfather. One method of ensuring this support was to include a clause in the marriage contract whereby the husband volunteered to maintain his wife's children, or specified certain aspects of care for which he would take responsibility. These stipulations appear to have been enforced even when they were not specifically attached to divorce if they fell within certain societal norms of what a stepfather would customarily provide. These included food, drink, and according to some jurists, lodging.[38]

Women who entered a marriage with children from another husband had contracted at least one other marriage and would therefore have experience with the process itself, as well as a more clearly defined idea about how to adjust the terms of a marriage to meet their own needs and those of their families. Studies from seventeenth-century Ottoman Cairo have found that women who put stipulations in their marriage contracts were more likely to have been previously married.[39] In most cases from Morocco, it is difficult to know if women with contract stipulations were divorced or widowed, except in the case of making provisions to care for their children, when this is clearly the case.

It appears from fatwas concerned with caring for stepchildren and the jurists' discussion of the topic that it was a fairly common practice for husbands to assume this responsibility. This fact challenges the common assumption that women were expected to give up physical custody of their children if they remarried.[40] This was apparently not the case in Marinid Morocco, however, where women worked to keep their children with them, and as we will see in the following chapter, several disputes arose around the household dynamics of these combined families.

Husbands and the Concession of Rights

What would motivate a man to voluntarily restrict his marital rights, such as the right to have multiple sexual partners? A simple explanation would be that a man wanted to offer more to his new wife than the minimum required by law, but such an assumption of good will is rarely afforded to Muslim men. Henry Toledano, in *Judicial Practice and Family Law in Morocco,* cites a statement from a twelfth-century Andalusi jurist who said that men granted women stipulations, such as the option to divorce herself, in exchange for financial concessions made in the dower.[41] Yet, agreeing to an exchange for material compensation does not appear to have been common practice in Marinid Morocco. The fatwas considered here hint at other compelling reasons a husband might surrender his rights or make voluntary financial concessions, ranging from love to fear.

As for the most part these fatwas deal with husbands who were disputing stipulations and trying to reduce their wives' rights, the sources do not reflect them in a positive light. An easily overlooked yet straightforward motivation for a husband agreeing to a stipulation is that he wanted to please his new wife, or, in the case of stipulations agreed to after a marriage, that he did so out of love for his wife. The jurists' discourse provides insight into why men agreed to this kind of stipulation. In a case from Fez in 1368, a husband whose wife had died demanded that he be reimbursed for everything he had spent on her children.[42] Although he had volunteered to provide this support, he produced a document saying that his wife had agreed to absolve him of this commitment. The two muftis who responded to the question took issue with his strategy and went beyond a strictly legal answer to remind him that this support was a gift he had given to the children. Ibn Atiyya al-Wansharisi, the mufti from the case of the woman willing to take financial compensation to accept a co-wife, answered that a husband's offer to support his stepchildren, whether before or after contracting the marriage, "is voluntary and a gift to make the wife happy."[43] Similarly, Abu Abdullah Muhammad al-Fishtali (d. 1375–76) suggested additional reasons why a husband might agree to take care of another man's children. He said that prior to the marriage, a husband might consent to such stipulations "in hopes of hastening an answer to his proposal, and to prompt [her] towards marrying him."[44] If he volunteered after contracting the marriage, it was "in the hope of good relations, and to enrich a beautiful companionship, and to ensure happiness," language similar to that of the notary documents from al-Andalus.[45] In reminding the husband why he spent the money in the first place, the muftis added a layer of moral rebuke to what was a clear-cut legal outcome, in which the husband had no recourse to financial compensation.

In theory, husbands could of course have been pressured to agree to stipulations, although only one case from Marinid Morocco reveals compulsion as a motive for agreeing to a stipulation.[46] Presumably a wide range of factors contributed to the inclusion of stipulations in marriage contracts, such as societal expectations, norms related to a particular social status, financial considerations, and pressure exerted by the wife or her family. We cannot, however, overlook the possibility that these stipulations were volunteered to in good faith by a husband who was willing to give up some of his rights to create a harmonious marital partnership and imagine a new family that included his wife's children.

Conclusion

The young woman from Taza faced significant challenges in marrying the man of her choosing because Islamic legal doctrine had placed control in the hands of her father. And yet, it was mechanisms built into Islamic law that enabled her to muster support from her community and local legal officials to get the marriage she wanted. Her vision for her own future did not match the process outlined by legal doctrine, yet the law accommodated her conceptualization and facilitated her marriage. Legal doctrine never fully defined what a fulfilling and happy marriage would look like; rather, it provided the structure and people filled in the details. While love was not the primary goal of marriage until recent centuries, in either the Muslim or Christian world, early Islamic history and the example of the Prophet Muhammad show that affection could definitely be a factor in selecting a spouse.

While legal doctrine established the basic terms of a marriage, these conditions were negotiable, allowing women to reframe what an ideal marriage and family looked like, and achieve it through legal tools supported by family, local legal officials, and the new husbands themselves. In practice, men often did *not* exercise their legal rights (for example, few fathers tried to force their daughters into marriage) or were restricted by contract stipulations that simultaneously increased the rights of a wife. In this way, couples could imagine and build more equitable and inclusive family configurations, likely drawing on more egalitarian strands of Islam that did not become part of legal doctrine. Such a picture departs from modern conceptions of Islamic law, which view its teachings as prescribing a sacred ideal for the family rather than a baseline of minimum rights afforded to women that could only be negotiated upward.

Contracting a marriage in Marinid Morocco was a process of negotiation, first between a woman and her family, and then between her family and her husband or husband's family. While Maliki law placed few limits on a father's authority to conduct his daughter's marriage, in practice, a process of consultation often took place. Women had multiple opportunities to intervene in selecting a suitable groom, negotiating a beneficial financial arrangement, and altering the rights typically assigned by the law to each party.[47]

The use of conditions in marriage contracts has been incorporated into modern family law in a variety of ways, with a range of consequences. They may provide a mechanism for reform, but they may also be more difficult for women to take advantage of.[48] The Moroccan family code (*Mudawwana*), including the 2004 reforms, allows provisions to be inserted into the marriage contract. Conditions favored by women in North Africa today include the right to work and study, in addition to longstanding concerns about polygamy.[49] A 2007 study, however, revealed that most women did not even know they had the right to impose conditions, and others did not make demands for fear the groom would withdraw from negotiations, among other concerns.[50] The NGO that conducted the study, Global Rights, argues that the use of marriage contracts with stipulations is a promising route to guaranteeing women's rights in countries that use forms of Islamic family law.[51] One suggestion raised in the group's report was that all marriage contracts include a standard set of conditions,[52] a practice that existed in al-Andalus five hundred years ago. The strategy of using conditions to address the concerns that women have with regard to marital rights, including the possibility of automatically including specific conditions in every contract, has historical precedence and legal legitimacy, and has the possibility to address the needs of women while satisfying Islamic legal requirements.

Contract stipulations provided a way to restrict the authority that Islamic law granted men in their relationships with their wives, using mechanisms from within the same legal tradition, and highlighting the fragility of the gendered construction of a husband's sexual authority in marriage. By altering the standard rules that governed a marriage, a couple could seek to create a union in which the rights of both spouses were more balanced than in the rules elaborated by Muslim jurists over the centuries. Stipulations inserted into a marriage contract or agreed to around the time of a marriage were a legal strategy available to women and their families to ensure both their financial stability and emotional well-being. Those stipulations that came to the attention of the legal system of Marinid Morocco, such as a husband agreeing to support his stepchildren or in-laws, to limit himself to monogamy, or to refrain from harming his wife or relocating her away from her family, did so when their validity was challenged, often when the husband tried to circumvent it.

Like the case of the young woman from Taza, these cases reveal a high degree of legal knowledge among the population and the ability to seek out further advice as needed. In all the cases examined here that restricted polygamy, with one exception, stipulations were attached to a divorce clause that ensured their legal enforceability. This fact indicates that the wives and their families either knew of this technicality or had received guidance from notaries or other officials about ways to circumvent standard Maliki doctrine on this issue. A case explored in the following chapter confirms this assumption, one in which a jurist chastised a woman for failing to include a clause in a divorce contract that allowed her to maintain custody of her children. In his opinion, the woman, like other women, should have been familiar with the technicalities of this law.

Examining how Islamic law was implemented in a particular time and place, in this case Marinid Morocco, suggests the pitfalls of drawing conclusions about premodern Islamic societies from legal concepts alone. The Maliki doctrine is clear: stipulations restricting a husband from rights in a marriage that were granted to him by the law were invalid and did not need to be enforced. Yet, by looking at sources that document how actual cases were handled by the most knowledgeable jurists of the time, we can see that husbands, wives, and their families found ways to imagine a different configuration of rights in a marriage, and that they used the legal mechanism of attaching consequences to stipulations to make them enforceable by law. Attending to the specific social and historical contexts in which Islamic law held sway can show us how women navigated and adapted its provisions to meet their needs, revealing them as active participants in the production of law rather than mere victims of it.

6

Divorce and Re-envisioning the Family

Taza Anecdote

After Qadi Iysa al-Turjali agreed to allow the young woman from Taza to marry the man of her choosing, the story might have ended there. The young woman had successfully navigated the system and found a way to remove herself from what she alleged was a toxic and abusive family environment. She had used complex legal knowledge to achieve this, circumventing her father's right to approve her marriage, or to force her into marriage. The story does not, however, end there. The father initially challenged the ruling, but did not find support. So, he waited three years to again protest the judge's ruling to the Marinid sultan and his council of legal scholars in Fez. The sultan directed the jurists to review the case and interviewed the judge and other legal officials of Taza. Based on the petitions the Fasi jurists received from the father, they unanimously recommended the annulment of the young woman's marriage to Ibn al-Turjuman, although each of them had slightly different critiques of al-Turjali's ruling. Yet, they lacked the authority to overturn the ruling, which could only be done by al-Turjali himself, the sultan, or a judge designated by the sultan.

Annulment and judicial divorces were uncommon ways to end a marriage. The most common type of divorce that appears in the fatwa sources of the time was actually a divorce oath, similar to the oath the father swore in front of witnesses that he would be divorced if he married his daughter to Ibn al-Turjuman, a type of divorce that will be discussed in the following chapter. We can assume marriages more commonly ended with a simple pronouncement of divorce by the husband, but unless there was contestation or ambiguity, this type of divorce did not require legal intervention and therefore would not be recorded in the sources.

Introduction

The case from Taza introduces us to two ways to end a marriage: annulment by a judge and a divorce oath that triggered an immediate divorce if the condition sworn upon was met. There were other ways to end a marriage, and although most of these means were controlled by men, women did have options when it came to seeking a divorce. An examination of cases involving divorce in this chapter and chapter 7 allows us to see in more detail a few aspects of women's agency and their engagement with the law introduced in the case from Taza. For example, disputes show women's knowledge of law and how they used it to enhance their rights and protect their interests with help from the jurists. These cases also continue the theme of chapter 5 and confirm, within the context of divorce, how Islamic law established the baseline for women's rights, but provided them with the tools to renegotiate the terms and protect their interests.

Through an examination of the ways in which both men and women approached the dissolution of marriage, with a particular focus on female-initiated divorce (*khul*), this chapter argues that, similar to marriage, divorce afforded women a process by which to renegotiate the rights provided by the law to obtain an outcome that more closely matched their vision for their family. Divorce was almost exclusively a male right, a symbol of a man's authority in the family. Masculinity was constructed through the patrilineal, patriarchal family structure, in which lineage was of the utmost importance and the children's lineage was traced through their father and his family. This notion of masculinity showed signs of fracture, however, when it came to *khul* divorce, in which a husband not only transferred the right to divorce to his wife, but in some cases gave up custody of his children and even allowed them to live with their mother's new husband, in exchange for his own financial benefit. This seemingly easy exchange or renegotiation of gendered rights destabilizes the fixed notion of masculinity and its associated privileges enshrined by legal sources.

As in other areas of legal and familial interactions, women used their knowledge of the law to help them rebalance their rights. The primary example is their willingness to give up financial support in exchange for retaining physical custody of their children. Similar to marriage contract stipulations, Islamic legal theory set the minimum standards for what a woman could expect, but provided her with the tools to alter the terms beyond those baseline rights.

Ending a Marriage in Marinid Morocco

Unlike in the medieval Christian world, it was extremely easy to obtain a divorce in the premodern Islamic world. Nevertheless, access to divorce was unequal, and while a man had the right to unilaterally divorce his wife with a simple statement, for any reason or no reason, a woman had fewer options to initiate a divorce. Sources from Marinid Morocco contain numerous disputes involving divorce, and al-Wansharisi's multivolume fatwa collection devotes an entire volume to the subject. Yossef Rapoport found high divorce rates for a similar time period in the Mamluk cities of Cairo, Jerusalem, and Damascus.[1]

Islamic law provided multiple avenues for initiating a divorce.[2] Relationships and the disputes that arose within them could be complicated by many factors and one troubled marriage might be subject to multiple types of divorce and subsequent reconciliations before a final separation or resolution. The most basic way to end a marriage was a straightforward pronouncement of repudiation (*talaq*), an option only available to men. Women had access to *khul*, a female-initiated divorce that required a husband's consent and involved a wife giving up certain financial rights, which might include part or all of her dower, in addition to maintenance and child support. Neither type of divorce required judicial intervention unless a particular aspect was disputed, at which point the case entered the legal system, and thus at times the historical record. While repudiation remained an exclusively male right, a husband did have the option of transferring this power to his wife through different types of delegated divorce, *tamlik*[3] or *takhyir*,[4] or through marriage contract stipulations.

Repudiation, or *talaq*, required a man to state that his wife was divorced. This pronouncement initiated a waiting period of three menstrual cycles *(idda)*, before the completion of which the wife could not remarry. A single divorce pronouncement (e.g., "I divorce you") could be revokable (*raj'i*), meaning a husband could return to the marriage during the waiting period. A divorce became final (*ba'in*) when the waiting period expired with no resolution, or after three pronouncements of divorce. The preferred method of divorce was to space these pronouncements over three menstrual cycles, giving a couple time to reconcile. However, a disliked, but accepted method was to specify a triple divorce in one utterance (e.g., "I divorce you, I divorce you, I divorce you," or "You are triply divorced.")

Marinid muftis were often consulted in cases of divorce in which the husband had used ambiguous wording instead of a straightforward pronouncement, such as "I divorce you," thus generating uncertainty over whether a divorce had in fact occurred. Men used a wide range of what was often highly creative phrasing to signal a divorce and legal scholars frequently had to decide if a particular phrase had the effect of ending a marriage. One example of a legally valid divorce pronouncement according to the Maliki school was for a man to state that a woman was prohibited (*haram*) to him.[5] Other, more questionable statements include: "You are divorced a thousand times";[6] "You are forbidden to me like pig's meat";[7] "Get out of my face, I have no need for you";[8] "I consider you like a dead person" (a statement that the muftis who responded to the question did not consider a divorce).[9] Men also claimed that despite a statement they had made, they had not intended to divorce their wives. Confusion over the number of divorces that had occurred, from a single divorce to a triple divorce, was another area of uncertainty that required legal consultation, especially if witnesses to the divorce did not agree on what had taken place. Misunderstandings also arose over the proper procedures for resuming a marriage after a non-final divorce. Husbands could contest their own divorces, claiming they had been coerced, usually by one wife pressuring her husband to divorce another wife.[10]

A triple divorce created a prohibition that prevented a couple remarrying unless the wife first married and divorced another man and completed the required waiting period. While a repudiation was extremely easy to initiate, it came with financial consequences for the husband. At the time of marriage, the dower (*sadaq*) was often divided into two parts, with one part given in advance and the other delayed.[11] Although in theory the marriage contract required the husband to pay the delayed portion by a specific date, records show that men frequently only paid it upon divorce or the death of one of the spouses.[12] Therefore, although husbands had easy access to divorce, they had to consider the financial consequences of their actions. Rapoport argues that the practice of dividing the dower evolved precisely to place a check on a husband's right to arbitrary repudiation, as he would have to surrender a large sum of money (i.e., the delayed part of the dower) at the time of divorce.[13]

The type of marriage dissolution that dominated the Taza case was annulment by a judge (*faskh*). A relatively rare method of ending a marriage, both women and men might seek this type of divorce to avoid the financial ramifications that came with other types of divorce. Most schools of Islamic law limited women's access to a judicial divorce to very specific, restrictive circumstances, such as a lengthy absence on the part of the husband, or sexual impotence.[14] The Maliki school, however, provided women with additional justifications for seeking a divorce. They included harm, an absence of four years, lack of financial support, certain defects that would impact sexual intercourse, or a serious illness, such as leprosy or a mental illness.[15] Marinid legal sources contain cases representing all types of divorce, although overall, judicial divorce appears to have been a rarity. A judicial divorce could also take longer than other types of divorce and may not have been worth the wait if there was another way to exit the marriage. While in the Maliki school harm was a valid reason for seeking a divorce, the rules for establishing the mistreatment that would enable a judge to grant the divorce were complicated, and the process could be drawn out, possibly requiring arbitration or other forms of family and community intervention.[16] There are no cases in the sources from Marinid Morocco that mention a judge granting a divorce in the case of harm, and few from the Islamic West overall.[17] Women did make allegations of beating and other forms of abuse, claims which often surfaced during divorce proceedings. Most of these cases, however, resulted in *khul*, where a woman sacrificed her financial rights in exchange for a divorce. On several occasions, after having been granted a *khul*, women attempted to establish the grounds of harm retroactively in order to recover whatever part of their dower they had given up in the *khul*.[18] This appears to have been a more common strategy for approaching a divorce when remaining in a marriage was impossible to tolerate, because it provided a quick exit and afterward, the divorced wife could seek to establish her claims of harm and her right to the full dower from a safely removed space. Family support was often evident in these cases, with fathers or other male family members intervening on behalf of a battered wife by challenging the husband or providing refuge for the wife. At times, the husband's family members also intervened to stop his abusive behavior.[19]

In some cases, a woman circumvented the rules by providing testimony that she had learned of her husband's death, or she simply remarried without following any of the required procedures.[20] In a case discussed by al-Sughayyir's students, a woman had been married for five years when a man appeared claiming he was her first husband and that they had never divorced. She said she thought he was dead and had therefore remarried. The jurists' answers did not indicate how they evaluated the status of her second marriage. The question put to them asked whether she should be punished for her alleged adultery and they responded that this should only happen if she confessed to that crime, as her belief that her husband was dead was sufficient to avoid any penalty for marrying another man while still married to the first.[21] Even without the excuse of an absent or dead husband, some cases show that women simply left their husbands, and remarried in a new place. In the previous chapter, we saw women petitioning a judge to marry, claiming that they had no guardian (*wali*). In the case of a wife who abandoned her first husband, a new marriage would only be challenged if her husband located her and brought the case to court. In this situation, the burden of proof was particularly high, and it was the first husband's responsibility to prove that his alleged marriage had taken place and had not been dissolved.[22]

What Women Wanted

What women wanted in divorce and how they got it is most visible in *khul* cases. This was a type of divorce that could be initiated by women. Maliki doctrine awarded a mother physical custody of her young children, girls for longer than boys, but these rights were contingent on her staying in the same place and remaining unmarried.[23] Cases show that for some women, their archetype of family meant keeping their children with them regardless of age, or whether they remarried or moved to another town. Women were able to negotiate to increase their custody rights using contract stipulations, in this case, divorce contract stipulations.

Scholars and activists often point to *khul* as a locus of women's agency within Islamic law.[24] This type of divorce involved concessions from the wife—which in the Moroccan context typically required a wife to give up the delayed portion of her dower (*kali*),[25] the amount her husband would have had to pay her if he initiated the divorce—often combined with waiving her right to maintenance or any other financial claims she had against her husband.[26] Only in a very small number of cases was returning the total dower a possibility.[27] Women did, however, make other concessions in a *khul* divorce, some of them financial. They frequently gave up their right to child support, and occasionally relinquished the payment owed by the husband for nursing an infant, usually in exchange for increasing their right to physical custody of the child. In this case, a woman essentially paid to be assigned rights that would otherwise belong to her husband.

Below the level of the elite, where large amounts of money and property changed hands at the time of marriage, surrendering the right to a future payment appears to have been an acceptable solution for an unhappy wife.[28] No evidence exists in the sources of women struggling to divorce by *khul*, or failing to convince their husbands to release them in exchange for what is sometimes referred to as a "ransom."[29] While a *khul* divorce was a negotiated settlement between the couple, it nevertheless required a husband's consent. Husbands seemed more than happy to agree, and in some cases even encouraged their wives toward this resolution, as it was in their own best financial interests. While obviously not in a woman's best financial interest, it nonetheless offered a way out of an unhappy marriage.

Disputes over *khul* appear frequently in sources from Marinid Morocco. This is similar to what Rapoport has found for the Mamluk East, where *khul* was the most common type of divorce.[30] While *khul* divorces appeared in court records from the Ottoman Empire,[31] dissolving a marriage like this in Morocco does not appear to have involved the courts, although it did require witnesses and a contract stating the agreed-upon settlement.[32] Consequently, it was a more expedient way for women to seek a divorce even when they had legal grounds to proceed with a court-ordered divorce.

Khul divorce makes it clear what women wanted beyond the basics provided by the law. In most cases, women used their legal knowledge to preserve what was most important to them, which was maintaining physical custody of their children at the expense of some financial rights. Moreover, they also desired a certain amount of autonomy to decide if they wanted to remarry or relocate, actions that usually meant the removal of their children. This is evident both in the stipulations they inserted into the divorce contracts and in the cases they later brought to clarify or contest the terms of the divorce. These conflicts in the aftermath of a *khul* also reveal women's expectations about what they were entitled to, which sometimes differed from the basic rights the law provided, and the challenges they could face when their lack of legal knowledge meant they risked losing custody of their children. The jurists understood that many women wanted to retain custody of their children in the case of divorce and assumed they would have the legal expertise to establish the conditions in their *khul* contracts accordingly. They also assumed that the women would voluntarily give up certain financial rights in return for partial autonomy in remarrying and relocating while maintaining custody of their children.

Khul divorces often came to the attention of jurists when the terms of the settlement were disputed. From these disputes, a picture emerges of what a standard settlement looked like, as well as the areas of tension where conflict most frequently arose. A question Abu al-Hassan al-Sughayyir was asked in the mid-fourteenth century revealed the assumptions of both mothers and jurists in these cases. In a *khul* divorce settlement, a mother committed to the financial maintenance of her daughter.[33] When she remarried, however, the paternal grandmother assumed custody of the child. The grandmother asked her son, the girl's father, for child support, but he refused, saying his ex-wife was responsible for this payment. The ex-wife, however, responded: "I took responsibility for it [maintenance] thinking that you wouldn't take her from me and even if I married she would stay with me, so return her to me and I will maintain her."[34] Evidently, she thought it unfair that she had lost her daughter and in protest, refused to continue paying for her maintenance. The mother lacked the legal erudition to understand that simply agreeing to pay to maintain her child was not enough; she needed to include additional contractual stipulations to ensure that her daughter remained with her.

The question presented to al-Sughayyir contained a follow-up question and its answer and was probably posed by the local mufti who originally handled the question and sought further advice from al-Sughayyir. The follow-up question was: "Can she be excused because of her ignorance thinking that she [i.e., the daughter] wouldn't be taken from her?"[35] The original mufti answered that her ignorance was not a valid excuse to abandon her responsibility for maintenance, as "women are not ignorant about the removal of the child from them when they marry, as you see that the ones who want this put stipulations in the *khul* contract stating that the child cannot be removed from them, whether they marry or stay single, travel or stay in the same place."[36] This is a significant statement from a jurist and reveals his belief that women had the necessary legal knowledge to navigate the conditions of a *khul* contract and therefore could not be excused from their obligations due to ignorance.[37] He also understood that it was a goal for many (but not all) women to keep their children from their first marriage, even if they remarried. The mother, in this case, apparently believed she would retain physical custody and had not known that she needed the extra condition to guarantee this, even after remarriage. It is also possible her appeal exaggerated her ignorance as part of a legal strategy. The jurists were unsympathetic to the mother's position, essentially saying that she should have known better. There was no doubt that she was still responsible for the child support she had agreed to in the *khul*.

The earlier comment from the unnamed jurist implies that ordinary women were expected to possess a certain amount of legal knowledge that would allow them to protect their interests through mechanisms provided by the law, although he does not indicate how they would have gained this understanding. His answer, however, details how women could protect the physical custody of their children by stipulating that it could not be relinquished even if they married or traveled, advice that would have returned to the questioner, and could have potentially educated other women about these technicalities. We know from other cases that women learned from the experiences of other women, in addition to consulting local jurists on an informal basis for professional advice, a process of self-education that will be discussed further in the following chapter. In the case from Taza, the young woman at its center had obtained the requisite legal knowledge to pursue a solid case against her father, in addition to an understanding of societal expectations and legal implementation, to the extent that she was not worried about confessing to *zina* despite the severe penalties laid out in legal doctrine.

In a similar case from the fourteenth century, a woman had known to stipulate that she would keep custody of her child even if she moved between the Moroccan cities of Meknes and Salé, but she later remarried and wanted to move to a different city, losing custody as a result.[38] Although the case does not mention it directly, she must have also included a stipulation that allowed her to keep her child if she remarried, as this was not the problem she faced in the case. Yet, the mufti stated that she was still required to pay her son's expenses, which she had committed to in the *khul* contract. The woman in this case lost custody of her child not because she lacked knowledge of how to draw up her *khul* to allow her to keep her child after remarriage or relocating, but because the contract limited her to two cities, which were perhaps all her ex-husband would agree to at the time of their divorce.

Certain gendered rights were transferred more willingly than others. While husbands had no qualms about a divorced wife assuming financial responsibility for their children, an obligation that was patently assigned to men by Islamic legal doctrine, fathers sometimes challenged an ex-wife's custody of their children if she remarried. Ziba Mir-Hosseini describes Maliki child custody laws as "matrifocal," with the mother and her female relatives given priority for custody.[39] Custody would not pass to the father's side of the family unless all possibilities on the mother's side had been exhausted, and children remained with their mother until a son reached maturity and a daughter's marriage was consummated.[40] In contrast, the other three schools of Islamic law required a mother to give up custody of her son at age seven and her daughter before puberty; in practice, however, children sometimes stayed with the mother even if she remarried.[41] The doctrine of all the schools, however, stated that a mother lost custody if she married a man who was not a close relative of the children (*mahram*), with only the Maliki school allowing the option to retain custody through divorce contract stipulation.[42]

The cases where *khul* contracts were disputed show that overwhelmingly, women had the knowledge to construct these documents in a way that allowed them to enhance the basic rights they were provided by Islamic law, and secure the family situation that they desired. This meant keeping custody of their children even if they remarried or moved cities, but it required them to renounce certain financial benefits. We saw the perspective of the new husband in the previous chapter who wanted to embrace his role as a stepfather. There was clearly some confusion among laypeople over whether a woman was allowed to retain physical custody (*hadana*) of her child even when she remarried if she had assumed financial responsibility for them. Some women mistakenly believed that when they agreed to financially support their children in a *khul* divorce, they were also being granted the right to maintain physical custody of the children, regardless of their marital status. Yet, the jurists expected women to understand legal technicalities well enough to leverage them to protect their ideal family unit. The mufti's response in Abu al-Hassan al-Sughayyir's case made clear that women needed to make sure to include an additional, explicit stipulation that they would keep physical custody over their child even if they remarried or moved. The jurists in these cases therefore seemed unsympathetic to women who lost custody of their children because they had failed to include the required stipulations. In the previous chapter, we saw that family configurations did not always match the recommendations contained in legal theory, with stepfathers agreeing to take over maintenance of their stepchildren. Islamic law allowed the flexibility for people to reimagine, or expand, how they wanted to shape the family unit.

Conclusion

The young woman from Taza knew what she wanted. She wanted to get married, and she was intent on marrying the man of her choosing. Although Islamic legal doctrine did not grant her full independence and instead expected her father to look out for her best interests, the law, in practice, allowed her to construct the marriage and family she had envisioned. The pressure to annul her marriage and the strong condemnation by the jurists of Fez was not directed at her but rather at the judge who had facilitated her marriage, Iysa al-Turjali. Luckily, al-Turjali withstood the pressure and refused to use his power to annul the marriage.

Women's legal knowledge was an ordinary, everyday part of their lives, their interactions with their families, and their encounters with the legal system. Such awareness, which the young woman from Taza utilized to evade her father's control over her marriage, also enabled women to navigate divorce and ensure that they retained physical custody of their children. They acquired this knowledge through the circulation of information within the community, in addition to informal consultations with jurists, a process that will be discussed in the following chapter. The jurists expected them to obtain a basic legal understanding of how to get what they wanted and use that information to secure their interests.

Islamic legal theory set the foundation for what would happen to children in the event of a divorce. These cases show that neither jurists nor laypeople viewed this foundation as sacrosanct or some kind of moral imperative, and people were free to re-envision the shape of their family. Women faced no judgment from the jurists or pressure to surrender their children to the father because that is what the law dictated, or because it was religiously or morally preferable. Fathers allowed their biological children to be raised by other men. Stepfathers were willing to accept children from an earlier marriage into their family and even pay to maintain them, which was not legally required. Gendered identities were reconstructed as rights were bartered. Women "bought" the masculine rights to end divorce, keep their children, and raise their children with a new husband, while taking on the masculine responsibility to financially support their children. People took a practical rather than a moral approach: if the law had the tools to accomplish what they wanted, then women could and should use those tools to their advantage. Marriage and divorce contracts included a mechanism for contract stipulations and were enforced the same way as other contracts, except for some types of marriage stipulations that required the additional enforcement mechanism of attaching them to divorce. If a woman wanted to retain custody of her child after she remarried, it was as simple as inserting a stipulation into the *khul* contract, assuming her husband agreed, in exchange for her assuming his financial responsibilities to the child. Premodern legal practice was distinct from the modern moralistic relationship to law today, where (some) people see legal principles as reflecting the unchanging natural order of things, enshrining an ideal vision as God intended, never to be revised or renegotiated.[43] The lived reality of Islamic law in premodern North Africa acted instead as an immersive background to life, providing the basic structure for relationships, yet remaining completely open to negotiation by women seeking rights beyond the basic minimum and using tools the law itself provided with the full support of the jurists, who ensured their attention to the technicalities of legal doctrine.

Fatwa records from Marinid Morocco provide valuable insight into different kinds of divorce strategies available to both men and women and show how people engaged with legal theory to achieve the kinds of marriages, divorces, and custody arrangements that fit their needs. Despite women's legal disadvantages in divorce regulations, they exercised a considerable amount of agency in negotiating dissolution settlements with their husbands, taking advantage of broken divorce oaths, seeking a divorce through the courts when it benefited them financially, and at times using tricks or mechanisms outside of strictly legal practices to protect their interests. Their knowledge of the law is especially visible in the case of *khul* contracts, which also reveal what was important to women; this was primarily being open to remarrying while keeping their children from their previous marriage with them, despite the associated financial concessions. These records show that both male- and female-initiated divorces were commonplace and handled mostly at a family and community level, and entered the legal system only when disputes arose around the terms of settlement, such as financial obligations or child custody.

7

Divorce Oaths and Legal Flexibility

Taza Anecdote

As the drama unfolded in the streets of Taza the night Ibrahim al-Anbaki found Ibn al-Turjuman at his house with the alleged intention of having sex with his daughter, al-Anbaki called for witnesses to help resolve the situation. When the witnesses confronted Ibn al-Turjuman, he told them that Ibrahim al-Anbaki had called him out of his own house and then took his clothes. When the witnesses were about to leave, Ibn al-Turjuman asked them to go back to al-Anbaki to try to get him to agree to his daughter's marriage. In the heat of the night's events, or perhaps because of a deeper grudge, when presented with this request, Ibrahim al-Anbaki swore a divorce oath to never marry his daughter to Ibn al-Turjuman.[1] With this impulsive act, he essentially tied his hands and made it impossible for him to ever allow his daughter's marriage to Ibn al-Turjuman without triggering his own divorce, which would require paying any outstanding part of the dower. According to Taza qadi Iysa al-Turjali's narrative, the father later told the judge to do what he saw fit, because if he himself allowed his daughter to marry Ibn al-Turjuman, his own marriage would end. What seems like a ludicrous statement made in anger was actually an exceedingly common pronouncement. The sources are full of men trying to recover their marriages after rashly making a divorce oath they later regretted.

Introduction

The oath sworn by Ibrahim al-Anbaki that he would be divorced if he married his daughter to Ibn al-Turjuman showed the witnesses just how serious he was about his resolve to prevent this marriage. This type of oath had clear consequences if broken (that is, divorce and whatever financial consequences followed), unlike an oath sworn to God, which should have been taken more seriously but had built-in means for expiation if broken.[2] Once made, an oath could not be retracted. A broken divorce oath triggered a divorce, with no way around it. A husband could swear an oath on his own behavior, on his wife's behavior, or on the occurrence of something completely unrelated to the marriage, but in all cases, his wife would be divorced if the condition was met.[3] Divorce by legally binding oath, which has received relatively little scholarly attention, appears with great frequency in legal sources from Morocco in the medieval period. The divorce oath certainly seems like the height of patriarchal privilege and disregard for a marriage, and if we read the legal doctrine alone, this might be our conclusion. And yet, the cases from Marinid Morocco reveal divorce oaths as an area particularly suggestive of legal flexibility toward women.

One reason was the existence and acceptance of multiple opinions on a number of points regarding divorce oaths in Maliki law. In some cases, this presented women with the flexibility to decide, in the wake of a broken divorce oath, whether to stay in a marriage, or to leave it. These cases show how jurists dealt with different opinions, reconciled them, and gave laypeople the opportunity to participate in the interpretation of Islamic law. In the Islamic East, the coexistence of different schools of Islamic law (*madhahib*) allowed for legal pluralism as people, jurists, and political powers exploited the differences between them, adding flexibility to the implementation of law there. Although the Maliki school was dominant in the Islamic West, the multiplicity of opinions within the school fostered flexibility there as well. These points of contention created both confusion and opportunities for couples working through their marital disputes. The cases show a complex and shifting landscape of volatile marital relationships, with creative strategies pursued by both husbands and wives. The wide range of real-life situations contained in the sources challenge simplistic assumptions about how men and women related to each other and to Islamic law. The existence of multiple opinions within the tradition, and the opportunity for ordinary people to choose which opinion to follow, allowed people to engage in a process of collaborative legal interpretation.

A second legal aspect that benefited women was the existence of informal legal spaces, a feature rarely visible in historical sources, and of which the fatwa sources only provide glimpses. Due to divorce oaths being confusing and contentious, and people having conflicting motivations, they often sought out informal legal opinions from local jurists before bringing a formal question to a mufti or a case in front of a judge. The fatwa records here preserve aspects of disputes that occurred before a formal written question was sent to a distinguished mufti from Fez or another regional center, and it is in these narratives that informal legal spaces become visible as people attempted to resolve their disputes or strengthen their cases with the help of neighborhood experts. Several of the cases discussed here mention that before a case reached a court or one of the prominent muftis of Fez, a husband, his wife, or the couple together sought legal advice from a mufti. This took the form of consultations with a local mufti or with legal students, who gave advice on the case presented to them. Women had access to these spaces and the oral advice removed a layer of formality from the process of consulting a mufti, as the parties did not have to enlist the services of a scribe to compose a written question for a more well-known mufti. Seeking legal advice from local Taza jurists, and possibly the judge too, probably explains how the young woman from Taza was able to construct such a solid case to remove her father's right to compel her to marry, and it was the judge himself who sheltered the young woman in his home when she ran away from her father. Both husbands and wives took advantage of these informal opportunities to try and resolve their situations before they reached a point that required further legal intervention.

The cases examined here illustrate an area of law in which men were granted exclusive authority to end a marriage, placing women at a distinct disadvantage because the fate of a marriage could be determined by a husband's single pronouncement, which was often spoken in anger. Yet, as will become evident in this chapter, women could at times turn the tables and use their husbands' rash actions to their advantage, such as when they forced their husbands to break their divorce oaths. This was significant, as a divorce initiated by a woman required her to make financial sacrifices, whereas a divorce initiated by a husband obligated him to make financial concessions to his wife. The fatwa sources show that while a husband could try to control his wife's behavior by swearing a divorce oath, his power in the relationship was contingent on his wife believing the gendered notion of her husband's authority. A wife could simply take control of this masculine privilege to end the marriage and force the husband to break an oath sworn on her behavior. On the surface, the divorce oath appears to put women in an extremely precarious situation, but in practice its consequences were mitigated, and it could even serve women as an additional exit strategy from an undesirable marriage with their financial rights intact.

Divorce Oaths in Action

Scholars have assumed that a key function of divorce oaths was to serve as a mechanism for men to control the behavior of their wives, as a man could swear that if his wife left the house or went to a specific place or carried out a certain action, she would be divorced.[4] In the sources from Marinid Morocco, however, divorce oaths contingent on a wife's behavior were the least frequent type of oath, and far from controlling her behavior, they often backfired completely. Men could also swear divorce oaths on other actions entirely unrelated to their marriage, as in the oath the father from Taza swore on his own daughter's marriage. When the condition was met, a divorce took place immediately. Divorce by conditional oath is the type of divorce that appears most frequently in the disputes in Marinid legal sources. This can partly be explained by confusion over the meaning of certain statements, as well as a lack of consensus within the Maliki school on some of the details of these oaths.[5] In many cases, divorce oaths took the power of divorce out of a husband's hands and transferred it to his wife or a third party, for reasons often completely unrelated to marriage or divorce. These statements jeopardized the stability of a marriage while simultaneously providing a woman with an additional route to divorce.

The oaths found in the Marinid sources covered a wide range of actions and behaviors. In line with a husband's greater control over when to end a marriage, these oaths could only be sworn by a man. Divorce was not necessarily the intended outcome of an oath, but it provided a dramatic platform upon which to make a grand gesture or convince another party of one's sincerity. Of the divorce oaths found in the sources used for this study, more than half dealt with a man's relationships outside of his family. The remainder were oaths sworn in the context of the family, with roughly half of these hinging on the wife's behavior, and the other half on the husband's own actions.

The practice documented in Mamluk Cairo, Damascus, and Jerusalem by Yossef Rapoport shows that divorce oaths were normalized in official dealings with the state or the courts, because they were considered a very serious type of pledge.[6] Because oath taking (and likewise oath breaking) was so commonplace, elaborate strategies were devised to bypass the consequences of these oaths. Instead of husbands controlling wives, Rapoport shows how divorce oaths were used by the state as a mechanism of control over its own officials. Leslie Peirce found similar evidence of divorce oaths being demanded by Ottoman officials, although this practice did not appear to be common, nor was it institutionalized as in the Mamluk context.[7] In Marinid Morocco, however, divorce oaths mainly arose in personal interactions between individuals, often in the context of business, and there is no indication that the state attempted to employ this method of control.

We have already seen one type of divorce oath in chapter 5, where they were attached to marriage contract stipulations to make them enforceable. While stipulations and divorce oaths were two distinct legal categories, the invalidity of inserting certain types of stipulations into a marriage contract according to the Maliki school, particularly those that restricted a husband's rights, made some legal maneuvering necessary. In order to make an invalid stipulation enforceable in a marriage contract, it was attached to a divorce initiated as soon as the condition was met, which essentially enforced the condition by way of a divorce oath. Therefore, a stipulation in a marriage contract that the husband would not take another wife was treated like an oath in which he swore that if he married another woman, his wife was automatically divorced. Other than the method of enforcement, however, stipulations and divorce oaths served very different purposes. Stipulations always concerned the relationship between a husband and wife and often expanded a wife's rights while restricting those of her husband, working to enhance the stability of a marriage. Divorce oaths, on the other hand, were a destabilizing force that frequently had nothing to do with a marital relationship, and when related to this relationship, they were often intended as a means by which to limit a wife's behavior and activities.

The Anatomy of an Oath

Oaths sworn on a wife's behavior often represented an attempt to restrict her mobility, while others showed annoyance with the relationship between a wife and her children from a previous marriage.[8] In the most common oaths targeting women's behavior, husbands swore that their wives would be divorced if they left the house or went to specific places. Other oaths were sworn in frustration over a particular behavior, such as a wife's refusal of sex.[9] Some oaths attempted to forbid women from engaging in certain economic activities outside of the home. Negotiations over mobility concerned both spouses, as we saw in the stipulations in which women attempted to preserve their right to work outside of the house, as well as the right to simply leave it. These cases also provide an idea of the possibilities for women's mobility, however, because if women were not going out, and in some cases working, their husbands would not feel the need to make this kind of oath.[10]

Two cases from Fez or nearby towns in the second half of the thirteenth century demonstrate, in great detail, the intricacies of disputes that prompted divorce oaths and subsequent legal negotiations. In the first, a wife lodged a complaint against her husband alleging that he was harming her, and that he was spoiling their "marital companionship."[11] With the pending case as leverage, she proposed to her husband that if he moved her from where they lived in the town of Moulay Idriss Zerhoun to the nearby city of Fez, she would drop the claim against him. In response, the husband swore that if he lodged her in Fez, she would be divorced. The wife left and went to Fez on her own. The case should have ended here with a simple divorce and without requiring the intervention of the legal system. Yet, the couple reconciled and needed to find a way to legally resume their marital relationship.

The wife stated that she had left her home due to fear of her husband, without his permission, and had intended to force him to break his oath and thus instigate a divorce. She also said that the divorce oath her husband had sworn was for a single, revocable divorce, not a triple divorce, which meant they could legally resume their marriage. The wife consulted a mufti to inquire about her legal status. Both husband and wife were under the assumption that a divorce had taken place and thus enlisted witnesses to testify to the resumption of their marriage. Complications arose, however, when the witnesses cast doubt on whether they could legally remarry. At this point, the prominent Fasi mufti from the early Marinid period, whose students included al-Sughayyir, Abu al-Fadl Rashid al-Walidi (d. 1276–77), was consulted.[12] Al-Walidi explained the different opinions within the Maliki school that would apply in this case and said that in these particular circumstances, each option offered the couple a legal way to continue their marriage.

In the second case from around the same time and place, a man called Abdullah bin Alal swore that his wife would be triply divorced if she passed a certain point on the road near Fez in order to visit her family.[13] She proceeded to do so, with the intention of making him break his oath. When the husband consulted a mufti to verify if his oath was broken, the mufti explained that there were two different opinions on the matter, and he could follow the opinion he preferred. The husband chose the opinion that said the oath was broken and he was therefore divorced. He later regretted his decision, however, and tried to find a way to remarry his wife. At this point, the mufti Rashid al-Walidi was once again consulted, and his answer confirmed that the husband must accept the divorce. Unlike in the first case, the wife here was not seeking to return to the marriage and stood by her earlier action which had initiated its dissolution.

These two cases from the early Marinid period provide an example of oaths intended to regulate a wife's mobility. In each case, the husband attempted to control his wife's movements and in doing so, placed the power of divorce in her hands. In both cases, the wife reacted by doing the exact thing that would initiate a divorce. Not only did these wives not obey, they forced their husbands into positions that the latter, in both cases, regretted. In one instance, the wife also later regretted the divorce and helped to facilitate a reconciliation. As these and other cases indicate, a divorce oath was not a highly effective strategy to discipline or control a wife, because it actually transferred the power to end the relationship to the wife, which was likely the reason this type of divorce oath appears less frequently in the sources.

A divorce was not necessarily the intention, as is illustrated by the numerous examples of husbands trying to avoid the consequences of a broken divorce oath. Rather, these oaths were pronounced in an attempt to confirm just how serious they were about whatever statement they were making, and to add a coercive element to that statement. In more than half of the cases examined here, a husband's oath to divorce his wife had nothing to do with his wife or his marriage but was articulated as a way of proving his sincerity and recognizing the seriousness of the matter, or to express his anger or frustration. Rapoport notes that "in a society in which public status was seen to be derived from power over women, slaves and children, men were expected to use their patriarchal privileges to bolster their commitments in the public sphere," meaning their exclusive control over divorce, which was exhibited through divorce oaths.[14] The wide range of oaths pronounced by men, in contexts ranging from chess games to business partnerships to interpersonal conflicts, formed a variety of circumstances that could provoke this type of oath. If such a pledge was kept, the man's marriage remained completely irrelevant to the situation at hand. Problems arose only when an oath was inadvertently broken, with the result that a husband involuntarily divorced his wife, or likewise when there was doubt over whether an oath had been broken.

At other times, men swore based on another person's actions, essentially taking the fate of their marriages out of their control. An example of an oath made conditional on the behavior of a third party was a domestic dispute presented to the chief judge of Fez, Abu Salim al-Yaznasni (d. 1392), the grandson of the mufti in the Taza case, Ibrahim al-Yaznasni.[15] In the course of a fight between a husband and wife that attracted the attention of the neighbors, the wife told her husband to call witnesses so that they could divorce by *khul*. The husband swore that witnesses would not enter his house that night. After the husband left, however, family members of both spouses who had heard news of the commotion came to the house in an attempt to mediate between the pair. As it happened, these family members were among the trustworthy people of the city who served as witnesses, and thus it appeared that the husband's oath was broken. Although the husband swore his oath during a fight with his wife, he did not make it conditional on either of their actions, but on the presence of witnesses in response to his wife's suggestion that they be summoned. Neither party claimed that the wife herself had called the family members to the house, but the fact was that they had arrived, and that they counted as the witnesses mentioned in the husband's oath. And so, instead of the *khul* divorce that the wife originally proposed, she was able to leave the marriage without renouncing any financial rights due to her husband's oath being pronounced in a moment of anger. As in the Taza case, the surrounding community, in this case family members of the angry couple, tried to intervene and help mediate the conflict.

What Women Wanted

What women wanted in these situations is rarely apparent in the sources. When women's wishes are legible, there seems to have been no preferred inclination, or course of action. Some women actively tried to make their husbands break their oaths, while other women were concerned with preserving their marriages. Other women simply were not visibly involved in the legal processes taking place around their marriage and were perhaps not even informed or consulted about the situation until a divorce occurred.

In some cases, women took advantage of a divorce oath, either by forcing it to be broken or by holding a husband liable if they knew a certain condition had been met. Al-Wansharisi, the compiler of the *Mi'yar*, complained that women were doing this frequently, and he blamed them for their bad intentions in forcing their husbands to break their oaths.[16] Most of these cases, such as the two presented to Rashid al-Walidi, involved women leaving the house after their husbands swore an oath forbidding it.[17] Other cases dealt with a mother's interactions with her children.[18]

Forcing a husband to break his oath in order for a wife to divorce herself came with its own complications due to the multiple opinions in the Maliki school as to whether an oath was broken if someone caused it to be broken intentionally, as in the two cases answered by Rashid al-Walidi earlier. This created a situation where people sometimes received the option to choose an opinion they wanted to follow, and women were also consulted in this process, a rare legal opportunity that will be discussed later. There were also a good number of cases in which women took great pains to make sure an oath was not broken, or made an effort to facilitate a new marriage, or the resumption of a marriage in case a divorce did occur.[19]

Relationship disputes were obviously complicated and in some cases it is not entirely obvious what motivated women to act or not, and what their true desires were. An example is the case from the late fourteenth century described earlier, where in the middle of a fight, a wife said she and her husband should call witnesses so she could divorce herself by *khul*, and her husband swore that if witnesses entered the house she was divorced.[20] The husband would not have brought this case to the mufti had he not wanted to reconcile with his wife. Although the source offers no information about the wife's interests concerning the outcome of this case beyond her initial request for a *khul* divorce, there would have been no dispute if she and her family had not interpreted the evening's events as a divorce. While she had begun the night asking for a *khul*, she did not try to force the divorce by calling witnesses. Nevertheless, she accepted the divorce when it occurred. This case indicates the complex motivations of women in many instances, where feelings toward a divorce may have been ambivalent.

These cases provide rare insights into what women desired in the event of divorce oaths, where a fundamental question is how women reacted to these oaths and what outcomes they preferred. It is impossible to generalize from these sources about what women wanted, nor can we assume that they always sought to leave a marriage, or that they always wanted to remain in it. Unfortunately, most cases do not give any intimation of the wishes of the women involved, and it is possible that their interests were not taken into consideration.

Divorce Oaths and Legal Flexibility

In addition to women assuming some control over the divorce process when a divorce oath was made contingent on their behavior, the existence of different opinions on certain points within the Maliki school provided an opportunity to negotiate a reconciliation or accept the termination of the marriage. If a case reached court, the judge would impose one opinion through his ruling, but before that happened people could take advantage of the legal flexibility that resulted from different views. The disagreements within the legal tradition centered around intention and whether it should be taken into account with regard to making and breaking oaths. If an oath fell into a category in which one opinion maintained that it had been broken while the other did not, this created a dilemma for the oath taker. He could end his marriage because his oath had been broken, according to one opinion, or continue his marriage on the assumption that the oath was unbroken, according to the other opinion. Wives could also be involved in the process of deciding which view to apply.

In the case from Moulay Idriss Zerhoun, in which the pair reconciled, the couple's options depended on three technicalities, one concerning the number of divorces specified and the other two related to the intention behind making and breaking the oath.[21] The husband had pronounced a divorce oath stating that if he lodged his wife in Fez, she was divorced. She proceeded to move to Fez on her own. On the surface, it would appear that the oath was broken. The couple reconciled, however, and the husband promised that she could continue to live in Fez.[22] When they sought witnesses to testify to the terms of the resumption of their marriage, the witnesses objected and claimed that they had been triply divorced, due to some writing they noticed in the marriage contract that had seemingly been erased. The case was then presented to the mufti Abu al-Fadl Rashid al-Walidi.

For al-Walidi, the witnesses' objection was legally irrelevant, and he argued that they had overstepped their bounds and usurped authority that belonged only to a judge. This fatwa was likely preserved by al-Wansharisi to illustrate a conflict in which a mufti criticized the professionalism and practices of the official witnesses. Instead, al-Walidi addressed the factors he deemed significant in the assessment of the couple's legal status.[23] Crucial to the case was that the wife stated that her husband had pronounced his oath for only a single divorce, leaving the option of reconciliation open during the waiting period. According to al-Sughayyir, a divorce oath by default initiated a triple divorce, meaning a final, irrevocable divorce.[24] The number of divorces, however, could be specified, leaving an opportunity to swear a divorce oath that would only cause a single divorce if broken. A triple divorce would create a situation in which the couple could only remarry after the wife had married and divorced another man, which was a major point of conflict in these cases as husbands sought to backtrack from the finality of the separation. The Marinid documents do not, however, show the high number of legal ploys for resolving these situations that can be observed in the Islamic East, such as sham marriages or other legal tricks.[25] In this case, the wife testified that her husband had explicitly sworn the oath about her not leaving the house as a single divorce, which cleared the way for the couple to return to their marriage if the opinion a divorce had in fact occurred was chosen.

Whether a divorce had even transpired depended on two points of disagreement in Maliki law, both involving the question of intention. The first concerned the specific phrasing of the husband's oath, in which he vowed that his wife was divorced if he lodged her in Fez. Technically, she had left on her own and lodged herself. Did this count as divorce? The preferred opinion in the Maliki school held that the intention behind the oath mattered. Rashid al-Walidi stated that in this case, it was clear that the husband's oath had meant that he did not want her to go to Fez, and the fact that he had specifically used the wording that he would not "lodge" her there was unimportant. Therefore, when she moved to Fez on her own, the oath was broken. The other opinion accepted by the Maliki school, however, to which al-Walidi pointed and that "the Iraqis" (meaning legal interpretations of the Hanafi school) also followed, placed more importance on the actual words, not the intention.[26] The husband said specifically that he would not lodge her and he had not, so therefore the oath was not broken, the couple was not divorced, and they could continue their marriage.

The second area of disagreement centered on the conditions of breaking the oath. The wife stated that she had moved to Fez with the intention of compelling her husband to break his oath. According to the opinion transmitted by Malik's disciple Ashhab ibn Abd al-Aziz (d. 820), an oath was not broken if someone had intentionally caused it to be broken. Yet, according to another of Malik's disciples, Abd al-Rahman Ibn al-Qasim (d. 806), the oath was considered broken if the condition on which it was contingent had indeed occurred, regardless of whether compulsion was a factor.[27] Therefore, if one followed the opinion of Ashhab, a divorce had not taken place, because the wife moved to Fez with the explicit intention of making her husband break his oath. On the other hand, if Ibn al-Qasim's opinion was favored, the oath was broken with the act of moving, regardless of the circumstances, in which case the couple could legally return to their marriage thanks to the wife's testimony that the oath was sworn on a single divorce. The mufti pointed out that according to any viewpoint, the couple was not irrevocably divorced.

The question presented to Abu al-Fadl Rashid on behalf of the couple touched on every possible point of law that could provide an opportunity for them to resume their marriage. This resumption was inevitable based on the evidence presented. They had clearly received guidance on how to construct their case and the fatwa mentions at least one previous consultation between the wife and a mufti. Equally important was the level of cooperation between the spouses. If the wife had not confirmed that the divorce was only a single divorce, or that she had intentionally caused her husband to break his oath, a divorce could have been enforced. The husband and wife approached the mufti with a collaborative strategy that strengthened their case beyond a doubt.

In the second case from the mid-thirteenth century, in which the couple did not reconcile, the husband, Abdullah al-Alal, had sworn that if his wife passed Wargha, near Fez, on the way to visit her family, she would be divorced.[28] After she passed this place, intentionally seeking to make him break his oath, he consulted a mufti. The mufti explained the opinions mentioned above, that according to Ibn al-Qasim, his oath was broken, as the compulsion was not taken into account, while according to Ashhab his oath was not broken. The husband asked the mufti to advise him on which opinion to follow, but the mufti said the husband should select the judgment himself, adding that one was the easy way out while the other was more difficult. The husband chose Ibn al-Qasim's more difficult opinion, which maintained that a divorce had occurred. He later regretted his choice and consulted local legal scholars, who informed him that in the opinion of some scholars, he had not broken his oath. At this point, the dilemma was presented to Rashid al-Walidi. He responded that because the husband had selected the opinion that mandated divorce, a divorce had taken place, and he was bound by it.[29] Al-Walidi noted, however, that if his wife had approached a mufti for an opinion first, and had chosen to apply the opinion that confirmed the divorce, the husband would have to abide by it, removing his choice in the matter.

These two fatwas reveal a legal space that existed at the community level, before the involvement of a court or the prominent jurists of Fez and other large urban centers. Local muftis were accessible to the population, who could consult them informally, without the need for composing a written question to one of the well-respected jurists whose opinions were preserved by al-Wansharisi and others. These oral fatwas would not have been preserved, and we only see traces of them in descriptions of disputes that escalated beyond the point where they could be resolved at this less formal level. We also saw in the first case, in which the couple reconciled, that it was the wife who first sought an opinion on her marital status, indicating that these legal spaces and consultations were also available to women. It is also possible that women educated in the legal sciences advised other women through similar oral consultations. Abdullah al-Abdusi's sisters, along with some other women of their generation, were described with the term *faqiha*, or legal scholar, which meant they were qualified to provide the same advice as a mufti.

In these informal consultations, we see law as a collaborative process, especially in the cases where there was no single, decisive opinion. Muftis presented the options to the petitioners and helped guide them toward a decision or advised them to make their own decision armed with the pertinent legal information. Research on the Islamic East shows that the existence of multiple legal schools provided a certain amount of flexibility for ordinary people, who could follow an opinion from the school that best met their needs.[30] Although the Maliki school was the sole legal school in the Islamic West during and after this period and there was no legal pluralism as in other areas of the Muslim world, differences of opinion within the Maliki school afforded a certain amount of elasticity. In this space of consulting a mufti before the direct involvement of a court, people could take advantage of these coexisting opinions to arrive at a resolution that worked for them, an option available to women as well as men.

In the cases above, spouses consulted muftis together or sought opinions on their own. In the first case, however, the wife was seeking advice on how to remain in her marriage. In two cases addressed by Abdullah al-Abdusi that consider the possibility a wife does not wish to remain in the marriage, al-Abdusi said that consulting the wife was obligatory if the husband followed the opinion that held no divorce had occurred.[31] This seems logical, and indeed critical, if we consider that if she favored the opinion the oath had been broken, remaining in the marriage would be impossible as she would understand herself to be living in a state of fornication, even if the husband considered the marriage to be valid.[32] If the wife held the opinion that the oath had been broken, al-Abdusi said that the matter would have to be decided by the judge. Although both opinions were valid within the school, judges, by the nature of their position, had to select one decision in a ruling, and the opinion that judges favored in their rulings was that the oath was broken, as this was the more favored (*mashhur*) of the two opinions within the Maliki school.

The pliability surrounding the rules of oath taking and oath breaking could also be subject to exploitation and abuse, a matter which concerned the jurists. In al-Wansharisi's compilation of the *Mi'yar*, directly after the case addressed by al-Walidi in which the couple did not reconcile, al-Wansharisi described a related case that had recently occurred (i.e., the late fifteenth century, more than two hundred years after al-Walidi's time) in which a woman had intentionally broken her husband's divorce oath.[33] In this situation, a husband swore that his wife, Umm al-'Izz, could not go out to visit her father; she then went to visit her father, intentionally causing her husband to break his oath. Taking advantage of the informal legal space, she sought advice, perhaps because she was seeking a way to reconcile, and was advised to follow (*taqlid*) the opinion of Ashhab, which maintained that an oath broken intentionally did not count as broken. In this case, the husband and wife mutually agreed to follow this opinion, and their decision was confirmed by an unnamed mufti. Somewhat unusually, however, the chief judge of Fez overruled the mufti and ordered him to withdraw his fatwa.[34] The couple was therefore required to proceed with a divorce mandated by the competing opinion of Ibn al-Qasim, which held that an oath was broken regardless of whether compulsion had been involved.[35]

In his comment, al-Wansharisi mentioned that in his time people frequently chose to follow the opinion of Ashhab, due to many women causing their husbands to break their oaths.[36] His critique here did not, however, take aim at the men making reckless oaths and not accepting the consequences when oaths were broken. Rather, he criticized what he saw as the bad intentions of the women who were deliberately breaking oaths. If the purpose of making an oath contingent on a wife's behavior was to regulate that behavior, and if she took the specified action anyway, and broke the oath and initiated a divorce, the husband was the clear loser. Choosing Ashhab's opinion that did not consider an oath broken if it had been broken intentionally enabled a husband to mitigate the potential damage to his life and finances caused by his wife's actions. The judge's public and official endorsement of Ibn al-Qasim's opinion was a warning to husbands who were swearing unreasonable or irrational oaths and to wives who seized the opportunity to break them. Knowing that the consequences of a broken oath would be enforced, couples would have to proceed more cautiously in their disputes if they had any interest in preserving their marriages.

In the Islamic West, there was no tolerance for the elaborate strategies invented by men in other parts of the Muslim world (at times with the guidance of the jurists) to circumvent the consequences of a broken divorce oath. In the Ottoman Empire, Colin Imber observed a change over time in the attitude of jurists toward oaths, with earlier jurists focusing on enforcing legal technicalities, while later muftis appeared to place more emphasis on seeking a resolution.[37] Muftis in Marinid Morocco worked with couples they must have considered to be acting in good faith and helped them to find resolution within the legal tradition, often drawing on the disagreements in opinion that provided them with interpretive discretion. These cases brought laypeople, including women, into the process of lawmaking, and gave them opportunities to engage in a direct and profound way with the legal tradition.

Conclusion

The divorce oath embodied men's privileged position over women in deciding when to end a marriage. It was the ultimate symbol of masculine power, particularly when deployed as a tactic to limit a wife's mobility or activities. Yet, sources that document how these oaths were made and broken in practice reveal both the fluidity of gendered identities and the flexibility of Islamic law, including women's active role in the decision-making process. Leslie Peirce argues that in the case of sixteenth-century Ottoman Aintab, "it was the people of Aintab who, negotiating with and through the court, were responsible for much of that interpretation."[38] A similar process in Marinid Morocco occurred largely outside of formal legal venues, by which ordinary people interpreted Islamic law with the guidance of the jurists, and took an active role in engaging with the legal tradition. Women assumed a key role in shaping these disputes by their actions and reactions, and through the consultative process with local jurists, they became key stakeholders and agents in the coproduction of Islamic law.

Men pronounced oaths in anger and in the course of disputes with other men in circumstances entirely unrelated to their marriages, thereby undermining their own gendered authority in the moment they attempted to proclaim it. In contrast to conditions in marriage contracts, which delegated the power of divorce to women if certain circumstances occurred, and served to stabilize partnerships, divorce oaths jeopardized marital stability. Two factors mitigated the potential damage caused by men flaunting their patriarchal privilege and destabilizing marriages through divorce oaths. First, broken oaths provided wives with the means to exit an unwanted marriage while preserving their financial rights, thereby turning a husband's impulsive behavior against him. Second, the fact that the Maliki school accepted the legitimacy of multiple legal opinions gave muftis the latitude to seek a resolution that could preserve the integrity of a marriage, if that was the goal of both spouses. These fatwas illuminate a fascinating consultative process whereby ordinary people were authorized to make interpretive decisions by choosing to follow one of the opinions recognized by the Maliki school. Wives were given a voice in the process, often through the existence of informal legal spaces, and indeed their involvement in the decision-making process was sometimes compulsory.

The sources that detail actual practice within a legal system help us to understand how the law worked. In the case of divorce oaths, the legal doctrine seemingly agreed upon during the Marinid period favored one opinion over the other. Without analyzing these sources, we would have no understanding of how this point was contested, negotiated, and perhaps in some cases abused by both women and men, with legal authorities providing the necessary framework to guide this diversity in interpretation.

8

Transgressions and Legal Accommodation

Taza Anecdote

As part of her strategy to remove her father's coercive power over her marriage, the young woman from Taza confessed to Qadi Iysa al-Turjali that she had committed *zina* and was no longer a virgin. This confession was a key element in the case that al-Turjali constructed to rule against the young woman's father, Ibrahim al-Anbaki, as it removed his ability to control her marriage. The father's narrative also contained an allegation of *zina* against his daughter. He described how Ibn al-Turjuman seduced her and would sneak into his house when he was gone, culminating in the dramatic nighttime scene where al-Anbaki ripped off al-Turjuman's clothes as the latter ran away.

Unfortunately, in handling this case, Qadi al-Turjali made a serious misstep: even though the young woman later withdrew her confession of *zina*, the qadi should still have made her observe a waiting period (*istibra*) as a measure of caution to prove that she was not pregnant, before allowing her to marry Ibn al-Turjuman. Perhaps al-Turjali skipped this requirement intentionally, fearing for the young woman's physical safety if she remained under the supervision of her father, or that he would force her into an unwanted marriage.[1] Regardless, it was this technicality that created the most serious threat to the continuation of the marriage.

Istibra was a legal mechanism that illustrates the pragmatic approach jurists took to women who strayed outside legal boundaries. Far from a punishment, it was a way to return women to a position from which they could marry. Rather than obsess over virginity or honor, jurists, families, and community members worked to provide a space for a woman to observe this waiting period, after which she could move on with her life, which usually involved marrying the man with whom she was suspected of committing *zina*.

Introduction

We have seen how women negotiated better conditions in marriage and divorce and how they used legal strategies and tools to temper male authority over them in the gendered legal doctrine of the family. The disputes recounted in the fatwas show that these interventions remained, for the most part, within social norms and legal boundaries. The law itself, reinforced by a robust support network of local jurists, community members, and, most importantly, family, allowed women to renegotiate the baseline terms set by the doctrine to realize the lives, families, and marriages that aligned more closely with their interests and expectations, while remaining within the safety of social norms and legal boundaries.

This chapter explores what happened when women trespassed these boundaries, often in contexts in which premarital sex (*zina*) was the defining factor but was rarely a direct or provable allegation. The legal doctrine set clear rules (*zina* was a *hadd* crime, or crime against God, and punishable) and at the same time built in a flexibility that favored avoiding accusations, let alone punishment. The requirements for proving *zina* were nearly impossible to meet and historically the punishment was almost never carried out. A confession was a different matter, as it removed the strict requirement of four witnesses testifying to actually having seen the point of penetration. Nevertheless, Prophetic example discouraged confession, and withdrawing a confession was favored. Faced with the reality that premarital sex may have happened, even if not provable, jurists took a pragmatic approach that required a woman to observe a waiting period analogous to the waiting period after a divorce or death of a husband (*idda*) to ensure that she was not pregnant by her previous husband before her remarriage.

The women in this chapter found themselves in a compromised position. In many cases they had defied family authority and landed in a seemingly sticky legal situation. And yet, the same legal system provided the framework to help them return to a place where they could resume their lives, aided by family, community, and local jurists. The jurists' concern was very clear: to bring illicit sex into legally valid terms and to clarify lineage. To do so, they first imposed a waiting period to ensure that no child had been conceived during the relationship, which had consequences for paternity and inheritance. At that point, the couple were free to marry. The jurists' responsibility was to attend to the technicalities of the process. Largely absent in these cases, from the perspective of the jurists or the community, was discourse on female sexuality, morality, virginity, or honor; concerns that define women's experience in modern legal contexts that make claims to the legacy of the Islamic legal tradition. Women were not shunned or made unmarriageable, and their transgressions did not destroy their lives or even seem to define them.

In chapter 2, the legal category of virginity was presented in the context of how much control a father had over his daughter's marriage. In cases where *zina* was suspected, where based on modern preoccupations we might imagine virginity would assume a central role, the category was surprisingly absent from the legal discourse. The gendered category at stake was lineage, the pillar that held up patriarchal notions of the family. Lineage was traced through the father, although children born outside of a valid marriage were instead assigned to their mother's lineage. The jurists' preoccupation in cases of suspected *zina* was safeguarding the lineage of the children by ensuring that the bride was not pregnant at the time of marriage. This is where *istibra* came in, to restore not virginity but lineage. Virginity when detached from the concept of honor was almost a side effect of the endeavor to preserve lineage and was likely more socially than legally relevant. In cases of suspected *zina*, the category of virginity could remain ambiguous, and did not need to be resolved; *istibra* ensured there was no pregnancy but made no claims about virginity.

I argue here that even when women ventured outside of legal boundaries, the law remained the defining feature of both the women's actions, and the reactions of the family, the community, and the jurists. The measures taken by the women, from running away to confessions of *zina*, may have constituted a subversion of family authority, or a manipulation of the legal system; however, it was also through legal avenues that the cases ultimately resulted in a marriage that was recognized by the community and the law. Through these steps, women forced jurists and the legal system to deal with situations that had not been clearly elaborated in Islamic law, and in this way helped to shape the law through the preservation of their actions in the legal records.[2]

Social Transgressions: Runaways and Elopement

The case from Taza was the most dramatic case of its kind and was unique in its level of detail. The woman ran away from her home and had either committed *zina* or falsely confessed to it to circumvent her father's authority as her marriage guardian. The woman from Taza is not, however, the only runaway to be found in the sources. There are six similar cases spanning the Marinid period, whose outcomes, in certain respects, are consistent with this case, suggesting that its less extreme elements were not isolated occurrences.[3] The actions taken by the women in these cases served as a way of choosing, or refusing, a particular husband and forcing her family to accept her decision. In each instance, the woman achieved the desired result, in what often resembled elopement. Likewise, successful outcomes were facilitated by the involvement of communities and the legal system. No other case met with the same kind of legal opposition from jurists as the case from Taza, primarily because no other woman faced as much resistance from her father or other family members.

Elopement was not unknown in the medieval Islamic world, nor in the medieval Christian world, although it rarely appears in legal sources.[4] The categories of elopement and abduction sometimes overlapped, and in some cases, elopement may have been disguised as abduction, as Judith E. Tucker suggests in some instances of marriage by capture in Ottoman Syria and Palestine, for example to help a woman avoid an unwanted marriage promise.[5] An Ottoman provincial legal code (*kanunname*) contained severe penalties for women who were consenting partners in an "abduction."[6] In Marinid Morocco, however, there seems to have been little need for the legal fiction of claiming abduction to avoid *zina* charges, and cases that involved forced abduction or rape were clearly distinct from consensual elopement.

The act of running away itself was a challenge to a father's authority, but not to the law, and therefore the jurists did not address it directly.

Islamic law lacks the concept of elopement, although the associated crime of *zina* is very thoroughly treated in doctrinal sources. There were mechanisms to deal with it when it occurred, however, and how it was addressed depended on the particular time, place, and legal context, as there was no set theory or doctrine to consult. From the other cases discussed here, we can see a more "typical" path to resolution than that in the Taza case.

Of the seven cases involving runaways in Marinid sources, one in the early Marinid period was answered by al-Sughayyir, followed by the case from Taza answered by his students, while a cluster of four similar cases were answered by Abdullah al-Abdusi (d. 1445) toward the end of the period.[7] This could either mean that women and families considered al-Abdusi a more sympathetic mufti when it came to issues of this type, or that more cases occurred at this time of political upheaval. A similar case from late fourteenth-century Bougie elicited responses from as far away as Tlemcen and Tunis.

A comparison of these other runaway cases to the Taza case is instructive. In several of them, including the Taza case, the community intervened to help resolve a potentially scandalous situation. In a case presented to al-Sughayyir, an orphaned woman ran away to the house of one man to avoid marrying another one.[8] The people of her town removed her from this man's house and brought her to the leader (*shaykh*) of the tribe. She was provided a safe space to complete her waiting period (*istibra*). At that point, she authorized the *shaykh* to perform her marriage to the man with whom she ran away. In the case of *zina*, this waiting period was called *istibra*, and was analogized to the shorter waiting period (one menstrual cycle) imposed on an enslaved woman when she changed owners, as male enslavers had a right to sexual relations with the women they enslaved. The *istibra* after *zina* was set at three menstrual cycles, like that after the divorce of a free woman, although some jurists maintained that it should only be one menstrual cycle.

An orphan, like a nonvirgin, was not subject to the coercive capacity of a father in marriage, a fact that could provide more room to negotiate or challenge the validity of a particular marriage guardian. In one case addressed to al-Abdusi, an orphaned woman refused a marriage contracted for her by one marriage guardian, claiming that she had not authorized him to conduct the marriage, and instead ran away with another man.[9] Al-Abdusi agreed that the first marriage would be invalid if she had been married without her consent. Another woman who ran away from a contracted marriage suggested another, somewhat flimsy, legal excuse to invalidate the contract and marry the man she ran away with.[10] While al-Abdusi did not provide her with a clear path to stay in her second marriage, he did place the burden of challenging it on the abandoned husband, and, as we saw in the case from Taza, judges were hesitant to annul an existing marriage without solid supporting evidence.

Although there was no accusation or even a suggestion of improper conduct in al-Sughayyir's case, observing a waiting period (*istibra*) was a standard precaution that occurred in many cases. In an example presented to al-Abdusi, a woman was removed from the house of the man she ran away with and completed her waiting period in the house of a neighbor, after which her father reluctantly agreed to marry her to the man.[11] A similar outcome occurred in a case from Bougie in the late fourteenth century, which is described later in the discussion of *zina*.[12]

In most cases, families were eventually swayed by the daughter's actions into accepting her choice or refusal of a husband, unlike in the case from Taza, where the father continued to press for the annulment of his daughter's marriage. In the other cases in which women ran away with a man, even when *zina* was an issue, the parties involved found a way to contract a marriage in accordance with the law. If the events had unfolded differently, without the animosity of the father or the missteps of the judge, the case from Taza might have had a similar legal outcome. This lack of resolution was unusual because in most cases some kind of agreement or uneasy truce was negotiated. In the case of al-Abdusi mentioned above, the father acquiesced to his daughter and contracted the marriage after the completion of his daughter's waiting period.[13] Yet, the father demanded a large gift from the groom for the marriage celebration, including "around 20 handfuls of butter, two animal loads of flour, a bull, clothes valued at thirty gold dinars, and eight dinars of food," which the groom had trouble fulfilling, thus delaying consummation of the marriage.[14] The bride ran away for the second time to her new husband's house and he gave her the clothes he had promised in the marriage contract, and she remained in his house at the time of the complaint. In this case, al-Abdusi ruled that it was permissible for her to stay with her husband if the marriage had already been consummated, and her husband had provided her with a dower adequate for someone of her status (*sadaq al-mithl*), completing the marriage requirements. A marriage could not be considered valid until a proper dower had been paid, but instead of holding the husband to the high dower he had promised originally, al-Abdusi merely required him to pay a dower that someone of her social status could expect to receive.

In another case, a daughter who had been betrothed to her cousin as a child protested the marriage when she came of age.[15] In this instance, the daughter's threat to run away was enough to convince her father to revoke the promised marriage. This strategy of threatening to run away in order to force her father to support her marriage choice indicated that the daughter had a certain amount of knowledge about how these cases played out. Women would have known from similar situations that it was unlikely they would face severe consequences, whether from the legal system or their own family, and that the suspicion *zina* had occurred would make it difficult for their families to arrange another marriage. This transmission of legal knowledge through both formal channels, such as consulting a mufti, or informal channels, such as word of mouth based on other women's experiences, provided women with the ability to navigate many legally complex situations in ways that were advantageous.

The jurists involved in these cases paid little attention to the defiant act of a woman running away from her family, even in the case of suspected *zina*. Instead, they took a pragmatic approach in searching for legal solutions, such as meeting the requirements of a valid marriage, or observing a waiting period in the case of *zina*. Punishments or consequences for *zina* were mentioned only in the case from Taza and only in passing, when the daughter confessed to *zina* in order to remove her father's right of guardianship over her. This fact stands in sharp contrast to modern implementations of Islamic law, which emphasize harsh punishments as a way to regulate women's sexuality.

The cases discussed above did not encounter the legal system because the women ran away with men they wanted to marry or to protest their marriage to a particular man. Running away in itself was not a crime, and the muftis were only brought into these cases later, after other disputes arose around a marriage. Otherwise, the community's intervention would have been sufficient to resolve the situation, both by intervening with a woman's family and by providing a path in accordance with legal norms, including observing a waiting period before contracting a legal marriage with a suitable dower. Rather, the cases were brought to the attention of the law for other reasons, such as technical requirements of the marriage contract not being fulfilled or competing claims from another suitor or deserted husband. Families, neighbors, and the legal authorities worked to resolve these potentially disastrous situations and return the couple to the path of a legally recognized marriage, overlooking the transgressions that had occurred, in every case except that of the father from Taza, who refused to allow his daughter to marry the man she insisted on marrying.

Zina in Theory

The most serious legal transgression in the case from Taza was *zina*, which here means fornication, although the term could also refer to adultery in the context of married parties. This crime was considered among the crimes against God (*hudud*) requiring the severe *hadd* punishment, a category of crime that targeted activities that destabilized public order, such as theft, highway robbery, drinking alcohol, and a range of sexual crimes.[16] With regard to fornication, the punishment according to the Maliki school was one hundred lashes for both parties, followed by a year or more of exile for the man.[17] Yet, evidentiary rules made this crime nearly impossible to prove. Establishing and proving an accusation of *zina* required four reliable male witnesses to testify to observing the act of penetration; moreover, bringing claims of *zina* with anything less than this proof meant severe corporal punishment for the accusers.[18] Additionally, a Prophetic hadith advised avoiding the *hadd* punishments in cases where there was any doubt (*shubha*), and jurists relied on this principle to avoid implementing these punishments where possible.[19] One other means of establishing *zina* was by confession, although this could later be revoked to avoid the *hadd* punishment, as we saw in the case from Taza. No one was ever obligated to confess to this crime, however, and confessions of *zina* were discouraged based on Prophetic example.[20]

Although in the modern period, extremist groups and states looking to boost their "authentic" Islamic credentials have embraced *hadd* punishments, including for *zina*, historical studies show very few instances of the *hadd* being applied for *zina*, and in most cases it was only because of a voluntary confession.[21] The strict evidentiary rules mandated by the Islamic legal tradition in addition to the jurists' directive to try and avoid this penalty explains the lack of punishment for *zina* during the medieval era. Some modern states, such as Pakistan, have codified the concept of *zina* and its punishment, but have at the same time incorporated completely different rules for procedure and evidence, such as accepting circumstantial evidence, which makes conviction for this crime significantly easier.[22]

Zina in the Medieval Muslim World

The Ottoman Empire has received the most scholarly attention because of the quality and accessibility of its legal sources, and many view the conclusions drawn from these studies as generalizable and representative of Islamic law. The Ottoman legal system was exceptional, however, as certain areas of law, including *zina*, were subsumed under state law, with the sultan's mandated punishments replacing those punishments found in Islamic law.[23] While evidentiary rules were relaxed to allow the possibility of finding someone guilty of *zina*, punishments were changed to a sliding scale of fines based on a person's social status and financial means.[24] Ottoman muftis could still use classical Islamic law to recommend stoning, but officials did not have to follow the recommendation.[25]

In her research on court records from Ottoman Aleppo from the sixteenth to the nineteenth century, Elyse Semerdjian found that "the shariʿa courts regularly recorded nonviolent, noncorporal punishments" in cases of immorality.[26] Often, the punishment for an offender was banishment from a neighborhood owing to accusations of immoral behavior that would not meet traditional Islamic legal standards of evidence. In her study of a town in sixteenth-century Anatolia, Leslie Peirce likewise found no record of corporal punishment for any crimes.[27] Cases of fornication occurred in this context mostly in rural areas.[28] One case from these records of confession to *zina* later led to a marriage and Peirce suggests that perhaps premarital sex was a strategy to push for a particular marriage.[29] While Peirce's evidence allows for only tentative conclusions, the North African cases of runaways and other instances of *zina* discussed later make it clear that in the Maghrib, premarital sex was indeed a way to force a family to accept an unwanted marriage, or to accelerate the marriage process. Like the earlier Moroccan examples, voluntary confessions of *zina* in the Ottoman context served a purpose. In the Ottoman case, however, these confessions could have been a strategy to seek a relatively light punishment, such as a fine, from the court, in order to avert the punishment that might be meted out by the family in a so-called "honor killing," an extrajudicial form of punishment that was legally condoned in the central Middle East, but did not exist as a social or legal category in the Islamic West.[30] In seventeenth- and eighteenth-century Ottoman Syria and Palestine, Judith E. Tucker found that the muftis favored requiring a man to pay a dower (*mahr*) as compensation for taking a woman's virginity, instead of delivering punishments defined by the religious or administrative legal system, which were usually based on doubt (*shubha*).[31] Significantly, however, cases of *zina* were rarely brought to court, which suggests extrajudicial mechanisms of resolution.[32]

In one of the few secondary sources to consider this topic for medieval North Africa, David S. Powers discusses two cases from the *Mi'yar* that deal with *zina* in fourteenth-century Morocco. One case, involving an allegation that a man had conceived a child with his daughter's slave, concerned paternity (with implications for inheritance) and not punishment, as the alleged father was deceased.[33] Interestingly, the judge in this complex case was Iysa al-Turjali, and as in the earlier case from Taza, he consulted Ibrahim al-Yaznasni for a second opinion. This case took place under the reign of the previous sultan, Abu Said Uthman (r. 1310–31), before the relationship between al-Turjali and the Fasi jurists was so badly damaged.

In another case analyzed by Powers, from a slightly earlier period, the jurist Musa al-Haskuri was accused of improperly continuing relations with his wife after divorce.[34] Abu al-Hassan al-Sughayyir, one of the muftis consulted, recommended lashing as a punishment for *zina*, but not stoning. He also recommended life imprisonment for the illicit behavior in light of al-Haskuri's status as a scholar and position as a mufti.[35]

Another mufti was consulted and recommended death by stoning, outraged that a fellow jurist would favor what he saw as a lighter sentence; however, the judge went with al-Sughayyir's opinion and the offending jurist was merely lashed.[36] The outrage in this case was directed at the jurist, al-Haskuri, and there was no discussion of punishment for his wife. This was an exceptional case due to the status of the offender and the fact that his crimes clearly warranted punishment; however, the evidence in the case would not have met the standards for *hadd* punishment for *zina*, and if al-Haskuri had not been a mufti issuing fatwas for others to follow, his case would most likely have been treated very differently.

Delfina Serrano Ruano examined an earlier case from twelfth-century Andalusia, in which the prominent Cordoban jurist Abu Walid Ibn Rushd the Elder (d. 1126) recommended stoning a woman in a case presented to him from Almeria.[37] Serrano argues, however, that Ibn Rushd's main legal strategy was to change the venue of the case and remove it from the jurisdiction of the local judge, as the mufti stated that only the chief judge had the authority to impose such a sentence.[38] Had the case reached the chief judge, the evidence against the woman would likely not have met the strict standards needed to impose this punishment. Serrano also notes that no instances of punishing *zina* by stoning have been found in historical sources for the premodern Islamic West.[39]

Zina in Marinid Morocco

Outside of the runaway cases, the sources contain few cases of *zina* from Marinid Morocco.[40] In *al-Durr al-Nathir*, our jurist from the early Marinid period, Abu al-Hassan al-Sughayyir, only responded to one question that explicitly addressed *zina*, in addition to the runaway case he answered. Aside from his cases dealing with runaways, al-Abdusi's collection contains no concrete cases of *zina*, although he answered one theoretical question regarding laws about *zina* another scholar asked him.[41] The *Mi'yar* contains only two cases of *zina* beyond the runaway cases that can be situated in Marinid Morocco, one being the jurist who improperly remarried his wife, in which al-Sughayyir gave an opinion, and another case that was presented to al-Sughayyir's students, including most of the same jurists who responded in the Taza runaway case.[42]

In the one case presented to al-Sughayyir, he was asked about the validity of a marriage contracted between a man and a woman who had committed *zina*. The woman had observed a waiting period of one menstrual cycle before they consummated their marriage.[43] Al-Sughayyir answered that the marriage was invalid because it was contracted during the waiting period, which should have been three menstrual cycles. The rest of his answer dealt with the issue of whether they could remarry after the marriage was annulled and he listed several competing opinions in the Maliki school on this matter, meaning that the couple had a legal pathway to remarry from among them. Similar to the cases involving runaways, neither the *zina* nor its punishment was the focus here; rather, al-Sughayyir's task was to determine the legal status of the marriage and any resulting children.

A waiting period was observed even in cases where *zina* was not directly alleged, if there was any possibility it had occurred, such as in cases of runaways where the couple had spent time alone together. This requirement was in line with the muftis' goal of facilitating a legal marriage and preserving lineage. The jurists rarely discussed *hadd* punishments in their answer and when they did, it was often because the question raised the issue. One example involved a scorned man whose wife had remarried in his absence and who clearly wanted her to suffer for her actions.[44] This type of case, discussed in chapter 5, reflected the uncertainties of a time when men might not return from their travels, or could be killed or captured in war. Typically, however, these cases were discussed under the rubric of valid marriage and divorce, and this case brought in the issue of *zina* only at the husband's insistence. The students of al-Sughayyir, most of the same jurists who were embroiled in the Taza case (including Ibrahim al-Yaznasni, Ibn Abd al-Karim, Abd al-Aziz al-Qayrawani, and Abu Diya Misbah al-Yalsuti), responded to this question, and while they all addressed the issue of punishment, for the most part they agreed that it should be averted according to the doctrine of doubt, as the woman said she thought her husband was dead at the time she had remarried. These same muftis from the sultan's council had likewise ignored the issue of punishment in the case from Taza, where their harshest judgment was reserved for the judge himself.

The case of al-Haskuri, the Fasi jurist who remarried his wife after an irrevocable divorce, is the only instance in the Marinid sources in which we know that a corporal punishment was carried out in a case related to *zina*.[45] As discussed earlier, however, the case was more about the abuse of his position and knowledge than about *zina* itself, as is evidenced by the fact that punishment for his wife, a partner in the invalid marriage, was never considered by the jurists.

It is clear from the Moroccan cases of runaways, and other cases of *zina*, that the offending parties judged the risk of punishment to be low. The *zina* confession of the woman in the case from Taza as a strategy to remove her father's guardianship is somewhat surprising, as a confession of *zina* is one of the few instances where application of the *hadd* punishment has been observed historically. The daughter in this case was evidently not concerned, however, or had calculated that the desired outcome was worth the risk.

The *Mi'yar* contains several cases related to *zina* from Algeria, Tunisia, and al-Andalus in the same period, which highlight some interesting parallels and allow us to make comparisons to the Moroccan cases. Two cases from neighboring Algeria also involved confessions of *zina* as a legal strategy, which further suggests the low risk of confessing to *zina* in certain circumstances. A case from fifteenth-century Algeria involved a strange voluntary confession from a widow who became pregnant three years after her husband died.[46] The Maliki school, unlike the other schools of jurisprudence, allowed a child born up to five years after the death of a husband or a divorce to be attributed to his father's lineage, based on the concept of a "sleeping fetus" (*raqqad*). What may seem like an absurdity to the modern reader was actually a feature of Maliki law that made it more flexible for women, and had the particular effect of shielding their transgressions after divorce or the death of their husband.[47] The woman from Algeria, however, claimed she was pregnant from *zina*, and that her dead husband was not the father of the child. Yet, the husband's brother said that the child obviously belonged to his deceased brother and alleged that the wife was only confessing to *zina* because there was bad blood between the widow and her brother-in-law. The question was complicated and contested, and circulated among several prominent figures in Algeria and Tunisia, including the Tunisian compiler of a great fatwa collection, Abu al-Qasim al-Burzuli (d. 1438). The issue they debated was whether the child belonged to his father's lineage and although they did not agree on the answer, the matter of *zina* was not addressed by any of them. The woman could have concealed her transgressions by claiming the child belonged to her late husband. Yet, keeping the child away from her husband's family was clearly her priority, even if it meant confessing to *zina*, and she would have known that the risk of punishment was minimal.

In another case, originating from Bougie or the surrounding area in the fourteenth century, a confession of *zina* served as a strategy to circumvent a divorce precipitated by a broken oath. In this case, which irritated jurists from as far away as Tunis and Tlemcen, a man audaciously insisted that he could not be triply divorced from his wife as a result of his broken oath, because their entire marriage was invalid.[48] He explained that he had committed *zina* with his wife when they ran away together before they were married and that he had continued his sexual relationship with her while she observed her waiting period at her father's house. Therefore, because she never completed a proper waiting period, their marriage was invalid from the start, which meant that he could not be permanently barred from marrying her as a result of his broken oath.

The muftis recognized the man's attempt to manipulate the law for his own purposes. He essentially confessed to years of *zina* to evade a broken divorce oath. One mufti expressed his annoyance by writing an explanation of why he would not answer this man's question.[49] Another mufti suggested that if the man really wanted to use *zina* as an excuse to avoid the triple divorce he should likewise accept the consequences for *zina*—that is, the *hadd* punishment.[50] This mention of the *hadd* reflected the mufti's exasperation with what another mufti from Bougie had indicated was a widespread societal problem involving men trying to legitimize sex with women whom they had divorced through broken oaths.[51] Interestingly, the *Mi'yar* contains five versions of this case and only two include details of the couple running away before premarital sex occurred, demonstrating the arbitrariness with which certain details were either left out in the original question or were edited out by later compilers—in this case, a vital piece of information that reveals a woman's agency in choosing a partner and taking action to be with him.[52] Similarly, one of the runaway fatwas presented to al-Abdusi was also preserved in a fatwa collection from the early twentieth century, and the later version omits the sentence about the woman running away with another man.[53]

Conclusion

The legal transgressions described in this chapter hardly represent every type of law-breaking; however, they provide a framework for exploring how Islamic law accommodated cases in which women strayed outside of legal norms. The case of the young woman from Taza, and other cases, show the support systems that worked in conjunction with the law, which became more visible when they were mobilized to deal with extreme or scandalous cases, including at the level of family, neighborhood, tribe, local religious scholars and officials, and central religious and political authorities. This type of case also highlights the aspects of law and dispute resolution that happened outside the courts, often without the need for formal legal intervention. This chapter demonstrates the extent to which the law intertwined with the daily lives of ordinary people in Marinid Morocco, including women, even in the context of their transgressions against it. Islamic law enshrined a father's right to make arrangements for his daughter's marriage, and this right was nearly impossible to challenge. In the rare cases when this authority was contested by an uncompromising daughter, however, the same legal tradition facilitated a resolution. Legal mechanisms enabled women to put their lives back together after running away or engaging in premarital sex, through the pathways created by cooperation between families, communities, and legal officials.

Islamic legal procedure made *zina* almost impossible to prove. The legal system of Marinid Morocco overwhelmingly seemed to give the benefit of the doubt in *zina* cases, and not solely through the formal legal doctrine of doubt (*shubha*). Accusations remained rare due to the severe punishments for false or unproven accusations of *zina*. When *zina* did come to the attention of the law, it was almost always in the context of a couple on a path toward marriage. For married people, the stakes would have been much higher, as the punishment of *zina* for married people was technically death; therefore, there would have been little incentive to come forward with a voluntary confession. Even in the case of the widow who confessed to *zina* in Algeria, however, the jurists only addressed the question posed by the petitioner, which concerned the paternity of her child. Unique to the North African context was the extensive discussion of the mechanism of a waiting period, the *istibra*, for making a legal marriage after a sexual transgression had possibly occurred. If everyone followed Islamic law correctly, *zina* would not occur, but because it did, jurists found a way to deal with it.

A perhaps surprising legacy of *istibra* is found in modern fatwas where Muslims from around the world can seek guidance from internet muftis. Numerous questions ask what a couple should do when they have had premarital relations (although in many of the questions, the couple is dealing with the additional complication of a pregnancy due to these relations).[54] The fatwas in response to these questions recommend the observation of *istibra* followed by marriage. Those posing these questions are not concerned with marriage laws of the modern state but rather with ensuring their marriage is legal according to traditional Islamic interpretations. These websites function in a similar way to premodern extra-legal spaces by helping a couple contract a valid Islamic marriage, which is more a matter of conscience when they are living under the secular laws of a modern nation state or even hybrid laws that draw on Islamic principles in a modern Muslim state.

Most premodern cases in which *zina* was an issue involved couples that families, communities, or the jurists if necessary, had helped to steer toward a legally recognized marriage. Such cases resemble fornication cases from the same period in Venice, in which marriages were often sanctioned after a couple had had premarital sexual relations.[55] Additionally, jurists dealt with the more complex questions surrounding the paternity of children resulting from these cases, detached from concerns of virginity. Their goal was to resolve such crises when they occurred in society, not to punish or make an example of people, except in extreme cases such as that of the jurist who flaunted the law for his own purposes. Along with running away, *zina* often seems to have been part of a strategy to bring about a marriage, and both society and the law found ways to accommodate these actions.

Although women remained largely excluded from the realm of legal interpretation and implementation, the women in these cases made their mark on the law as they sought resolution through the tools available to them in the Islamic legal tradition. Concerns brought by women and the solutions the muftis provided to these questions were gathered in fatwa collections, which in turn could be used as a source for updating jurisprudential texts, often in the form of commentaries.[56] Even if fatwas were not incorporated into other legal genres, however, collections such as the *Mi'yar*, a work that was intended to serve as a guide for judges and has had more longevity than many works of substantive law, have remained important sources through to the present, preserving the concerns of women in Marinid Morocco and other periods of North African and Spanish history as examples for both legal scholars and laypeople.

Conclusion

This book has told the story of the young woman from Taza and other women whose disputes with family members brought them into contact with the law. Here, law has served as both the archive for women's lives and family relationships and a subject worthy of study in its own right. While women were the main focus of this book, their actions have also helped to illuminate a number of features of Islamic law that would not have been visible without women's persistent challenges to specific male rights and other actions that required jurists to devise creative and pragmatic accommodations. Using gender as a category of analysis has allowed for the disentanglement of assumed relationships and identities, showing the contingency of gendered identities and the precarity of binaries such as man/woman.

These cases allow us to draw some conclusions about the lives of women in Marinid Morocco, the practical application of the Maliki school of Islamic law, and how women's lives were shaped by law and in turn shaped it. A broad takeaway about the nature of Islamic law is that legal doctrine established basic rights for women, and women could negotiate, to a certain extent, to increase these rights or prioritize one right over another (for example, giving up financial support in exchange for maintaining physical custody of children).[1] While the family defined in legal doctrine was polygynous and men largely controlled the right to divorce, and while the bond between a woman and her children could be easily severed, the sources show that women consistently fought to keep their marriages monogamous, were willingly handed the power to initiate divorce themselves, and made financial concessions to keep their children after divorce. The family and associated rights laid out by Islamic law were not approached as sacred ideals, but rather as a starting point for negotiations.

Women drew on more egalitarian models of marital relations found in the Quran and sunna that existed alongside the legal rules that elevated a man's position in marriage. This bargaining for greater rights for women deployed tools and strategies from within the Islamic legal tradition, aided by the jurists.

The legal system that developed in and around Marinid Fez responded to the needs of society, including the concerns brought by women, and accommodated women's needs through sophisticated engagement with the Islamic legal tradition. Women challenged men's authority over them from within the same system that granted men their privileged familial status. They confined their husbands to monogamy using carefully worded contract stipulations, or by taking the right of divorce into their own hands by intentionally breaking a divorce oath. When no leeway existed in the law, such as in the case of a father's control over his daughter's marriage, women sometimes resorted to extralegal actions to force a resolution. While a daughter who ran away with a man she wanted to marry posed a serious challenge to a father's authority and was cast under the shadow of *zina*—one of the crimes treated most seriously in Islamic law because of its potential threat to societal order—communities and legal officials nevertheless worked through legal mechanisms to bring these situations back into a legally recognized framework. The legal system approached these transgressions pragmatically and focused on finding a solution that restored order to the community, using techniques such as the implementation of a waiting period (*istibra*) to safeguard paternity and the inheritance rights of children if the couple married, instead of occupying themselves with punishment, or the regulation of women's sexuality. Through their actions, women carved out a space for themselves in the legal discourse, inserting their concerns into the Islamic legal tradition, and demanding that their needs be addressed.

This legal accommodation did not mean that the law was being improperly implemented by jurists in the Islamic West, nor does it expose a large gap between theory and practice. For example, when it came to *zina*, the jurists of course understood the legal theory, but they also understood the high evidentiary standards needed to establish this crime. Therefore, the focus shifted to bringing the situation back into a legal framework to ensure the rights of children to lineage and inheritance, which typically led to a legally valid marriage. Legal theory was translated in practice to respond to the real-life situations that arose in the community, and to the needs of its members. Jurists considered the differences of opinion in Maliki doctrine on key points and this flexibility often worked to women's advantage, as legal officials helped them find resolutions to their problems. In informal legal spaces, jurists even authorized laypeople to select the opinion that they wanted to apply, drawing them into the interpretive process. In the case of broken divorce oaths, the muftis could make it obligatory to consult a wife about which opinion she wanted to follow. These facts point to the existence of collaborative law-making in spaces outside of formal legal structures that were invisible in theoretical legal sources and court records. Law, in this estimation, is located not just in books of legal theory, but at the point where legal theory is lived, interpreted, and negotiated within specific communities at particular times and places. This comprehensive view of law also helps us understand why Islamic law has remained relevant in multiple cultural and political contexts over the centuries.

The Marinid dynasty's patronage of learning contributed to a legal culture in which law pervaded people's lives and infused and defined their relationships. Newly established madrasas educated increasing numbers of jurists who shared their knowledge at home with their family members, including women, as well as with the larger community. The state refrained from intervening in the legal system unless legal harmony was threatened by disputes between the jurists themselves, and in these cases the rulers pushed the jurists to resolve the issues on their own rather than risk further social and legal instability by issuing unilateral legal directives. This confirms the Marinid dynasty's strength and its confidence in its position as upholder of the Islamic faith and Maliki orthodoxy, without needing to concede to the gendered anxieties of the jurists in Fez as they sought to promote a competing vision of orthodoxy contingent on masculine authority in the family.

Ordinary people used their knowledge of the law in their daily interactions and disputes, from the bedroom to the courtroom, and women were intimately familiar with the legal strategies they could use to limit men's authority over them. The sources also reveal support structures outside of the courts—from family to neighbors to tribe, among others—that helped uphold legal principles and resolve disputes. These records thus illuminate not only women's relationship to the law, but also their relationships and interactions within the family and beyond. In addition, informal legal spaces served as a venue where ordinary people, including women, could consult with local scholars and seek advice on how to resolve a conflict or approach more formal legal structures, such as the court system or a prominent mufti.

Reading theoretical texts alone obscures the dynamic world of interpretation, accommodation, and dispute resolution mechanisms that existed outside of formal legal structures. Law as it is understood here is found at the intersection of doctrine and practice, in the ongoing application of legal principles to real-life problems, and embedded in the support system provided by families, communities, and local institutions. Law, very simply, is historically produced. These sources allow us to see how people actually used the law, and particularly how women were able to exploit ambiguities within legal doctrine to make it work for them. Of course, the fatwa records have limitations, and the highly selective editing and compilation process of the fatwa collections used here makes it impossible to address certain types of questions, such as the frequency of the different types of cases that ended up in court and other quantitative analyses. Nevertheless, unlike court records, the sources used in this study capture a world of law-making that occurred outside of the courts, in which ordinary people constantly engaged with the law and brought Islamic legal principles into both disputes and dispute resolution without the need for legal authorities.

The approach taken here to the study of women's engagement with Islamic law understands women as deeply connected to their families, communities, and legal structures, and makes agency visible even when it was exercised within a legal system that gave women fewer rights in the context of the family and put them under male authority. This approach could also serve scholars of women's engagement with modern Islamic legal systems to avoid marginalizing the stories and voices of women who choose to work within these systems, or who do so out of necessity—that is, to avoid recognizing agency only when women challenge Islamic legal principles. Women's legal agency should not only be measured in situations where they transgress the law or circumvent it.[2] Likewise, viewing the law in terms of gendered binaries obscures the insidious ways in which modern systems especially put certain categories of women, such as those who are poor or uneducated, or single mothers, at a legal disadvantage.

From an examination of Islamic legal theory, it might appear that the purpose of this legal system was to grant men extensive rights in their relationships with women and allow them to enforce their authority over these women. And this was essentially how the male jurists who elaborated the law in the early Islamic period envisioned it. In the context studied here, however, the law seemed to be approached more as a tool that had the capacity to limit men's absolute authority. A recent volume, *Men in Charge? Rethinking Authority in the Muslim Legal Tradition,* examines various aspects of the textual bases for men's authority in Islamic law, focusing on the dual concepts of *wilaya* and *qiwama,* the first of which grants a father authority over his daughter, and the second which defines the hierarchical relationship between husband and wife.[3] However, as the editor Ziba Mir-Hosseini acknowledges, the authors do not consider how these concepts have been implemented or negotiated historically.[4] This book offers a practical analysis of the actual ways in which men's authority in the family was lived as a social and legal reality in the context of a comprehensive premodern Islamic legal system. It shows that while men's authority was recognized and respected by jurists as defined by the legal sources and was vigorously protected by men themselves against any challenges, in practice, women relied on the law and legal authorities to confront and restrict men's rights to find a balance that more closely reflected their needs and interests. And in many cases, gendered rights were easily traded or even exchanged for financial compensation, thus highlighting the fluidity of gendered categories.

Women's relationship to Islamic law is a divisive and contested topic in the modern period, with examples of extreme brutality carried out against women (and others) in the name of Islamic law pitched against fervent feminist efforts to save women from legal oppression.[5] Modern discussions of Islamic law, whether by religious conservatives or secular feminists, Muslim or otherwise, often take as their starting point contemporary implementations of what is identified as "sharia." These are for the most part hybrid creations selectively drawn and adapted from Islamic legal principles and then shaped into the form of Western legal codes, practiced in an institutional structure borrowed from former European colonizers, and staffed by officials trained in Western legal theory, not Islamic law. Significantly, these codes are relegated to family law (also referred to as personal status law) and deal with issues relating to women and the family, such as marriage, divorce, child custody, and inheritance.

Based on modern conditions, secular feminists tend to project back the assumption of a timeless, unchanging, antagonistic relationship between women and Islamic law.[6] Likewise, conservatives tend to take modern Islamic legal codes as representative of a timeless, unchanging, sacred Islamic law. Kenneth M. Cuno, in *Modernizing Marriage,* describes this phenomenon in the case of Egypt, where the construction of "a postcolonial narrative of national awakening and recovery of the true bases of Islam legitimated twentieth-century Muslim family law as both modern and authentic, obscuring the way it is shaped in the colonial process," an observation which has significant implications for other postcolonial Muslim nations and their legal systems, including Morocco.[7] Modern debates are based on a nationalized and codified iteration of Islamic law that bears little resemblance to the institutions, structures, practices, and relationships that existed before the break that came with modernity and colonialism, and have often had the effect of weakening women's legal position.[8] Significantly, societal and familial structures have also changed drastically in the modern period, and layers of support that worked in conjunction with the law have been removed. As Ziba Mir-Hosseini argues in the case of Morocco, "the grafting of Maliki law onto a modern legal system in Morocco has created a situation in which the patriarchal elements of the Shariʿa are reinforced, while the classical leeways are reduced."[9] In Mir-Hosseini's assessment, the main victims of these reforms are poor women.

Modern Islamic law codified the position of "man/husband as head of the family, to be obeyed and even revered."[10] At the same time, it became both a repository for tradition and a sacred connection to a glorious past, backed up by the power of the state and highly politicized. Rather than the premodern dynamic, flexible system that incorporated and accommodated women, modern law became sacred and untouchable, with men's authority now cloaked in a divine mandate, projected as an ideal that modern Muslims should strive for. Women have become subject to a system that has lost its flexibility in codification and at the same time has been stripped of the protections of family and community that supported premodern legal practice. Today, women's efforts to negotiate further rights are contested and suspect. In the modern version of "sharia," the codified rights are the maximum women can hope for, not the starting point for discussion. As Hallaq notes, "at the end of the day, the Sharia has ceased to be even an approximate reincarnation of its historical self."[11]

Notes

Bibliography

Index

Notes

Prelude

1. The source for this lengthy legal battle is al-Wansharisi, *al-Mi'yar*, 3:59–82.

2. The documents related to this case consist of two petitions presented on behalf of the father, one to Sultan Abu al-Hassan and the other to the jurists of Fez; a summary of the case submitted to the jurists of Fez by the judge disputing the facts of the father's petitions; a question submitted to the jurists after the death of al-Turjali asking that the case be re-evaluated; responses from the jurists to the questions directed to them; a letter on behalf of the father from one of the jurists to the judge who was appointed following al-Turjali's death; and a fatwa by an unknown jurist that addressed the issues of the case and also critiqued the responses of the other jurists.

1. Introduction

1. Mahmood, *Politics of Piety*, 5.
2. Tucker, *Women, Family, and Gender*, 24.
3. Mahmood, *Politics of Piety*, 5.
4. Scott, "Gender," 1053–75; this language paraphrases the insightful comments of Antoinette Burton on an earlier iteration of this study.
5. See Mir-Hosseini, Al-Sharmani, and Rumminger, eds. *Men in Charge?* for an exploration of these underpinnings of men's authority in legal texts.
6. Tucker, *Women, Family, and Gender*, 34.
7. Beattie and Stevens, *Married Women and the Law*, 10.
8. Beattie and Stevens, *Married Women and the Law*, 5.
9. Phipps and Youngs, *Litigating Women*, 2.
10. Phipps and Youngs, *Litigating Women*, 2.
11. Phipps and Youngs, *Litigating Women*, 4.
12. Hardwick, *Sex in an Old Regime City*, 8–12.
13. Hardwick, *Sex in an Old Regime City*, 8.
14. McClanan and Encarnación, *The Material Culture of Sex*, 3.

15. Kim, *The Emotions of Justice*, 5–6.

16. Kim, *The Emotions of Justice*, 6.

17. Kim, *The Emotions of Justice*, 20.

18. For example, Ali, *Marriage and Slavery in Early Islam*, argues that early (male) Muslim jurists analogized marriage contracts to sales contracts and particularly slave ownership, partly as a result of the centrality of this institution in their particular historical and societal context.

19. Abou El Fadl, "Emergence and Sources."

20. I am grateful to the anonymous reviewer who encouraged me to engage with and expand this framework, which is crucial to understanding law and tying together my various arguments.

21. Abou El Fadl, *Reasoning with God*, xxxii.

22. Admiral, "Navigating Consent," 69–86.

23. Rosen, *The Anthropology of Justice*, 5.

24. On hadith, see Brown, *Hadith*, and for the relation of law and hadith, see chapter 5, "The Function of Prophetic Traditions in Islamic Law."

25. Wadud-Muhsin, *Qur'an and Woman*, v–vi.

26. Mernissi, *The Veil and the Male Elite*.

27. Ahmed, *Women and Gender in Islam*, 63.

28. Ahmed, *Women and Gender in Islam*, 63.

29. Ali, *Marriage and Slavery*, 31–38.

30. Mernissi, *The Veil and the Male Elite*, 192.

31. On how men influenced interpretations of the Quran, see Wadud-Muhsin, *Qur'an and Woman*. For women's role in hadith transmission, see Sayeed, *Women and the Transmission of Religious Knowledge in Islam* and Nadwi, *al-Muhaddithat*.

32. I owe the term "coproduction" to Antoinette Burton. Leslie Peirce makes a similar argument in *Morality Tales*, 1–2.

33. Thanks to Antoinette Burton for this wording.

34. Scott, "Gender," 1056, 1067.

35. Peirce, *Morality Tales*, 149.

36. Peirce, *Morality Tales*, 354.

37. Peirce, *Morality Tales*, 176–208.

38. Tucker, *In the House of the Law*, 36.

39. Tucker, *In the House of the Law*. Although in *In the House of the Law* Tucker draws on Scott's definition of gender to help elaborate her conceptualization of gender in Islamic law (10), in her later book, *Women, Family and Gender*, while she continues to engage with the concept of gendered legal norms, she no longer explicitly cites Scott's conceptualization to help with the analytical work.

40. Holmes Katz, *Women in the Mosque*, 8, 197.

41. Scott, "Gender," 1070.

42. Najmabadi, "Beyond the Americas," 11–21; Scott, "*AHR Forum:* Unanswered Questions," 1424. Thank you to the anonymous reviewer who pushed me to think in this direction.

43. Najmabadi, "Beyond the Americas," 18, emphasis added.

44. Katz, *Women in the Mosque*, 3.

45. Peirce, *Morality Tales*, 149.

46. Abou El Fadl, *Speaking in God's Name*, 297–98 and 481; Anchassi, "Status Distinctions and Sartorial Difference," 125–55.

47. Anchassi, "Status Distinctions," 18. For more on reasons for this ruling and early debates on the topic, see full article.

48. Mernissi, *The Veil and the Male Elite*, 182–87. This destabilization of the category of "woman" also occurs in other areas where assumptions are made about Muslim women, for example, about gendered seclusion. When rules and social norms about seclusion are examined in multiple historical contexts, it becomes clear that the category of woman fractures along the lines of social status. The seclusion expected for elite or upper-class women necessitates increased mobility for women of lower social statuses who move in the streets for work or to take care of their families and cater to the needs of women who are unable to move so freely. Huda Lutfi mentions, for example, women who served as peddlers in medieval Cairo, going door to door so that elite women did not need to leave the house. "Manners and Customs," 106.

49. Abu-Lughod, "Do Muslim Women Really Need Saving?," 788.

50. Abun-Nasr, *A History of the Maghrib*, 104.

51. Le Tourneau, *Fez in the Age of the Marinides*, 13–14; Ibn Marzuq, *El Musnad*, 336.

52. Al-Manouni, *Waraqat*, 234. In the Islamic East, the Mamluks in Egypt were also in a position to carry out a similar role.

53. Al-Manouni, *Waraqat*, 234.

54. Recent scholarship on these dynasties includes Messier, *The Almoravids and the Meanings of Jihad* and Allen James Fromherz, *The Almohads: The Rise of an Islamic Empire*. See also Maribel Fierro, *The Almohad Revolution* and Fierro, "Proto-Malikis, Malikis, and Reformed Malikis in al-Andalus," 57–76.

55. For an overview of this scholarship, see Bourqia and Gilson Miller, eds., *In the Shadow of the Sultan*.

56. Technically, "fatwa" refers only to the mufti's response, but I will use fatwa sources more loosely to refer to the case record, including questions, answers, petitions, and related documents.

57. See, for example, French summaries from the *Mi'yar* in Amar, "La pierre de touche des Fétwas de Ahmad al-Wanscharisi"; Idris, "Le mariage en occident musulman," 12 (1972): 45–62, 17 (1974): 71–105, 25 (1978): 119–38; and Lagardère, *Histoire et société*. One

early English-language source that discusses women and law in Morocco using a non-fatwa source is Toledano's *Judicial Practice and Family Law in Morocco.* The ambitious title implies that it has comprehensively covered topics of interest to the current research. However, for the most part, Toledano's study is simply an annotated translation of an eighteenth-century legal work from a very particular legal genre, with no connection to the context of local society, the family, or women.

58. Zomeño, *Dote y Matrimonio*, which draws on Idris, "Le mariage en occident musulman," 32 (1970): 157–67.

59. Arbuh, *Awda' al-Mar'a*.

60. Katz, *Women in the Mosque*, 198.

61. Powers, *Law, Society, and Culture*, 229.

62. Powers, *Law, Society, and Culture*, 232.

63. Hendrickson, *Leaving Iberia*.

64. Shatzmiller, *Her Day in Court*.

65. Fatha, *al-Nawazil al-Fiqhiyya wa al-Mujtama'*, 23, 9; Benmira, *al-Nawazil wa al-Mujtama'*, 19. See also Hajji, *Nadharat fi al-Nawazil al-Fiqhiyya*.

66. Fatha, *al-Nawazil al-Fiqhiyya*, 20.

67. Tucker, "'And God Knows Best,'" 175.

68. Tucker, *In the House of the Law*, 184.

69. Trouillot, *Silencing the Past*, 48.

70. See chapter 8 for a discussion of these cases.

71. Mir-Hosseini, *Marriage on Trial*, 15.

72. See, for example, pioneering work on seventeenth-century courts in Anatolia: Jennings, "Women in Early 17th-Century Ottoman Judicial Records," 53–114.

73. Tucker, *In the House of the Law*; Peirce, *Morality Tales;* and Rapoport, *Marriage, Money and Divorce in Medieval Islamic Society.*

74. Ruggles, *Women, Patronage, and Self-Representation*; Makdisi, *The Rise of Colleges*, 45; Hallaq, *An Introduction to Islamic Law*, 69–70.

75. Peirce, *Morality Tales*, 382.

76. Peirce, *Morality Tales*, 1.

77. This is evident in sweeping statements such as, "According to *Sunni* prescriptions, boys normally remain in the care of their mothers until age seven, and girls until seven or nine, at which time they move to the custody of their father or, in the absence of their paternal grandparents, until marriage," which ignores distinctions in (Sunni) Maliki custody law. Zilfi, "'We Don't Get Along,'" 286, emphasis added. Similarly, Esposito generalizes Hanafi custody law as universal to Muslim families and societies. Esposito with Natana J. DeLong-Bas, *Women in Muslim Family Law*, 35–36.

78. Edmund Burke III and David N. Yaghoubian advocate the use of "social biography" to understand the worlds and activities of ordinary people; the story of the young woman from Taza benefits from this approach, but more broadly, the stories here

make up composite social biographies. "Middle Eastern Societies and Ordinary People's Lives," 6.

79. An example of how this can be recorded in the sources is a case from the early Marinid rule in Fez, where a mufti responding to a question about a divorce mentioned that the wife had originally sought an opinion from a local mufti before the case reached the qadi's court. See al-Wansharisi, *al-Mi'yar*, 4:509–12.

80. For biographical information on al-Wansharisi, see Vidal Castro, "Ahmad al-Wansarisi (m. 914/1508)." The *Mi'yar*'s complete name is *al-Mi'yar al-Mu'rib wa al-Jami' al-Mughrib 'an Fatawi Ahl Ifriqiyya wa al-Andalus wa al-Maghrib,* which translates to "The Comprehensive Criterion [for evaluation or judgment] and the Extensive Collection of Fatwas of the People of Ifriqiyya and al-Andalus and al-Maghrib." This indicates that al-Wansharisi's objective was to serve as a reference for legal practitioners. Vidal Castro, "El *Mi'yar* de al-Wansarisi (m. 914/1508)," 214.

81. Fatha, *al-Nawazil al-Fiqhiyya,* 10; Powers, *Law, Society, and Culture,* 6.

82. Powers, *Law, Society, and Culture,* 8.

83. Al-Sijilmasi, *al-Durr al-Nathir 'ala Ajwiba Abu al-Hassan al-Saghir.* The editor's spelling (i.e., diacritics) of the collection's title (*al-Nathir* instead of *al-Nuthayyir*) and the mufti (*al-Saghir* instead of *al-Sughayyir*) does not follow established spelling for these two names. Ibn Hilal also compiled his own fatwa collection, *Nawazil al-Fiqh* (Salé: Mu'assasa al-Khizana al-'Ilmiyya al-Sbihiyya, lith. #759).

84. One manuscript with few fatwas that overlap with fatwas in the *Mi'yar* is Abdullah al-Abdusi, *Ajwiba Fiqhiyya* (Rabat: al-Khizana al-Hasaniyya, ms. 14056). The opinions of al-Abdusi from a wide range of sources were recently compiled and edited into a coherent collection by Hisham al-Muhammadi: al-Abdusi, *Ajwibat al-Abdusi.* A comprehensive list of sources for Abdullah al-Abdusi's fatwas can be found on pages 71–79 of this book.

85. Al-Satti was sent as an emissary to Hafsid Tunis on behalf of Sultan Abu al-Hassan and succeeded in arranging a marriage between the ruler and the daughter of the Hafsid sultan. Ibn Marzuq, *El Musnad*, 217; al-Zarakshi, *Tarikh al-Dawlatayn al-Muwahhidiyya wa al-Hafsiyya*, 78. When Ibn Marzuq himself was sent on behalf of Sultan Abu Inan to ask for the hand of a Hafsid princess, she refused (97).

86. Hallaq, "Was the Gate of *Ijtihad* Closed?," 18.

87. Awass, *Fatwa and the Making and Renewal of Islamic Law,* 3.

88. Hallaq, "From *Fatwas* to *Furu'*," 55.

2. "I Refuse Anyone but Him"

1. Al-Wansharisi, *al-Mi'yar*, 3:59–62. See chapter 3 for more context on al-Turjali. We know he died around the time of the legal dispute, so most likely in 1339, or the following year.

2. Al-Wansharisi, *al-Mi'yar*, 3:59.

3. Ali, *Marriage and Slavery*, 33.

4. Spectorsky, *Women in Classical Islamic Law*, 67–69; Ali, "Marriage in Classical Islamic Jurisprudence," 18–19.

5. Ali, *Marriage and Slavery*, 32.

6. Al-Wansharisi, *al-Mi'yar*, 3:60.

7. Even a husband's claim that his wife was not a virgin on his wedding night had no legal significance, although it would have different social connotations depending on the time and place. See Tucker's analysis of a mufti's response to such a case in "'And God Knows Best,'" 171–75.

8. Al-Wansharisi, *al-Mi'yar*, 3:59–60.

9. Ali, *Marriage and Slavery*, 33.

10. This concept is known as *'aḍl* in Islamic legal doctrine.

11. Sahnun Ibn Sa'id al-Tunnukhi, *al-Mudawwana al-Kubra*, 3:817–18.

12. Al-Wansharisi, *al-Mi'yar*, 3:59.

13. The Maliki school allowed a father to compel his virgin daughter to marry, even if she was not a minor. Ali, "Marriage in Classical Islamic Jurisprudence," 17–18.

14. Al-Wansharisi, *al-Mi'yar*, 3:60–61. Some cases quote participants in local dialect, while some filter voices through more formal legal language, as in this case.

15. Al-Wansharisi, *al-Mi'yar*, 3:60.

16. Al-Wansharisi, *al-Mi'yar*, 3:61.

17. This oath indicates that he was married and must have sworn on his marriage to his daughter's stepmother, as in his own petition he stated that his children did not have a mother.

18. Al-Wansharisi, *al-Mi'yar*, 3:60.

19. There is no mention of a dower in this case, although one would have been required to make the marriage legal.

20. Al-Wansharisi, *al-Mi'yar*, 3:61.

21. Al-Wansharisi, *al-Mi'yar*, 3:75.

22. Written al-Abnaki in text; most likely a typo.

23. Al-Wansharisi, *al-Mi'yar*, 3:75.

24. Al-Wansharisi, *al-Mi'yar*, 3:76–78.

25. Al-Wansharisi, *al-Mi'yar*, 3:76–77. It was not a requirement that two people who had committed fornication marry each other, and there were differing opinions on the practice, with some jurists even arguing that it was forbidden, including one of the local muftis from Taza; however, it was a fairly common practice, and several additional cases in which this occurs will be discussed below. See al-Sughayyir's explanation of these opinions in al-Sijilmasi, *al-Durr al-Nathir*, 1:128.

26. Al-Wansharisi, *al-Mi'yar*, 3:72.

27. It was easy for a man to withdraw from a contracted marriage and although typically he would have owed half the dower to the bride; in this case, the father's petition to

the jurists mentioned that he forgave the dower, which meant the groom would have owed nothing. Al-Wansharisi, *al-Mi'yar,* 3:77.

28. Al-Wansharisi, *al-Mi'yar,* 3:77.

29. Al-Wansharisi, *al-Mi'yar,* 3:77.

30. Previous studies have shown how reconstruction of a woman's encounter with the Islamic legal system can be revealing about gender, justice, and agency. See, for example, Toledano's description of the case of Shemsigul, an enslaved woman navigating the court system in nineteenth-century Cairo: "Shemsigul," 48–63. Toledano argues that "although as a woman and a slave she belonged to a doubly oppressed group, Shemsigul did ultimately receive justice in the courts" (62).

31. Titaou, "Jabrut al-Qadi wa Fatat Taza," 64–67.

32. Al-Wansharisi, *al-Mi'yar,* 3:60.

33. Al-Wansharisi, *al-Mi'yar,* 3:65.

34. Abu al-Hassan al-Sughayyir (d. 719/1320–21). Ibn Yahya al-Wansharisi, *Kitab Wafayat al-Wansharisi,* 18; bin Muhammad Ibn al-Qadi, *Jadhwat al-Iqtibas,* 472; Naji, *Abu al-Hasan al-Sughayyir,* 102–4.

35. Naji, *Abu al-Hasan al-Sughayyir,* 104, 135.

36. Al-Sijilmasi, *al-Durr al-Nathir.*

37. Ibn Marzuq, *El Musnad,* 215–23.

38. Ibn Battuta, *The Travels of Ibn Battuta,* 4:927.

39. These five jurists were al-Qayrawani, al-Yaznasni, Misbah, Abd al-Karim, and al-Satti. Ibn Marzuq, *El Musnad,* 139–40.

40. Ibrahim bin Muhammad al-Yaznasni (d. 794/1392) was a judge for the Marinids and al-Wansharisi preserved many of his fatwas in *al-Mi'yar.* See Ahmad Baba al-Tinbakti, *Nayl al-Ibtihaj,* 40, 53, 266; Ahmad Baba al-Tinbakti, *Kifayat al-Muhtaj,* 85; Makhluf, *Shajarat al-Nur,* 1:218; Ibn al-Qadi, *Jadhwat al-Iqtibas,* 86.

41. Abu Abdullah Muhammad bin Sulayman al-Satti (d. 750/1349–50). See Ahmad Baba, *Nayl al-Ibtihaj,* 408–10; Ibn Marzuq, *El Musnad,* 215–16; Makhluf, *Shajarat al-Nur,* 1:221; Ahmad Baba, *Kifayat al-Muhtaj,* 316–18; Abu Abdullah bin Sulayman al-Satti, *Sharh Mukhtasar al-Hawfi.* Samirah al-Terrab mentions that al-Satti taught and gave fatwas in Taza, *Taza wa Iqlimuha,* 318.

42. Ibn Marzuq, *El Musnad,* 215.

43. Abu Diya Misbah bin Muhammad bin Abdullah al-Yalsuti (d. 750/1349–50). See Ahmad Baba, *Nayl al-Ibtihaj,* 608–9; Ibn al-Qadi, *Jadhwat al-Iqtibas,* 336.

44. Very little biographical information is available about him. See Ibn Marzuq, *El Musnad,* 139, and al-Wansharisi, *al-Mi'yar,* 13:379.

45. Abd al-Aziz al-Qayrawani (d. 750/1349–50), also sometimes referred to as al-Qarawi. Ahmad Baba, *Nayl al-Ibtihaj,* 269–70; Makhluf, *Shajarat al-Nur,* 1:221; Ibn Marzuq, *El Musnad,* 139–40; Ibn al-Qadi, *Jadhwat al-Iqtibas,* 1:451.

46. Abu al-Rabii Sulayman bin Abdun al-Sarifi (d. 750/1349). Death date taken from Powers, *Law, Society, and Culture,* 125. For al-Sarifi's fatwas, see al-Wansharisi, *al-Mi'yar,* 1:16, 8:14.

47. Sahnun, *al-Mudawwana*, 3:817–18.

48. Al-Wansharisi, *al-Mi'yar,* 3:65. As the muftis indicated, the Maliki school was not in complete agreement over whether a father could still compel his daughter to marry if she had lost her virginity due to *zina*, rather than in a marriage. A century later, Abdullah al-Abdusi noted that the school's more popular opinion was that a father could still force his daughter into a marriage if she had lost her virginity because of *zina*, the opinion referred to by al-Yaznasni. Al-Abdusi, *Ajwibat al-Abdusi,* 485–86.

49. Al-Sughayyir describes this waiting period in al-Sijilmasi, *al-Durr al-Nathir,* 1:127–28.

50. Sahnun, *al-Mudawwana*, 365–86.

51. Mir-Hosseini, *Marriage on Trial*, 178, also locates this term's origin in the context of slavery, although she states that in the modern period it is only observed for one month, the shorter waiting period that was typically observed by enslaved women.

52. If the jurists' main concern was to find a way to make the marriage legal, as in the cases discussed below, they would have discussed other options, such as annulling the current marriage and recontracting it, although this might have been an impossible solution given the father's continued opposition.

53. For example, Misbah mentioned that Ibn al-Turjuman had hidden the daughter in his father's house, an incident that was never raised in the questions themselves. Al-Wansharisi, *al-Mi'yar,* 3:62.

54. The documents present conflicting timelines, so these ages are estimates.

55. In addition to the case of the young woman from Taza, Ibn Atiyya was also mentioned in the case of followers of the doctrine of Ibn Tumart. Al-Wansharisi, *al-Mi'yar,* 2:453–61. Ibn Atiyya's father was noted as Shaykh Abu al-Abbas bin Atiyya.

56. Ahmad Ibn Muhammad al-Maqqari, *Nahf al-Tib: Min Ghusn al-Andalus al-Ratib,* 5:253. For more information about the Maqqari family, see Adil, *Memorializing al-Maqqari.*

57. Al-Wansharisi, *al-Mi'yar,* 3:66.

58. Al-Wansharisi, *al-Mi'yar,* 3:66.

59. Al-Wansharisi, *al-Mi'yar,* 3:67.

60. Abu-Odeh, "Honor Killings," 917–20.

61. Abu-Odeh, "Honor Killings," 917.

62. Abu-Odeh, "Honor Killings," 917–20.

63. Al-Wansharisi, *al-Mi'yar,* 3:72.

64. Al-Wansharisi, *al-Mi'yar,* 3:65.

65. Al-Wansharisi, *al-Mi'yar,* 3:80–81.

66. Al-Wansharisi, *al-Mi'yar,* 3:64.

67. Al-Wansharisi, *al-Mi'yar,* 3:64.

68. Al-Wansharisi, *al-Mi'yar,* 3:60.

69. Al-Wansharisi, *al-Mi'yar,* 3:73.

70. Al-Wansharisi, *al-Mi'yar,* 3:78.

71. Al-Manouni, *Waraqat,* 442; Abun-Nasr, *A History of the Maghrib,* 137.

72. Abun-Nasr, *A History of the Maghrib,* 110. Al-Manouni, *Waraqat,* 458–59, mentions Ahmad bin Shaib al-Jazna'i from Taza, while al-'Alawi al-Bahi, *'Ulama' Taza,* 44, adds al-Satti, al-Zawawi, al-Hawari, and al-Sabagh as jurists from Taza who the sultan brought to Tunis. Ahmad Baba, *Nayl al-Ibtihaj,* 409.

73. Ahmad Baba, *Nayl al-Ibtihaj,* 409.

74. Ibn Battuta, *The Travels of Ibn Battuta,* 4:923.

75. Ibn Battuta, *The Travels of Ibn Battuta,* 4:922–23.

76. Abun-Nasr, *A History of the Maghrib,* 130.

77. Ibn Battuta, *The Travels of Ibn Battuta,* 4:925.

78. Abd al-Rahman Ibn Khaldun, *al-Tarif bi Ibn Khaldun,* 45; Abun-Nasr, *A History of the Maghrib,* 130.

79. For example, Abu Abdullah al-Rundi (d. 740/1339–40) died of the plague after accompanying the sultan on various campaigns: Ibn Marzuq, *El Musnad,* 216. Al-Qayrawani and Abu Diya Misbah also died the same year, but their biographers specify that they died in Fez: Ibn al-Qadi, *Jadhwat al-Iqtibas,* 451, 336.

80. Titaou, "Jabrut al-Qadi," argues that al-Turjali colluded with Ibn al-Turjuman, who he casts as a powerful man manipulating the local justice system.

3. Judicial Authority, Community, and Lawmaking

1. On the sultan as arbiter, see Khaneboubi, *Les Premiers Sultans,* 101.

2. See, for example, Khaneboubi, *Les Premiers Sultans,* 21–22, 206; Kably, "Legitimacy of State Power," 20–24.

3. See Burke III, *The Ethnographic State,* 1–17, for a description of how and why these themes were important to the colonial government. Scholarship on religion includes Cornell, *Realm of the Saint,* Kugle, *Rebel between Spirit and Law,* Munson Jr., *Religion and Power in Morocco,* and Geertz, *Islam Observed.*

4. In a rare English-language political history of the Marinid period, Maya Shatzmiller investigates the Marinid state, arguing for the importance of the dynasty's Berber (Amazigh) identity in creating an "Islamic" state: *The Berbers and the Islamic State.* For an overview of current debates in the Amazigh movement and a guide through the complex landscape of "Berber" activism, see Soulaimani, "Writing and Rewriting Amazigh/Berber Identity," 1–16.

5. Spanish scholars who studied earlier Moroccan dynasties took less of an interest in the Marinids, as unlike the Almoravids and the Almohads they no longer controlled what later became Spain.

6. Al-Manouni, *Waraqat*, 430. An authoritative reference for the Marinid period is Muhammad al-Manouni's *Waraqat 'an Hadarat al-Mariniyyin* (Documents about the Marinid Civilization), which is a meticulous accounting of the sources for writing Marinid history and serves as a guide for scholars investigating this history.

7. Laroui, *The History of the Maghrib*, 214; Al-Manouni, *Waraqat*, 435.

8. Examples of this are Muhammad Muqirr's investigation of clothing practices in the Marinid period up until the Saadi period: Muqirr, *al-Libas al-Maghribi*. In addition to his research on premodern women, Mohammed Yassir al-Hilali explores the social organization of Morocco in the fourteenth and fifteenth centuries, theorizing the applicability of Marxist conceptualizations of class in this context: Yassir al-Hilali, *Mujtama' al-Maghrib al-Aqsa*. Ibrahim Anwar investigates knowledge transmission in Marinid Morocco and Hafsid Tunis, comparing different institutions of learning with a particular focus on the *kuttab*, or Quranic school: Anwar, *Naql al-Ma'rifa*. An earlier example of intellectual history is Mohamed Benchekroun's study of intellectual life during the Marinid and Wattasid periods, which is a descriptive compilation of entries detailing the life and work of scholars from this period: Benchekroun, *La vie intellectuelle marocaine*. Hamid Titaou analyzes the impact of war on society from the thirteenth to fifteenth centuries, including its impact on women and families, from direct participation in war efforts to hardships brought on by absent husbands: Titaou, *al-Harb wa al-Mujtama'*. Another promising area of research is regional studies of cities and other areas under Marinid control, including rural areas.

9. Abdelhadi Tazi, "Fii Tarikh Taza (On the History of Taza)," *Daouat al-Haq* 241 (October 1984), https://www.habous.gov.ma/daouat-alhaq/item/6284.

10. These renovations were taking place when I visited Taza in June 2022.

11. Nassima Chahboun, "Taza, the Medina of Shimmering Words and Pale Stones," Patrimoine d'Orient, June 10, 2021, https://patrimoinedorient.org/index.php/en/2021/06/10/taza-the-medina-of-shimmering-words-and-pale-stones/.

12. Tazi, "Fii Tarikh Taza."

13. Al-Manouni, *Waraqat*, 244.

14. Al-Manouni, *Waraqat*, 312.

15. Africanus, *The History and Description of Africa*, 2:545–46.

16. Al-Bahi, *'Ulama' Taza*, 37.

17. Tazi, "Fii Tarikh Taza."

18. Ibn Battuta, *The Travels of Ibn Battuta*, 4:925.

19. Al-Bahi, *'Ulama' Taza*, 53.

20. Mohammad bin Ahmad al-Amrani, "Makanat Taza al-'Ilmiyya min Khilal al-Nusus al-Tarikhiyya wa al-Intajat al-Adabiyya wa al-Fiqhiyya" (The Intellectual Position of Taza from Historical Sources and Literary and Legal Production), *Daouat al-Haq* 286 (1991). http://www.habous.gov.ma/daouat-alhaq/item/7466. Accessed July 7, 2022.

21. Al-Wansharisi, *al-Mi'yar,* 3:60. There is no biographical information available for the mufti of Taza, Abu Muhammad Abdullah al-Batu'i.

22. Al-Wansharisi, *al-Mi'yar,* 3:61. Of the jurists consulted, only Ibn Atiyya is mentioned elsewhere.

23. Al-Bahi, *'Ulama' Taza,* 53.

24. Although some scholars understand Abu Asbagh al-Turjali and Abu Mahdi al-Turjali to be two different people, all the evidence from the available sources and related timeline makes it fairly clear that these names refer to the same person.

25. Abu Zayd Abd al-Rahman bin al-Qadi, *al-Fajr al-Sati',* 1:231–32; Abd al-Hadi Hamitu, *Qira'at al-Imam Nafi',* 3:108–9. Al-Terrab mentions that Ali bin Muhammad bin Ibrahim bin Fatah al-Qaysi was Qadi of Taza in 731/1331, but this could be referring to a judge who was not the chief judge. *Taza wa Iqlimuha,* 326.

26. Al-Wansharisi, *Kitab Wafayat,* 20.

27. Al-Wansharisi included a short biography of Ibn al-Baqal in *al-Mi'yar,* after a number of fatwas were answered by this mufti: al-Wansharisi, *al-Mi'yar,* 12:290–91. He also includes a series of twenty-nine questions posed to Ibn al-Baqal by another mufti, and his twenty-nine fatwas in response. Al-Wansharisi, *al-Mi'yar,* 12:263–90.

28. Al-Maqqari, *Nahf al-Tib,* 5:244–46; Ibn Abdullah Lisan al-Din Ibn al-Khatib, *al-Ihata fi Akhbar Ghranata,* 2:225. Al-Abili also taught al-Maqqari the Elder and Ibn al-Khatib.

29. Ibn al-Qadi, *al-Fajr al-Sati',* 1:231–32; Hamitu, *Qira'at al-Imam Nafi',* 3:108–9.

30. Al-Wansharisi, *al-Mi'yar,* 7:82.

31. Likewise, a Muhammad al-Turjali is mentioned as taking his oath of office to become a notary public in the early fifteenth century, another position embedded within the legal system: al-Terrab, *Taza wa Iqlimuha,* 354.

32. Al-Wansharisi, *al-Mi'yar,* 4:93, 3:96–97.

33. Al-Wansharisi, *al-Mi'yar,* 10:361.

34. The case of the young woman from Taza is al-Wansharisi, *al-Mi'yar,* 3:59–82, while the other case is al-Wansharisi, *al-Mi'yar,* 10:360–67, and has been analyzed in detail by Powers, *Law, Society, and Culture,* 22–52.

35. Al-Wansharisi, *al-Mi'yar,* 10:360–67; Powers, *Law, Society, and Culture,* 22–52.

36. Powers, *Law, Society, and Culture,* 49.

37. Powers, *Law, Society, and Culture,* 51.

38. Date of death unknown. See Ahmad Baba, *Nayl al-Ibtihaj,* 456; and Ibn al-Qadi, *Jadhwat al-Iqtibas,* 1:238.

39. Al-Wansharisi, *al-Mi'yar,* 2:453–61.

40. Al-Wansharisi, *al-Mi'yar,* 2:460.

41. Khaneboubi, *Les Premiers Sultans,* 111.

42. Ibn Marzuq, *El Musnad,* 292.

43. Ibn Marzuq, *El Musnad*, 139–40.

44. Al-Manouni, *Waraqat*, 543–69, summarizes a manuscript on Morocco in the time of Sultan Abu al-Hassan, including his daily routine and contact with scholars: *Masalik al-Absar fi Mamalik al-Amsar*, by Ibn Fadl Allah al-'Amri (d. 1348/749).

45. Dunn, *The Adventures of Ibn Battuta*, 3.

46. Ibn Battuta, *The Travels of Ibn Battuta,* 4:927.

47. Ibn Battuta, *The Travels of Ibn Battuta,* 4:928–29.

48. Ibn Battuta, *The Travels of Ibn Battuta,* 4:929.

49. Al-Wansharisi, *al-Mi'yar,* 3:69.

50. Al-Wansharisi, *al-Mi'yar,* 3:66.

51. Al-Wansharisi, *al-Mi'yar,* 3:62.

52. Al-Wansharisi, *al-Mi'yar,* 3:61–62; Abu al-Walid Muhammad bin Rushd (d. 520/1126), also known as al-Jadd (or the Elder). A jurist, qadi, and author of books of jurisprudence from Cordoba, he was also the grandfather of Ibn Rushd (d. 595/1198), known in Europe as Averroes.

53. Ibn Battuta, *The Travels of Ibn Battuta,* 4:927.

54. Scott draws on Foucault's conceptualization of "power as dispersed constellations of unequal relationships, discursively constituted in social 'fields of force'" ("Gender," 1067).

55. Khaneboubi, *Les Premiers Sultans,* 100.

4. Women, Men, and Legal Knowledge

1. Al-Wansharisi, *al-Mi'yar,* 3:59; Sahnun, *al-Mudawwana al-Kubra,* 3:817–18.

2. Al-Wansharisi, *al-Mi'yar,* 3:60.

3. For community participation in legal culture, see Peirce, *Morality Tales.*

4. Sayeed, "Muslim Women's Religious Education," 99.

5. Sayeed, *Women and the Transmission,* 177–78.

6. El Bouhsini, "La place reserve."

7. Kara, *al-Nisa' fi Fida'*. Histories of women in al-Andalus have a certain amount of comparative value and utilize some of the same sources as those available for Moroccan women's history; see, for example, Marín, *Mujeres en Al-Ándalus.*

8. Abdelhadi Tazi, *al-Mar'a fi Tarikh al-Gharb al-Islami.*

9. Latif, *al-Usra fi Maghrib al-'Asr al-Wasit.*

10. Yassir al-Hilali, "Nadharat al-Mujtama'," 76–98. The issue of the journal in which this article appears contains other articles on women's history in Morocco. See also Yassir al-Hilali, "Masadir Tarikh al-Mar'a al-Maghribiyya," 117–27. Among the secondary sources of note are two volumes on Moroccan women's history based on conferences held at the University of Kenitra: *Pour une histoire des femmes au Maroc,* University of Ibn Tufayl, 2001, and *Tarikh al-Nisa' al-Maghribiyyat: al-Iqsa' wa Rudud al-Fa'il—Histoire des femmes au Maghreb: Réponses à l'exclusion,* University of Ibn Tufayl, 1999.

11. Kara, *al-Nisa' fi Fida'*, 48.

12. Ibn Umar Ibn Rushayd and ibn Muhammad al-Jilani, *Istida'at al-ijazah.*

13. Benchekroun, *La Vie Intellectuelle,* 292.

14. Zarruq, *al-Kunnash.*

15. Ibn Ghazi, *al-Rawd al-Hatun.*

16. Zarruq, *al-Kunnash*, 13–14.

17. Zarruq, *al-Kunnash*, 13.

18. Al-Terrab, *Taza wa Iqlimuha*, 323.

19. Ibn Ghazi, *al-Rawd al-Hatun,* 63.

20. Ibn Ghazi, *al-Rawd al-Hatun,* 63.

21. Al-Manouni, *Waraqat,* 271–74.

22. Al-Terrab, *Taza wa Iqlimuha,* 296.

23. Africanus, *The History and Description*, 3:456–57. Language revised for clarity.

24. Al-Manouni, *Waraqat,* 271.

25. Berkey, *The Transmission of Knowledge*, 7, 28.

26. Latif, "Ornate Visions of Knowledge and Power," 169.

27. Makdisi, *The Rise of Colleges*, 9.

28. Chamberlain, *Knowledge and Social Practice*, 69–90.

29. Hallaq, *An Introduction to Islamic Law*, 39.

30. Ibn al-Sa'i, *Consorts of the Caliphs*, 62, 66.

31. Makdisi, *The Rise of Colleges*, 238.

32. Berkey, *The Transmission of Knowledge,* 61–62.

33. Berkey, *The Transmission of Knowledge,* 65.

34. An exception to this is the school in Sabta/Ceuta founded by hadith scholar Abu al-Hassan al-Shaari (d. 1251), which specialized in hadith studies and where women also studied, including the daughter of the founder: Kara, *al-Nisa' fi Fida'*, 51. This school, although still operating in the Marinid period, was founded at the end of the Almohad period, and did not focus on Islamic law like the Marinid madrasas.

35. Anwar, *Naql al-Ma'rifa*, 46.

36. Al-Manouni, *Waraqat,* 239–44; Latif, "Ornate Visions of Knowledge and Power," 5.

37. Al-Manouni, *Waraqat,* 239

38. Ibn Marzuq, *El Musnad*, 336.

39. Shatzmiller, "Les premiers Mérinides," 115–18.

40. Shatzmiller, "Les premiers Mérinides," 112. Shatzmiller also argues that these madrasas had an ethnic component and that the goal of the Berber/Amazigh Marinids was to train more Berber/Amazigh jurists and displace the Arab religious elite of Fez. Shatzmiller, *The Berbers and the Islamic State,* 91–92; Shatzmiller, "Les premiers Mérinides," 92.

41. Laroui, *The History of the Maghrib*, 214.

42. Berkey, *The Transmission of Knowledge*, 21–23.

43. Anwar, *Naql al-Ma'rifa*, 22.

44. Berkey, *The Transmission of Knowledge*, 169.

45. Anwar, *Naql al-Ma'rifa*, 25.

46. Anwar, *Naql al-Ma'rifa*, 25–26.

47. Al-Manouni, *Waraqat*, 293. For background information on Sahnun, see Brockopp, "Sahnun B. Sa'id," 65–84. For Ibn Abi Zayd's biography, see Makhluf, *Shajarat al-Nur*, 1:96. For al-Baradhi'i's biography, see Makhluf, *Shajarat al-Nur al-Zakiyya*, 1:105.

48. Anwar, *Naql al-Ma'rifa*, 25. Some sources alternatively spell it as al-Asda mosque.

49. Ibn al-Qadi, *Durrat al-Hijal fi Ghurrat Asma al-Rijal*, 295; Ibn al-Qadi, *Jadhwat al-Iqtibas*, 319; Ibn Ja'far al-Kattani, *Salwat al-Anfas*, 2:130; Ibn Ishaq al-Jundi, *Mukhtasar al-'Allamah Khalil.*

50. Fadel, "The Social Logic of Taqlid and the Rise of the Mukhtasar," 197–98.

51. Makdisi, *The Rise of Colleges*, 284.

52. Editor Muhammad al-Zahi transcribed this chain of transmission in Ibn Ghazi, *Fihris Ibn Ghazi*, 70–71n4.

53. Ibn Ghazi, *Fihris Ibn Ghazi*, 70n4. Ibn Ghazi mentioned that he only "heard some of the *Mudawwana*" from al-Qawri (Ibn Ghazi, *Fihris Ibn Ghazi*, 66), so he would not have been authorized to teach it as a part of this chain of transmission (*isnad*).

54. Ibn Ghazi, *Fihris Ibn Ghazi*, 66.

55. Ibn Battuta, *The Travels of Ibn Battuta*.

56. Berkey, *The Transmission of Knowledge*, 161; Sayeed, "Muslim Women's Religious Education."

57. Berkey, *The Transmission of Knowledge*, 162–80.

58. Sayeed, *Women and the Transmission*, 26–27.

59. Sayeed, *Women and the Transmission*, 186–91. For more on women's hadith transmission, see Nadwi, *al-Muhaddithat*; and Abou-Bakr, "Teaching the Words of the Prophet," 306–28.

60. Roded, *Women in Islamic Biographical Collections*, 2.

61. An example of this is volume 12 of Ibn Abd al-Rahman al-Sakhawi, *al-Daw' al-Lami'*.

62. Roded, *Women in Islamic Biographical Collections*, 58.

63. Roded, *Women in Islamic Biographical Collections*, 80–85. For more on Sufi women, see Abu 'Abd al-Rahman al-Sulami, *Early Sufi Women*.

64. Ávila, "Las mujeres sabias," 139–84; Fierro, "Mujeres Hispano-arabes en Tres Repertorios Biograficos," 177–82.

65. Hassan, "Reflections, Narrations, and Judgments," 323–51; Yacoob, "Women and Education in the Pre-Modern Middle East"; and al-Sa'adi and Abou-Bakr, *al-Mar'a wa-al-Hayat al-Diniyya*. For the Maghrib, see Admiral, "Finding the *Faqihat*," 37–61.

66. Hassan, "Reflections, Narrations," 323–51.

67. Hassan, "Reflections, Narrations," 344–48.

68. Ibn al-Sa'i, *Consorts of the Caliphs.*

69. Peirce, *The Imperial Harem*, 140–41.

70. Peirce, *The Imperial Harem*, 142.

71. Ávila, "Las mujeres sabias," 147, 143.

72. Kara, *al-Nisa' fi Fida'*, 52.

73. Abdelhadi Tazi, *Jami' al-Qarawiyyin*, 2:443.

74. Rausch, "Ishelhin women transmitters," 173–92.

75. Sal, "Qadaya al-Mar'a al-Taziyya," 159–75.

76. Gannun, *Al-Nubugh*, 1:202.

77. Gannun, *Al-Nubugh,* 1:215. The woman is Aisha bint al-Jiyar.

78. Gannun, *Al-Nubugh,* 1:203.

79. For a brief biography and comprehensive source list, see Francisco Vidal-Castro, "Ibn Rushayd," in *Encyclopaedia of Islam, Three*, eds. Kate Fleet, Gudrun Krämer, Denis Matringe, John Nawas, Everett Rowson, accessed August 24, 2022, http://dx.doi.org/10.1163/1573-3912_ei3_COM_32193.

80. Ibn Marzuq, *El Musnad*, 104; Ibn al-Khatib, *Al-Ihata*, 135–43; Haddadi, *Rihlat Ibn Rushayd.*

81. Al-Wansharisi, *al-Mi'yar*, 11:48; quotes Ibn Juzayy, quoting al-Tusi.

82. Haddadi, *Rihlat Ibn Rushayd.*

83. Al-Manouni, *Waraqat*, 237, 250, 305.

84. Ibn al-Qadi, *Jadhwat al-Iqtibas*, 522.

85. Ibn al-Qadi, *Jadhwat al-Iqtibas*, 522. For Ibn Salmun's biography, see Ibn al-Qadi, *Jadhwat al-Iqtibas*, 434–35.

86. Ibn Abd al-Rahman al-Bashr, ed., *Uns al-'Ashaq*. Ibn al-Qadi, *Jadhwat al-Iqtibas*, 522–29, also preserves some of Sara al-Halabiyya's poetry in her biography. Garulo, "Una Poetisa Oriental," 153–77.

87. Garulo, "Una Poetisa Oriental," 174; Ibn al-Qadi, *Jadhwat al-Iqtibas*, 522.

88. Garulo, "Una Poetisa Oriental," 158.

89. Garulo, "Desde Siria," 51.

90. Ibn al-Khatib, *al-Ihata*, 4:13–18.

91. Ibn al-Khatib, *al-Ihata*, 4:13–14.

92. Ibn Marzuq, *El Musnad*, 104, 218.

93. Ibn Marzuq, *El Musnad*, 219; Makhluf, *Shajarat al-Nur al-Zakiyya,* 1:220–21.

94. Al-Wansharisi, *al-Mi'yar*, 2:499.

95. For more on Umm Hani, see Admiral, "Finding the *Faqihat.*" Martin, *Muslim Brotherhoods in Nineteenth-Century Africa*, 26, mistakenly connects Umm Hani al-Abdusi to a Fulani saint who was also named Umm Hani and who made a prophesy about a coming religious reformer. The original Arabic text that Martin cites does not make this connection. Bello bin Uthman Fodi (d. 1837), *Infaq al-Maysur*, 81, simply narrates from al-Thaqib that "the pious Fulani saint Umm Hani" made a prophesy. A 1948 work

connected the two Umm Hanis and Martin may be drawing from this text without citing it directly: Abdullah Iluri, *Al-Islam fi Nigeria,* 84. I have found no evidence to support this connection between the Fulani Umm Hani and the Umm Hani from the Abdusi family active in Fez in the fourteenth and fifteenth centuries.

96. For biography of Musa al-Abdusi, see Ahmad Baba, *Nayl al-Ibtihaj,* 604–5; Ahmad Baba, *Kifayat al-Muhtaj,* 481–82; Ibn al-Qadi, *Jadhwat al-Iqtibas,* 346–47; Makhluf, *Shajarat al-Nur,* 1:234–35; Ibn Ahmad ibn Husayn Ibn Qunfudh, *Uns al-Faqir,* 24–26; Ibn al-Ahmar, *Rawdat al-Nisrin,* 50. For biography of Muhammad al-Abdusi, see Ahmad Baba, *Nayl al-Ibtihaj,* 480. For biography of Abu al-Qasim al-Abdusi, see Ahmad Baba, *Nayl al-Ibtihaj,* 270–74; Ahmad Baba, *Kifayat al-Muhtaj,* 199–201; Ibn al-Qadi, *Durrat al-Hijal,* 3:281–82; al-Sakhawi, *al-Daw' al-Lami',* 11:139; al-Wansharisi, *Kitab Wafayat,* 88–89; Makhluf, *Shajarat al-Nur al-Zakiyya,* 1:252. For biography of Abdullah al-Abdusi, see Zarruq, *al-Kunnash,* 18–19; al-Wansharisi, *Kitab Wafayat,* 93; Ibn Ghazi, *al-Rawd al-Hatun,* 32; Al-Sakhawi, *al-Daw' al-Lami',* 5:67; Ahmad Baba, *Nayl al-Ibtihaj,* 231–32; Ahmad Baba, *Kifayat al-Muhtaj,*167–68; Ibn al-Qadi, *Durrat al-Hijal,* 3:53; Ibn al-Qadi, *Jadhwat al-Iqtibas,* 2:425; al-Kattani, *Salwat al-Anfas,* 3:384–85; Makhluf, *Shajarat al-Nur,* 1:255.

97. Ahmad Baba, *Nayl al-Ibtihaj,* 271.

98. Ahmad Baba, *Nayl al-Ibtihaj,* 271–72.

99. Abu Abdullah Muhammad al-Ansari al-Rassa', *Fihrist al-Rassa',* 60, 63; Vidal Castro, "El *Mi'yar* de al-Wansarisi," 325; Abu al-Qasim ibn Ahmad al-Burzuli, *Fatawa al-Burzuli.*

100. Zarruq, *al-Kunnash,* 18–19.

101. Ibn Ghazi, *al-Rawd al-Hatun,* 32.

102. Zarruq, *al-Kunnash,* 18–19. This is what Kugle is referring to when he mentions that Zarruq's grandmother studied with *her own* sister and "another scholarly woman," (erroneously referring to Umm Hani and Fatima al-Abdusi), an error found in the original text that he cited. Kugle, *Rebel Between Spirit And Law,* 47. Katz further adds to the confusion by incorrectly citing Kugle to state that it was Zarruq's mother (not grandmother) who attended Abdullah al-Abdusi's classes with her own sister and another "scholarly woman," rather than Abdullah's sisters Umm Hani and Fatima. Katz, *Women in the Mosque,* 126.

103. Zarruq, *al-Kunnash,* 11–18.

104. Zarruq, *al-Kunnash,* 19.

105. Ibn Ghazi, *al-Rawd al-Hatun,* 60; Ahmad Baba, *Nayl al-Ibtihaj,* 548.

106. Abd al-Rahman bin Muhammad al-Sijilmasi Ibn Zaydan, *Ithaf Alam al-Nass,* 3:689; Ibn Ghazi, *al-Rawd al-Hatun,* 62.

107. Ibn Ghazi, *al-Rawd al-Hatun,* 63.

108. Al-Wansharisi, *al-Mi'yar,* 2:499.

109. Marín, "Derecho Islámico medieval," 37.

110. Admiral, "Living Islamic Law," 212–34.

111. Hassan, "Reflections, Narrations," 348.

112. Agrama, "Ethics, Tradition, Authority," 14.

113. Zarruq, *al-Kunnash,* 16.

114. Al-Abdusi, *Ajwibat al-Abdusi*, 476.

115. Recent studies have challenged this assumption, such as Ahmed, "Learned Women," 470–84.

116. Thanks to my colleague Ben Wright for helping me appreciate the importance of women's "input" into the formation and activities of these jurists, and not just how it impacted their "output."

5. Negotiating Marital Life

1. Al-Wansharisi, *al-Mi'yar,* 3:60–61.

2. In the North African context, the sources use both the terms *'aqd al-nikah* (marriage contract in the literal sense) and *'aqd al-sadaq* (literally, dower contract) to refer to a marriage contract that included standard information, financial agreements, and any additional stipulations.

3. There is no evidence from other studies, or from the primary sources of this study, of marriage contract stipulations being used to restrict women's rights in the premodern Islamic world; however, this is not surprising, as legal and social understandings of marriage granted men far greater rights by default.

4. See, for example, Buskens, "Recent Debates," 70–131. The articles in the 2004 *Mudawwana* relating to the requirement of a marriage guardian are articles 19, 20, and 21. "The Moroccan Family Code (*Moudawana*): An Unofficial English Translation of the Arabic Text," trans. Global Rights, accessed March 24, 2016, http://www.wluml.org/sites/wluml.org/files/moudawana-english.pdf.

5. Some of these cases include al-Wansharisi, *al-Mi'yar,* 3:113, 3:133, 3:137, 3:262, and 3:300. In al-Wansharisi, *al-Mi'yar,* 3:183, a woman initially asked a judge to marry her, but then later stated she did not want to marry the particular man they had agreed upon.

6. Al-Wansharisi, *al-Mi'yar,* 3:294, 3:112. A fatwa in *al-Mi'yar* (10:125) advised the marriage of virgins, even if their fathers were absent, due to fear of sexual transgressions.

7. Several examples of this type of case are listed in al-Wansharisi, *al-Mi'yar,* 3:112–13.

8. This is equivalent to *mahr,* the term used more frequently in the Islamic East.

9. Ali, *Marriage and Slavery,* 50.

10. Sahnun, *al-Mudawwana,* 3:841–41. According to Wael Hallaq, "The Malikites void such contracts before consummation of the marriage, but not subsequently." See his *Shari'a*, 278. After consummation, the contract itself would remain valid, but the stipulations would be considered invalid; Ali, "Marriage in Classical Islamic Jurisprudence," 23. See also Spectorsky, *Women in Classical Islamic Law,* 89.

11. Malik ibn Anas, *Muwatta al-Imam Malik,* 3:196–97; Malik ibn Anas, *Al-Muwatta*, 478–79.

12. Malik ibn Anas, *Muwatta al-Imam Malik,* 3:196–97; Malik ibn Anas, *Al-Muwatta,* 478–79.

13. Tucker, *Women, Family, and Gender,* 62.

14. Sonbol, "A History of Marriage Contracts in Egypt," 90.

15. Sonbol, "A History of Marriage," 101–2.

16. Tucker, *Women, Family, and Gender,* 62–63.

17. Tucker, *Women, Family, and Gender,* 62. Abdal-Rehim also found that when women in Ottoman Egypt reconciled with their husbands after a non-final divorce, they often included stipulations in the new agreements, presumably to address the issues that had led to divorce in the first place ("The Family and Gender Laws," 107).

18. Abdal-Rehim, "The Family and Gender Laws," 103.

19. Abdal-Rehim, "The Family and Gender Laws," 103.

20. Zomeño, "The Islamic Marriage Contract," 145.

21. Zomeño, "The Islamic Marriage Contract," 144.

22. Zomeño, "The Islamic Marriage Contract," 145.

23. Zomeño, "The Islamic Marriage Contract," 144.

24. In other circumstances, women's rights were additionally restricted in exchange for another benefit using contractual stipulations. One of these situations was in *khul* contracts, which set out the terms of female-initiated divorce, which will be discussed further in chapter 6. In these agreements, women often gave up financial rights in return for maintaining custody of their children. Women occasionally agreed to additional stipulations, such as not remarrying for a certain amount of time; however, the jurists did not enforce these stipulations. Likewise, in bequest (*wasiya*) documents drawn up by a husband to provide for his family after his death, wives served as executors in charge of their children's financial needs, but at times were restricted by these contracts from remarrying (many of these cases are found in al-Wansharisi, *al-Mi'yar,* vol. 10).

25. Al-Wansharisi, *al-Mi'yar,* 3:278–79.

26. Tucker, *Women, Family, and Gender,* 62.

27. Zomeño, "Abandoned Wives," 111–26.

28. Al-Wansharisi, *al-Mi'yar,* 4:121. This is a rare case in which we learn how the fatwa was implemented after it was issued. Written below al-Yaznasni's response is a note indicating that the judge of Meknes, Muhammad bin Abd al-Rahman bin Abd al-Aziz al-'Afiya, who had presumably requested guidance in a case being heard in his court, received the fatwa and ruled according to it: al-Wansharisi, *al-Mi'yar,* 4:121. The fatwas included in the *Mi'yar* and other fatwa collections have often been stripped of this follow-up information, but in the infrequent cases where the information is retained, we are able to follow the fatwa back to the requesting judge and observe his ruling in the case.

29. Al-Wansharisi, *al-Mi'yar,* 4:321.

30. See Mernissi, *The Veil and the Male Elite,* 192–93, for a description of the use of stipulations in marriage contracts by the Prophet Muhammad's great-granddaughter, Sukayna.

31. Mernissi, *The Veil and the Male Elite*, 192.

32. Al-Wansharisi, *al-Mi'yar,* 3:52–55. Ibn Atiyya was not related to the compiler of *Mi'yar,* who referred to him as "our countryman," i.e., from the same area in Algeria.

33. Al-Wansharisi, *al-Mi'yar,* 3:52.

34. Al-Wansharisi, *al-Mi'yar,* 3:54, quoting Ibn Yunes.

35. Al-Wansharisi, *al-Mi'yar,* 3:54.

36. Meriwether, "The Rights of Children," 223.

37. This will be discussed further in the following chapter.

38. If a husband volunteered to provide a higher level of care for his stepchildren, however, he was not necessarily held to his commitment. One example is a case in which a husband had volunteered to maintain his wife's children with slaves and take care of all their needs aside from clothing (al-Wansharisi, *al-Mi'yar,* 3:21). The mufti Abdullah al-Abdusi wrote that he was not obligated to maintain them at this level, or even provide them with lodging, but was only required to provide their food and drink. In a case from al-Andalus in the same time frame, it was the wife herself who gave her permission for her husband to cease maintaining her children by a different man (al-Wansharisi, *al-Mi'yar,* 3:21). The mufti consulted, however, did not allow the wife to consent to remove the husband's obligation to her children. He argued that the stipulation was for the children's benefit and was therefore their right, not their mother's, and because of this the mother could not revoke it.

39. Tucker, *Women, Family, and Gender,* 62.

40. Abdal-Rehim has found that this practice was not always followed in Ottoman Egypt: "There was a general acceptance of children from previous marriages, who were normally left with their mother and did not seem to be an obstruction to her remarriage, even when she was being remarried to a man other than the father of her child" ("The Family and Gender Laws," 110). Other historical studies have found women retaining custody of children beyond the age when they would technically be returned to the care of the father or the father's family; however, there is no mention in these cases of the consequences of the wife remarrying: Tucker, *In the House of the Law,* 130.

41. Toledano, *Judicial Practice*, 39. The jurist quoted by Ibn Hilal al-Sijilmasi is Ibn al-Attab.

42. Al-Wansharisi, *al-Mi'yar,* 3:339–41.

43. Al-Wansharisi, *al-Mi'yar,* 3:340.

44. Al-Wansharisi, *al-Mi'yar,* 3:341.

45. Al-Wansharisi, *al-Mi'yar,* 3:341; Zomeño, "The Islamic Marriage Contract," 144.

46. Al-Wansharisi, *al-Mi'yar,* 4:97–98.

47. Zomeño, "*Kafa'a* in the Maliki School," 87–106, discusses one of the rare instances of a marriage being challenged after it had taken place based on the doctrine of suitability, in two questions answered by Abdullah al-Abdusi, originally from al-Wansharisi, *al-Mi'yar,* 3:84–86.

48. Modern Iranian family law chose to include a specified list of stipulations as a standard part of a marriage contract to enforce certain rights for women: Mir-Hosseini, *Marriage on Trial*, 55; modern Egyptian law restricts them. Sonbol, "A History of Marriage," 90.

49. Global Rights: Partners for Justice, "Conditions, Not Conflict," http://www.globalrights.org/sites/default/files/docs/Conditions_not_Conflict_Marriage_Contract.pdf, 62–63.

50. "Conditions, Not Conflict," 47, 77.

51. "Conditions, Not Conflict," 5.

52. "Conditions, Not Conflict," 81.

6. Divorce and Re-envisioning the Family

1. Rapoport, *Marriage, Money, and Divorce*, 5.

2. My discussion of doctrine draws from Spectorsky, *Women in Classical Islamic Law*, 105–41, for the formative period, and 158–64 for the classical period. Tucker, *In the House of the Law*, 78–100; Tucker, *Women, Family, and Gender*, 84–104; Esposito, *Women in Muslim Family Law*, 27–37.

3. Ibn Rushd, *The Distinguished Jurist's Primer*, 2:85. While the majority of jurists accepted the validity of a delegated divorce, some jurists maintained that a man's authority over divorce could not be transferred to a woman.

4. Ali, "Marriage in Classical Islamic Jurisprudence," 25–27. There were differing opinions on whether this divorce was irrevocable (Ibn Rushd, *The Distinguished Jurist's Primer*, 2:85–86).

5. Ibn Rushd, *The Distinguished Jurist's Primer*, 2:92.

6. Al-Wansharisi, *al-Mi'yar*, 4:156.

7. Al-Wansharisi, *al-Mi'yar*, 4:196.

8. Al-Wansharisi, *al-Mi'yar*, 4:199.

9. Al-Wansharisi, *al-Mi'yar*, 4:265. Interestingly, this and other statements were made as a reaction to a wife refusing to have sex with her husband, which challenges assumptions drawn from legal doctrine that a wife must always be available sexually to her husband, with no requirement for consent. For analysis of consent and women refusing sex, see Admiral, "Navigating Consent."

10. Al-Abdusi responded to two cases of this type: al-Abdusi, *Ajwibat al-Abdusi*, 218, also in al-Wazzani, *al-Nawazil al-Jadida al-Kubra*, 4:325; and al-Abdusi, *Ajwibat al-Abdusi*, 221–22, also in al-Wansharisi, *al-Mi'yar*, 4:101–2.

11. Yossef Rapoport traces the evolution of this practice in "Matrimonial Gifts," 1–36.

12. Zomeño, *Dote y Matrimonio*, 228–29. Fatwa records from Marinid Morocco confirm this practice. In the case of the death of the wife, the payment would go to her heirs.

13. Rapoport, "Matrimonial Gifts," 12.

14. Khalil Ibn Ishaq al-Jundi, *Maliki Law*, 104; Tucker, *Women, Family, and Gender*, 92–95.

15. Esposito, *Women in Muslim Family Law*, 34; Tucker, *Women, Family, and Gender*, 93.

16. Cases of harm in al-Andalus often involved monitoring of the couple by a trusted member of the community. For an overview of how these cases were handled in Andalusia, see Fierro, "Ill-Treated Women," 323–47. The process for obtaining a divorce based on harm is described in detail in Khalil Ibn Ishaq al-Jundi, *Maliki Law*, 119–21.

17. In a case from fourteenth-century Andalusia, in which the wife had run away from her husband, the mufti, Ibn Lubb (d. 1381) advised the judge to grant a divorce on the grounds of harm, provided the wife's claims could be proven (Al-Wansharisi, *al-Mi'yar*, 2:432–33). Among the husband's offenses in this case was forcing his wife into prostitution, causing the ruling to clearly fall into the category of harm. In another case (*al-Mi'yar*, 3:319), from an unknown time and place , a couple went through arbitration but still hated each other. The woman was willing to relinquish rights in a *khul*, but her father objected. The mufti said that if arbiters had evidence the husband was harming her then it should be a divorce wherein he renounced financial rights; if she was responsible for the harm, then it should be a divorce in which she gave up hers. Another case was initiated based on competing complaints from a couple about the other's behavior, with the husband complaining that his wife went out too much, and the wife insisting that he did not maintain her sufficiently (i.e., with money) and that he hit her (*al-Mi'yar*, 3:131). The wife requested to be placed in the house of a righteous person, which might indicate that the case originated in Andalusia, as Fierro notes that this was the more common way of dealing with cases there, instead of appointing arbiters to intervene ("Ill-Treated Women," 332).

18. Powers analyzes a case of this type from twelfth-century Lisbon, found in *al-Mi'yar*, 4:4–5, in "Women and Divorce," 29–45. In this case, however, Powers suggests that her father encouraged her to remain in the marriage until sufficient proof could be gathered to prove harm and recover her sizable dower. In this case, it also appears that the husband beat his wife in an effort to provoke a *khul* divorce so that the assets he had gifted in the marriage would be returned. In another case, it was a wife's second husband who alleged harm when he attempted to claim the assets his wife had given up in a *khul* divorce from her first husband (al-Wansharisi, *al-Mi'yar*, 4:139–40).

19. One example is a case found in al-Abdusi, *Ajwibat al-Abdusi*, 227–28, and in al-Wansharisi, *al-Mi'yar*, 4:106–7, where the husband's brother put himself between the pair so the wife could escape.

20. In al-Sijilmasi, *al-Durr al-Nathir*, 1:263–70, al-Sughayyir responded to a question about a woman who had moved with her father to a new town near Fez and was seeking a divorce from her husband, whom they claimed was not only absent but mentally ill. The

case, however, may have been hypothetical, as it presented several scenarios as to what might really be going on; alternatively, it could have been a question attempting to find a way out of the marriage for the woman depending on how al-Sughayyir responded to the different situations. In 1466–67, al-Qawri also answered a seemingly theoretical question put to him by Ahmad al-Wansharisi, the compiler of the *Mi'yar,* about a married man who had intercourse with a woman knowing that she was already married; in this case, because of his foreknowledge, the discussion revolved around punishment (*al-Mi'yar,* 3:41). In another case, a wife divorced herself in her husband's absence using a condition in her marriage contract, and remarried (*al-Mi'yar,* 3:109–10). While her second husband was absent, she tracked down her first husband and resumed marital life with him, without telling him that she had divorced him and was now married to another man. Her case came to the attention of the law when her first husband discovered he had been living with her and had children with her without being legally married.

21. Al-Wansharisi, *al-Mi'yar,* 2:430–32. The question is repeated, although the wording is somewhat different in *al-Mi'yar,* 3:37–39.

22. Al-Abdusi discusses the strict evidentiary procedures that would need to be followed in a case of this type presented to him; see al-Abdusi, *Ajwibat al-Abdusi,* 453, and al-Abdusi, *Ajwiba Fiqhiyya,* 489. David S. Powers analyzes a case of this kind from the twelfth century in "Four Cases," 383–409. The original case is from al-Wansharisi, *al-Mi'yar,* 3:41–43. Another, similar case is *al-Mi'yar,* 3:46, where the mufti (al-Qabisi) recommended that the wife be returned to her first marriage, although without incurring the punishment for adultery. As the wife had remarried in another location, it may have been difficult to enforce this recommendation, even if a judge ruled according to his recommendation.

23. An exception to this rule permitted a woman to marry a man who was a close relative (*mahram*) of the children, for example, the brother of her deceased husband.

24. Zuhur Arbuh, in *Awda' al-Mar'a,* for example, *only* discusses this type of divorce in her cataloging of cases involving women from *al-Mi'yar,* as it fits her overall narrative of Islamic law advancing women's rights, although al-Wansharisi's *al-Mi'yar* contains an enormous amount of fatwas covering all types of divorce.

25. This deferred portion of the dower was also referred to as "*sadaq mu'ajjal.*"

26. Zomeño, *Dote y Matrimonio,* 254. For an example of cases with disputes over the amount, see al-Sijilmasi, *al-Durr al-Nathir,* 1:236, in which returning the *kali'* was agreed on, but an additional sum was disputed.

27. In one case, a woman offered to return her dower in exchange for a *khul* divorce, but later withdrew the offer (al-Wansharisi, *al-Mi'yar,* 4:12–13), while in another, an orphan with no guardian to guide her relinquished the entire amount, but the mufti said her ex-husband had to return it because she was not mature (*rashida*) and had been married for less than one year: al-Abdusi, *Ajwibat al-Abdusi,* 218; also in al-Wazzani, *al-Nawazil*

al-Jadida, 4:324. Khalil Ibn Ishaq states that if a woman was not capable of managing her own affairs, the property had to be returned, but she would remain divorced (*Maliki Law,* 113). In only one case from Marinid Morocco did a woman return her entire dower, and her husband may even have attempted to claim the additional assets she had acquired from a previous husband (al-Wansharisi, *al-Mi'yar,* 4:14–15). This is technically legal based on a statement by Malik: "There is nothing objectionable in a woman giving to her husband more than he gave her in order to remove herself from the marriage." Malik ibn Anas, *Al-Muwatta,* 505. Yet, it was clearly not a common practice.

28. While the Moroccan sources do not reveal much about social status, a study of court records from Ottoman Istanbul in the eighteenth century shows that this type of divorce was common among the middle classes. See Zilfi, "We Don't Get Along," 275.

29. Zilfi, "We Don't Get Along," 273.

30. Rapoport, *Marriage, Money, and Divorce,* 69.

31. Abdal-Rehim, "The Family and Gender Laws," 106. Zilfi also mentions that *khul* in Ottoman Istanbul was registered by the courts, although she suggests that some cases may have been handled privately ("We Don't Get Along," 294).

32. This is illustrated by a number of cases where problems arose with a *khul* due to a lack of contracts or witnesses: al-Wansharisi, *al-Mi'yar,* 4:12, 4:13, 4:14 (Granada), 4:336, in which a woman denied a *khul* agreement, and the man had no proof (Tunisia), and 4:99, where a man who did not want a *khul* to proceed swore that witnesses could not enter his house.

33. Al-Sijilmasi, *al-Durr al-Nathir,* 1:242–43.

34. Al-Sijilmasi, *al-Durr al-Nathir,* 1:242.

35. Al-Sijilmasi, *al-Durr al-Nathir,* 1:242.

36. Al-Sijilmasi, *al-Durr al-Nathir,* 1:242.

37. In a case from Tunis in the fourteenth century, a woman put exactly this condition in her *khul* contract, although she specified that she would only retain custody of her child if she remarried within the first two years following the divorce. al-Wansharisi, *al-Mi'yar,* 4:11; the mufti Ibn Arafa (d. 1400) responded.

38. Al-Wansharisi, *al-Mi'yar,* 4:7–8; the mufti here was al-Wanghili, a fourteenth-century contemporary of al-Qabab.

39. Mir-Hosseini, *Marriage on Trial,* 146.

40. Khalil Ibn Ishaq al-Jundi, *A Manual of the Law,* 320. The order of custody was changed in the 2004 *Mudawwana* to include the father after the mother.

41. Linant de Bellefonds, "Hadana." Abdal-Rehim has found that this practice was not always followed in Ottoman Egypt: "There was a general acceptance of children from previous marriages, who were normally left with their mother and did not seem to be an obstruction to her remarriage, even when she was being remarried to a man other than the father of her child" ("The Family and Gender Laws," 110).

42. Linant de Bellefonds, "Hadana," i.e., a *mahram*, meaning someone close enough that they were forbidden from marriage. Rapoport, "Legal Diversity," 222.

43. An example of this is modern Maliki internet fatwas that take a very rigid approach to this topic: "Questions and Answers Related to Child Custody," *The Madinan Way*, https://www.themadinanway.org/single-post/2017/10/17/questions-answers-related-to-child-custody, accessed March 27, 2024. In response to a question about a woman losing custody when she remarried, the mufti responded: "The reason is that according to the standard view in the Maliki madhhab, a custodian's right to custody is voided if he/she travels with the child to a town outside the proximity of the father's homeland unless the distance is less than forty-eight Hashimite miles. As for the fact that the new father is caring, this has no bearing on the situation." In this context, there is no room for flexibility.

7. Divorce Oaths and Legal Flexibility

1. This is mentioned in the father's narrative in al-Wansharisi, *al-Mi'yar*, 3:77; Iysa al-Turjali's narrative specifies that it was a divorce oath (*al-Mi'yar*, 3:60).

2. A similarly binding oath was one sworn on the manumission of a slave, which had the automatic result of freeing the slave if broken. Although an oath sworn to God, if broken, could be expiated by certain actions or good deeds, such as feeding the poor, fasting, or manumitting a slave, the consequence of an oath made on divorce was always divorce, and there was no possible expiation to atone for breaking the oath. For an overview of oaths, see Ibn Rushd, *The Distinguished Jurist's Primer*, 1:492. Rapoport, in *Marriage, Money, and Divorce*, chapter 5, describes Ibn Taymiyya's arguments that divorce oaths should have expiation like oaths to God, which led to his arrest and trial, in addition to the refutation of his opinion by his fellow jurists.

3. Islamic law also recognized several standard oaths that resulted in divorce, such as a husband's pledge of abstinence (*ila*) that lasted more than four months, and an arcane oath held over from pre-Islamic times in which a husband compared his wife to his mother's back (*dhihar*).

4. For example, Ali, "Marriage in Classical Islamic Jurisprudence," 24. Judith E. Tucker notes that in seventeenth- and eighteenth-century Ottoman Syria and Palestine, husbands sometimes used divorce oaths as a way to assume control over their wives, to force them into obedience (*In the House of the Law*, 101).

5. Muhammed Fadel in "The Social Logic of Taqlid and the Rise of the Mukhtasar" argues that the creation of the genre of "mukhtasar" was intended to identify one rule that everyone agreed upon to remove some of the uncertainty that existed within the divergent views of the vast legal tradition.

6. Rapoport mentions that the Mamluk period was probably the first time a divorce oath was required in a legal court in place of the standard oath sworn in legal proceedings (*Marriage, Money, and Divorce*, 93).

7. Peirce, "'She Is Trouble . . . ,'" 292.

8. It may or may not be significant that al-Sughayyir addressed many more oaths about controlling a wife's behavior than al-Abdusi dealt with two centuries later.

9. Admiral, "Navigating Consent."

10. Al-Wansharisi provides contemporary opinions from jurists about women's mobility in urban areas (*al-Mi'yar,* 2:499).

11. Al-Wansharisi, *al-Mi'yar,* 4:509–12.

12. For al-Walidi's biography, see Ahmad Baba, *Nayl al-Ibtihaj,* 179–80; Ahmad Baba, *Kifayat al-Muhtaj,* 132; Ibn al-Qadi, *Jadhwat al-Iqtibas,* 1:196; Ibn Qunfudh, *Uns al-Faqir,* 23–24; Ibn al-Qadi, *Durrat al-Hijal,* 1:273–74; al-Kattani, *Salwat al-Anfas,* 3:262; Makhluf, *Shajarat al-Nur al-Zakiyya,* 1:201. Most biographical sources agree that al-Walidi died in 1276–77 in Fez, although the editor of the critical edition of *al-Halal wa al-Haram,* Abd al-Rahman al-Idrisi, argues that it is more likely he died in 1296: Abu al-Fadl Rashid al-Walidi, *al-Halal wa al-Haram,* 46–48.

13. Al-Wansharisi, *al-Mi'yar,* 4:428–29.

14. Rapoport, *Marriage, Money, and Divorce,* 89.

15. Al-Wansharisi, *al-Mi'yar,* 4:99.

16. Al-Wansharisi, *al-Mi'yar,* 4:430.

17. See also al-Wansharisi, *al-Mi'yar,* 4:428–29, 4:429, 4:509–12; al-Sijilmasi, *al-Durr al-Nathir,* 1:185–88, where the husband stated, "You are for the mosque if you go out."

18. Al-Wansharisi, *al-Mi'yar,* 4:91.

19. Al-Sijilmasi, *al-Durr al-Nathir,* 1:44; al-Wansharisi, *al-Mi'yar,* 4:417; al-Abdusi, *Ajwibat al-Abdusi,* 220, and al-Wansharisi, *al-Mi'yar,* 4:88; al-Sijilmasi, *al-Durr al-Nathir,* 1:179.

20. Al-Wansharisi, *al-Mi'yar,* 4:99.

21. Al-Wansharisi, *al-Mi'yar,* 4:509–12.

22. Al-Wansharisi, *al-Mi'yar,* 4:509.

23. Al-Wansharisi, *al-Mi'yar,* 510–11.

24. Al-Sijilmasi, *al-Durr al-Nathir,* 1:177. Al-Sughayyir attributed the opinion to Asbagh ibn al-Faraj ibn Said (d. 840), a student of Ibn al-Qasim.

25. See, for example, Rapoport, *Marriage, Money, and Divorce,* 94–96.

26. Hanafis held that intention was irrelevant, while Hanbalis considered it relevant. Tucker, *Women, Family, and Gender,* 91.

27. Sahnun, *al-Mudawwana,* 2:652–53. In front of a judge, al-Abdusi pointed out that in another case, a couple would not have the freedom to choose to follow one opinion or the other; rather, the judge had to rule using one opinion, and it would be based on whichever opinion carried more weight in the Maliki school. al-Abdusi, *Ajwibat al-Abdusi,* 237; also in al-Wazzani, *al-Nawazil al-Jadida al-Kubra,* 4:111. Therefore, in these cases, resolving oaths and consequences at a community level, or with the help of a mufti

provided more flexibility than would be found in a court. The opinion that would be favored in this case was that of Ibn al-Qasim. Fadel quotes Ibn al-Qasim as saying, "It is as if Ashhab and I had studied with two different scholars" (from Qadi Iyad), highlighting the differences of opinion that existed between these two students of Malik ("The Social Logic of Taqlid," 218).

28. Al-Wansharisi, *al-Mi'yar,* 4:428–29.

29. Al-Wansharisi, *al-Mi'yar,* 4:429.

30. Rapoport, "Legal Diversity in the Age of Taqlid," 210–28.

31. Al-Abdusi, *Ajwibat al-Abdusi*, 175; also in al-Wazzani, *al-Nawazil al-Jadida al-Kubra*, 2:446, repeated 4:67, and al-Abdusi, *Ajwibat al-Abdusi*, 237; also in al-Wazzani, *al-Nawazil al-Jadida al-Kubra*, 4:111. This requirement might indicate change over time, or it could simply have been an anomalous practice by al-Abdusi.

32. The consequences of this could be fatal, because if a woman knew an oath had been broken and therefore she had been divorced, and her husband tried to force himself on her, she had the right to kill him like she could any other man who tried to force himself on her (although there are two opinions on this point, the one favored by the school is that she can kill him). Khalil Ibn Ishaq, *A Manual of the Law,* 190.

33. Al-Wansharisi, *al-Mi'yar,* 4:429–30.

34. This is the only case I have come across with this dynamic between a mufti and a judge. As chief judge, however, he was well within his authority to clarify the law that should have been followed in his jurisdiction.

35. Al-Wansharisi, *al-Mi'yar,* 4:430. This could be significant, for example indicating a shift in practice away from accepting both opinions as valid and enforcing one dominant opinion. Khalil favored Ibn al-Qasim's opinion, but clearly this fact was not decisive in determining which opinion jurists would follow. Further research would need to examine legal texts from a later period to determine whether this opinion remained dominant after this point.

36. Al-Wansharisi, *al-Mi'yar,* 4:430.

37. Imber, "'Involuntary' Annulment of Marriage," 70.

38. Peirce, *Morality Tales,* 1.

8. Transgressions and Legal Accommodation

1. Thanks to the University of Texas at Dallas spring 2022 Islamic Law and Society class (and Pale Almissouri specifically) for raising this possibility during our discussions of this fatwa.

2. For more on *zina* in the Marinid period, see Admiral, "Transgressing the Boundaries," 299–309.

3. These cases are: al-Sijilmasi, *al-Durr al-Nathir,* 1:82–84; al-Abdusi, *Ajwibat al-Abdusi,* 195–96, also in al-Wansharisi, *al-Mi'yar,* 3:92–93; al-Abdusi, *Ajwibat al-Abdusi,* 190–91, also in al-Wansharisi, *al-Mi'yar,* 3:89–90; al-Abdusi, *Ajwibat al-Abdusi,* 205–6,

also in al-Abdusi, *Ajwiba Fiqhiyya,* 445; al-Abdusi, *Ajwibat al-Abdusi,* 192–94, also in al-Wansharisi, *al-Mi'yar,* 3:90–91. One of these cases took place in nearby Algeria, although jurists from Tlemcen to Tunis responded (al-Wansharisi, *al-Mi'yar,* 4:476–77). Five other cases of women running away with men are contained in *al-Mi'yar,* in other times and places or where no information locates them in time or space. In three of the cases it is mentioned that they are able to marry (al-Wansharisi, *al-Mi'yar,* 3:347–48, 4:474, and 5:181–82), while in another the outcome is unclear due to issues with the observation of *istibra* (al-Wansharisi, *al-Mi'yar,* 4:475). In *al-Mi'yar* (4:523) it is revealed that a runaway couple had a child together, but the question is about paternity and it does not mention if they were legally married. A number of other cases involved married women running away with other men, as discussed in the previous chapter.

4. For elopement in medieval Britain, see Dunn, *Stolen Women,* 98–119, where it had a complicated legal relationship to abduction and rape; and Owen and Jenkins, eds., *The Welsh Law of Women.*

5. Tucker, "Questions of Consent," 132. Elopement cases were possibly more frequent in the countryside, which may explain why they do not appear often in the legal sources. For example, Peirce mentions that abduction took place in rural areas, although there is no indication that these may have been elopement cases (*Morality Tales,* 359). These categories continue to overlap in the modern period, such as in the case of Central Asian abduction marriages that are usually elopements. See Bowring, "Law," 2:417. See also Vogel, *Islamic Law and Legal System,* 265; and, for Somaliland, Anderson, *Islamic Law in Africa,* 51–52. In modern Indonesia, elopement is not disguised as abduction; see Hooker, *Indonesian Islam,* 148.

6. Semerdjian, *"Off the Straight Path,"* 38.

7. An interesting observation here (thanks to Hisham al-Muhammadi, editor of al-Abdusi's collection) is that the three cases presented to al-Abdusi also appear in the *Mi'yar* without attribution to any mufti, and from comparing them to al-Abdusi's collection they can be attributed to him. It is possible to pinpoint other fatwas in the *Mi'yar* based on the individual collections of other muftis.

8. Al-Sijilmasi, *al-Durr al-Nathir,* 1:82–84. "Orphan" (*yatima*) in Islamic law referred to someone whose father was dead, although their mother might still be alive. It is used in this way here to reflect its usage in the sources and the technical significance associated with this category.

9. Al-Abdusi, *Ajwibat al-Abdusi,* 195–96; also in al-Wansharisi, *al-Mi'yar,* 3:92. The version included in the *Mi'yar* does not identify the mufti.

10. Al-Abdusi, *Ajwibat al-Abdusi,* 190–91; also in al-Wansharisi, *al-Mi'yar,* 3:89–90. As above, the version included in the *Mi'yar* does not identify the mufti. Another version is included in al-Wazzani, *al-Nawazil al-Jadida al-Kubra,* 3:354, with the part about the woman running away omitted.

11. Al-Abdusi, *Ajwiba Fiqhiyya,* 445; al-Abdusi, *Ajwibat al-Abdusi,* 205–6.

12. Al-Wansharisi, *al-Mi'yar,* 4:476–77.

13. Al-Abdusi, *Ajwiba Fiqhiyya,* 445; al-Abdusi, *Ajwibat al-Abdusi,* 205–6.

14. Al-Abdusi, *Ajwiba Fiqhiyya,* 445; al-Abdusi, *Ajwibat al-Abdusi,* 205–6.

15. Al-Abdusi, *Ajwibat al-Abdusi,* 192–94; also in al-Wansharisi, *al-Mi'yar,* 3:90–91. As earlier, the version included in the *Mi'yar* does not identify the mufti.

16. Peirce, *Morality Tales,* 333, suggests that the "threat of drastic punishment was thus intended more as preventative than as penalty."

17. Peters, *Crime and Punishment in Islamic Law,* 60. All schools agreed on the number of lashes; three of four agreed they were to be followed by exile (not Hanafis); Malikis only banished males. Malikis were the only school to accept pregnancy as proof of *zina,* but they had a flexible doctrine with regards to pregnancy, considering anywhere from six months to five years as a possible period of gestation. Serrano Ruano, "La Lapidación," 450–51. Therefore, even if a child was born years after a divorce or the death of a husband, it would be attributed to that man's lineage.

18. Peters, *Crime and Punishment in Islamic Law,* 14–15. A false accusation of *zina,* which included a case where the testimony of all four witnesses was not accepted, subjected the accusers to punishment for another *hadd* crime: slander (*qadhf*) punishable by eighty lashes. Peters, *Crime and Punishment in Islamic Law,* 15.

19. Peters, *Crime and Punishment in Islamic Law,* 22.

20. Peters, *Crime and Punishment in Islamic Law,* 68.

21. Quraishi, "Her Honor," 287–320; Quraishi, "What if Sharia Weren't the Enemy?," 173–249. Peters identifies only one known instance of stoning in the Ottoman Empire. In this case, from Istanbul in 1680, a woman was stoned for having an affair with a Jew. The sultan's presence at the stoning also points to its exceptional nature. *Crime and Punishment in Islamic Law,* 93.

22. Quraishi, "Her Honor," 310–13.

23. Semerdjian, "*Off the Straight Path,*" chapter 2.

24. Imber, "*Zina* in Ottoman Law," 180–83.

25. Imber, "*Zina* in Ottoman Law," 190.

26. Semerdjian, "*Off the Straight Path,*" xvii.

27. Peirce, *Morality Tales,* 311.

28. Peirce, *Morality Tales,* 359.

29. Peirce, *Morality Tales,* 362–63.

30. Peirce, *Morality Tales,* 365. Also see Imber, "*Zina* in Ottoman Law," 180.

31. The term for dower more commonly used in North African sources is *sadaq,* and that is the term I use in this study. Tucker, *In the House of the Law,* 164. There is no indication, however, that these cases led to marriage as in the Moroccan context.

32. Tucker, *In the House of the Law,* 166.

33. Powers, *Law, Society, and Culture,* 23–52. This case is from al-Wansharisi, *al-Mi'yar,* 10:360–67.

34. Powers, *Law, Society, and Culture,* 53–94. This case is from al-Wansharisi, *al-Mi'yar,* 4:493–509.

35. Powers, *Law, Society, and Culture,* 62–65.

36. Powers, *Law, Society, and Culture,* 81.

37. Serrano Ruano, "La Lapidación," 449–73.

38. Serrano Ruano, "La Lapidación," 456.

39. Serrano Ruano, "La Lapidación," 469.

40. While there are more cases of *zina* from earlier periods, this is not necessarily meaningful or significant.

41. This is the opinion cited above in reference to the Taza case about whether a nonvirgin due to *zina* can still be compelled by her father to marry. Al-Abdusi, *Ajwibat al-Abdusi,* 485–86.

42. The muftis were very clear about when an act of sexual intercourse outside of marriage could be considered consensual, and cases of rape are not considered here under the *zina* framework. While the Powers paternity case discussed above did discuss *zina,* it was not central to the case as the man in question was dead, and therefore it is not considered here.

43. Al-Sijilmasi, *al-Durr al-Nathir,* 1:127–30.

44. Al-Wansharisi, *al-Mi'yar,* 2:430–32. The question is repeated, although with somewhat different wording, in al-Wansharisi, *al-Mi'yar,* 3:37–39.

45. Powers, *Law, Society, and Culture,* 53–94. This case is from al-Wansharisi, *al-Mi'yar,* 4:493–509.

46. Al-Wansharisi, *al-Mi'yar,* 4:477–78.

47. Mir-Hosseini discusses how this concept can provide women with flexibility in issues of paternity (*Marriage on Trial,* 143–45).

48. There are multiple versions of this fatwa scattered throughout al-Wansharisi, *al-Mi'yar* (3:58–59, 4:275–76, 4:308, 4:476–77, and 4:478–79).

49. The mufti from Bougie was Ali bin Uthman; al-Wansharisi, *al-Mi'yar,* 4:476.

50. The Tilimsani mufti Abu al-Fadl Qasim al-Uqbani (d. 1427); al-Wansharisi, *al-Mi'yar,* 4:476.

51. Al-Wansharisi, *al-Mi'yar,* 4:476.

52. Al-Wansharisi, *al-Mi'yar,* 3:58–59, 4:275–76, 4:308, 4:476–77, and 4:478–79.

53. Al-Wazzani, *al-Nawazil al-Jadida,* 3:354.

54. Islamweb.net is one site that has answered many such questions in both English and Arabic. An example is the question "Committed Zina with her husband a month and a half before marriage"; the answer recommends separation, observance of *istibra,* and remarriage. It also notes the disagreement among scholars over whether the waiting period is one or three menstrual cycles: https://www.islamweb.net/en/fatwa/117411/committed-zina-with-her-husband-a-month-and-a-half-before-marriage, accessed September 24, 2024.

55. See Ruggiero, *The Boundaries of Eros*, chapter 2: "Fornication and then Marriage." A further variation in the context of Renaissance Venice was that rape also often led to marriage. Ruggiero, *The Boundaries of Eros,* 31.

56. Wael Hallaq, "From *Fatwas* to *Furu'*," 61.

Conclusion

1. This same argument could also be made using the sources of Islamic law themselves, such as the Quran and sunna of the Prophet, both of which allow polygynous marriage as an option, but do not present it as an ideal. The only premodern exception where women gave up rights (aside from the exchange of financial rights to retain physical custody of children) was in the case of sisters giving up inheritance rights to brothers, which came in the context of a mutual support system.

2. Mahmood, *Politics of Piety,* 5, 14.

3. Mir-Hosseini et al., *Men in Charge?,* 1.

4. Mir-Hosseini, "Muslim Legal Tradition," 17.

5. Some explicit examples of these issues are found in the critical works of Abou El Fadl, *Reasoning with God,* 113–19; Hirschkind and Mahmood, "Feminism, the Taliban, and Politics of Counter-Insurgency," 339–54; and Quraishi, "What if Sharia," 173–249. Lila Abu-Lughod's *Do Muslim Women Really Need Saving?* critiques the broader debates surrounding Muslim women.

6. See, for example, Sadiqi, "The Central Role," 329. The Moroccan personal status code became closely identified with the feminist movement in the late 1980s and early 1990s. When Sadiqi references the "bitter disappointment" of feminists with this code, implemented in 1957 after Moroccan independence, who understood it as a "betrayal" of women, she does not specify if she is referring to women in the 1950s, the 1980s, or the present day (and does not cite a source that clarifies what she is referring to). The underlying assumption is that (Muslim) women in all times and places would see Islamic law as the enemy.

7. Cuno, *Modernizing Marriage,* 7.

8. Cuno and Desai, *Family, Gender, and Law;* Cuno, *Modernizing Marriage;* Tucker, *In the House;* Tucker, *Women, Family, and Gender;* Sonbol, *Women, the Family, and Divorce Laws.* Abou El Fadl in *Speaking in God's Name,* 16, identifies the multiple reasons for what he calls the "disintegration of the traditional dynamics of Islamic jurisprudence" as "the increasing centralization of state power, the nationalization of the private endowments (*awqaf*), that supported and funded the law guilds, the withering away of law guilds and their replacement with state-owned secular law schools, the adoption of the civil law system into a large number of Muslim countries, the development of enormous hegemonic state bureaucracies that co-opted and transformed many jurists into salaried employees, and the experience of colonialism that often methodically

dismantled the traditional institutions of Islamic law under the guise of the imperative of modernization."

9. Mir-Hosseini, *Marriage on Trial*, 198.

10. Hallaq, *An Introduction to Islamic Law*, 123.

11. Hallaq, *An Introduction to Islamic Law*, 170.

Bibliography

Primary Sources

al-Abdusi, Abdullah. *Ajwibat al-Abdusi*, edited by Hisham al-Muhammadi. al-Mamlaka al-Maghribiyya: Wizarat al-Awqaf wa-l-Shu'un al-Islamiyya, 2015.

al-Abdusi, Abdullah. *Ajwiba Fiqhiyya.* al-Khizana al-Hassaniyya, Rabat, ms. 14056.

Africanus, Leo. *The History and Description of Africa and of the Notable Things Contained Therein,* edited by Robert Brown. 2 vols. Cambridge: Cambridge University Press, 2010.

Ahmad Baba al-Tinbakti. *Kifayat al-Muhtaj li-Ma'rifat man laysa fi al-Dibaj.* Beirut: Dar Ibn Hazm, 2002.

Ahmad Baba al-Tinbakti. *Nayl al-Ibtihaj bi-Tatriz al-Dibaj.* Tripoli, Libya: Manshurat Kulliyat al-Da'awa al-Islamiyya, 1989.

al-Bashr, Muhammad bin Abd al-Rahman, ed. *Uns al-'Ashaq wa Nuzhat al-Sha'iq wa Riyad al-Muhibb al-Wamiq.* Beirut: Dar al-Kutub al-Ilmiyyah, 2012.

Bello, Muhammad. *Infaq al-Maysur fi Tarikh Bilad Takrur,* edited by Bahia al-Shadhili. Rabat: Manshurat Ma'hd al-Dirasat al-Ifriqiya, 1996.

Ibn al-Ahmar. *Rawdat al-Nisrin fi Dawlat Bani Marin,* edited and translated by Miguel Ángel Manzano. Madrid: Consejo Superior de Investigaciones Científicas, 1989.

Ibn Battuta. *The Travels of Ibn Battuta, A.D. 1325–1354, vol. 4.* Translated by H. A. R. Gibb. London: The Hakluyt Society, 1994.

Ibn Ghazi, Muhammad ibn Ahmad. *al-Rawd al-Hatun fi Akhbar Miknasat al-Zaytun.* Rabat: al-Matba'a al-Malakiyya, 1964.

Ibn Ghazi, Muhammad ibn Ahmad. *Fihris Ibn Ghazi,* edited by Muhammad al-Zahi. Tunis: Dar Bu Salama lil Taba'a wa al-Nashr wa al-Tawzi'a, 1984.

Ibn Khaldun, Abd al-Rahman. *Al-Tarif bi Ibn Khaldun: wa Rihlatihi Gharban wa Sharqan.* Beirut: Dar al-Kitab al-Lubnani, 1979.

Ibn al-Khatib, Muhammad Ibn Abdullah Lisan al-Din. *Al-Ihata fi Akhbar Ghranata.* 4 vols. Cairo: Maktabat al-Khanji, 1973–77.

Ibn Marzuq. *El Musnad: Hechos Memorables de Abu L-Hasan Sultan de Los Benimerines.* Translated by María J. Viguera. Madrid: Instituto Hispano-Árabe de Cultura, 1977.

Ibn al-Qadi, Abu Zayd Abd al-Rahman. *al-Fajr al-Sati' wa al-Diya' al-Lami' fi Sharh al-Durar al-Lawami'*, edited by Ahmad ibn Muhammad al-Bushaykhi. 4 vols. Marrakesh: al-Matba'a wa al-Waraqa al-Wataniyya, 2007.

Ibn al-Qadi, Ahmad bin Muhammad. *Durrat al-Hijal fi Ghurrat Asma al-Rijal*, edited by Muhammad al-Ahmadi Abu al-Nur. 3 vols. Cairo: Dar al-Turath, 1970.

Ibn al-Qadi, Ahmad bin Muhammad. *Jadhwat al-Iqtibas fi Dhikr man Halla min al-A'lam Madinat Fas.* Rabat: Dar al-Mansur li al-Tab'ia wa al-Waraqa, 1973.

Ibn Qunfudh, Ahmad ibn Husayn. *Uns al-Faqir wa Izz al-Haqir*, edited by Muhammad Fasi and Adolphe Faure. Rabat: al-Markaz al-Jami'i lil Bahth al-Ilmi, 1965.

Ibn Rushd. *The Distinguished Jurist's Primer: A Translation of Bidayat al-Mujtahid.* Translated by Imran Ahsan Khan. 2 vols. Reading: Centre for Muslim Contribution to Civilization, 1994–96.

Ibn al-Sa'i. *Consorts of the Caliphs: Women and the Court of Baghdad.* Translated by Shawkat M. Toorawa et al. New York: New York University Press, 2017.

Ibn Zaydan, Abd al-Rahman bin Muhammad al-Sijilmasi. *Ithaf Alam al-Nass bi Jamal Akhbar Hadarat Miknas*, edited by Ali Umar. 5 vols. Cairo: Maktaba al-Thaqafa al-Diniyya, 2008.

Al-Kattani, Muhammad ibn Ja'far. *Salwat al-Anfas wa Muhadithat al-Akiyas bi man Ukbira min al-Ulama wa al-Sulaha bi Fas*, edited by Muhammad Hamza bin Ali al-Kattani. 4 vols. Casablanca: Dar al-Thaqafa, 2004–06.

Khalil Ibn Ishaq al-Jundi. *Maliki Law: Being a Summary from French Translations of the Mukhtasar of Sidi Khalil.* Translated by F. H. Ruxton. Westport, CT: Hyperion Press, 1980.

Khalil Ibn Ishaq al-Jundi. *A Manual of the Law of Marriage from the Mukhtasar of Sidi Khalil.* Translated by Alexander David Russell and Abdullah al-Mamun al-Suhrawardy. Lahore: Law Pub. Co., 1979.

Khalil Ibn Ishaq al-Jundi. *Mukhtasar al-'Allamah Khalil fi Fiqh al-Imam Malik.* Sayda, Lebanon: Maktabat al-'Asriyya, 2003.

Makhluf, Mohammad. *Shajarat al-Nur al-Zakiyya fi Tabaqat al-Malikiyya.* 2 vols. Cairo: al-Maktaba al-Salafiyya, 1930.

Malik ibn Anas. *Al-Muwatta: The Recension of Yahya b. Yahya al-Laythi (d. 234/848)*, edited and translated by Mohammad Fadel and Connell Monette. Cambridge, MA: Harvard University Press, 2019.

Malik ibn Anas. *Muwatta al-Imam Malik: bi Riwayat Yahya al-Laythi.* 5 vols. Dubai: Majmu'at al-Furqan al-Tijariyya, 2003.

al-Maqqari, Ahmad ibn Muhammad. *Nahf al-Tib: Min Ghusn al-Andalus al-Ratib.* Edited by Ihsan Abbas. 8 vols. Beirut: Dar al-Sadir, 1968.

al-Rassa', Abu Abdullah Muhammad al-Ansari. *Fihrist al-Rassa'*, edited by Muhammad al-'Anabi. Tunis: al-Maktaba al-'Atiqa, 1967.

Sahnun ibn Sa'id al-Tanukhi. *Al-Mudawwana al-Kubra li Malik Ibn Anas al-Asbahi: Riwayat Sahnun ibn Sa'id al-Tanukhi 'an 'Abd al-Rahman ibn Qasim*, edited by Hamdi al-Damardash Muhammad. 9 vols. Mecca: Al-Maktaba al-'Asriyya, 1999.

al-Sakhawi, Muhammad ibn Abd al-Rahman. *Al-Daw' al-Lami' li Ahl al-Qarn al-Tasi'.* 12 vols. Beirut: Dar al-Jili, 1992.

al-Satti, Abu Abdullah bin Sulayman. *Sharh Mukhtasar al-Hawfi*, edited by Yahya Bu Aruru. Beirut: Dar Ibn Hazm, 2009.

al-Sijilmasi, Ibrahim ibn Hilal. *al-Durr al-Nathir 'ala Ajwiba Abu al-Hassan al-Saghir*, edited by Ahmad bin Ali Abu al-Fadl al-Diamati. 2 vols. Casablanca: Markaz al-Turath al-Thaqafi al-Maghribi, 2011.

al-Sijilmasi, Ibrahim ibn Hilal. *Nawazil al-Fiqh.* Salé: Mu'assasa al-Khizana al-'Ilmiyya al-Sbihiyya, lith. #759.

al-Walidi, Abu al-Fadl Rashid ibn Abi Rashid. *Al-Halal wa al-Haram*, edited by Abd al-Rahman al-Imrani al-Idrisi. Rabat: Wizarat al-Awqaf wa al-Shu'un al-Islamiyya, 1990.

al-Wansharisi, Ahmad ibn Yahya. *Al-Mi'yar al-Mu'rib wa al-Jami' al-Mughrib 'an Fatawi Ahl Ifriqiyah wa al-Andalus wa al-Maghrib*, edited by Muhammad Hajji. 13 vols. Rabat: Wizarat al-Awqaf wa al-Shu'un al-Islamiyya lil-Mamlaka al-Maghribiyya, 1981.

al-Wansharisi, Ahmad ibn Yahya. *Kitab Wafayat al-Wansharisi*, edited by Muhammad bin Yussef al-Qadi. Cairo: Sharika Nawabagh al-Fikr, 2009.

al-Wazzani, al-Mahdi. *al-Nawazil al-Jadida al-Kubra fi ma li Ahl Fas wa Ghayrihim min al-Badw wa al-Qura al-Musammat bi al-Mi'yar al-Jadid al-Jami' al-Mu'rib 'an Fatawi Muta'akhirin min 'Ulama' al-Maghrib.* 12 vols. Rabat: Wizarat al-Awqaf wa al-Shu'un al-Islamiyya lil-Mamlaka al-Maghribiyya, 1996–2000.

Zarruq, Ahmad. *al-Kunnash: Suwar min al-Dhikrayat al-Ula*, edited by 'Ali Khushaim. Tripoli, Libya: al-Munsha'at al-Sha'biyya, 1980.

Secondary Sources

Abdal-Rehim, Abdal-Rehim Abdal-Rahman. "The Family and Gender Laws in Egypt during the Ottoman Period." In *Women, the Family, and Divorce Laws in Islamic History,* edited by Amira El Azhary Sonbol, 96–111. Syracuse, NY: Syracuse University Press, 1996.

Abou-Bakr, Omaima. "Teaching the Words of the Prophet: Women Instructors of the Hadith (Fourteenth and Fifteenth Centuries)." *Hawwa* 1, no. 3 (2003): 306–28.

Abou El Fadl, Khaled. "Emergence and Sources." *LAW 338: Islamic Jurisprudence,* UCLA School of Law, Los Angeles. August 31, 2010.

Abou El Fadl, Khaled. *Reasoning with God: Reclaiming Shari'ah in the Modern Age*. Lanham, MD: Rowman & Littlefield, 2014.

Abou El Fadl, Khaled. *Speaking in God's Name: Islamic Law, Authority and Women*. Oxford: Oneworld, 2001.

Abu-Lughod, Lila. *Do Muslim Women Need Saving?* Cambridge, MA: Harvard University Press, 2013.

Abu-Lughod, Lila. "Do Muslim Women Really Need Saving? Anthropological Reflections on Cultural Relativism and Its Others." *American Anthropologist* 104, no. 3 (2002): 783–790.

Abun-Nasr, Jamil M. *A History of the Maghrib in the Islamic Period*. Cambridge: Cambridge University Press, 1987.

Abu-Odeh, Lama. "Honor Killings and the Construction of Gender in Arab Societies." *The American Journal of Comparative Law* 58 (2010): 911–52.

Adil, Sabahat. "Memorializing al-Maqqari: The Life, Work, and Worlds of a Muslim Scholar." PhD diss., The University of Chicago, 2015. ProQuest (3724435).

Admiral, Rosemary. "Finding the *Faqihat:* Women's Legal Scholarship and Biography in Premodern Morocco." *Journal of North African Studies* 29, no. 1 (2024): 37–61.

Admiral, Rosemary. "Living Islamic Law: Women and Legal Culture in Marinid Morocco." *Islamic Law and Society* 25, no. 3 (2018): 212–34.

Admiral, Rosemary. "Navigating Consent: On Women's Sexual Agency in the Premodern Islamic West." *Journal of Feminist Studies in Religion* 39, no. 1 (2023): 69–86.

Admiral, Rosemary. "Transgressing the Boundaries: *Zina* and Legal Accommodation in the Premodern Maghrib." In *The Routledge Handbook of Islam and Gender,* edited by Justine Howe, 299–309. London: Routledge, 2020.

Agrama, Hussein Ali. "Ethics, Tradition, Authority: Towards an Anthropology of the Fatwa." *American Ethnologist* 37, no. 1 (2010): 2–18.

Ahmed, Leila. *Women and Gender in Islam: Historical Roots of a Modern Debate.* New Haven: Yale University Press, 1992.

Ahmed, Sumayya. "Learned Women: Three Generations of Female Islamic Scholarship in Morocco." *The Journal of North African Studies* 21, no. 3 (2016): 470–84.

Ali, Kecia. *Marriage and Slavery in Early Islam.* Cambridge, MA: Harvard University Press, 2010.

Ali, Kecia. "Marriage in Classical Islamic Jurisprudence: A Survey of Doctrines." In *The Islamic Marriage Contract: Case Studies in Islamic Family Law,* edited by Asifa Quraishi and Frank E. Vogel, 11–45. Cambridge, MA: Harvard University Press, 2008.

Amar, Émile. "La pierre de touche des Fétwas de Ahmad al-Wanscharisi. Choix de consultations des faqihs du Maghreb." *Archives Marocaines: Publication de la Mission Scientifique du Maroc* 12 (1908): 365–97.

al-Amrani, Mohammad bin Ahmad. "Makanat Taza al-ʿIlmiyya min Khilal al-Nusus al-Tarikhiyya wa al-Intajat al-Adabiyya wa al-Fiqhiyya" (The Intellectual Position of Taza from Historical Sources and Literary and Legal Production). *Daouat al-Haq* 286 (1991). http://www.habous.gov.ma/daouat-alhaq/item/7466. Accessed July 7, 2022.

Anchassi, Omar. "Status Distinctions and Sartorial Difference: Slavery, Sexual Ethics, and the Social Logic of Veiling in Islamic Law." *Islamic Law and Society* 28 (2021): 125–55.

Anderson, J. N. D. *Islamic Law in Africa.* London: H. M. Stationery Office, 1954.

Anwar, Ibrahim. *Naql al-Maʿrifa fi al-Maghrib al-Mariniyya wa Ifriqiyya al-Hafsiyya (ila muntasaf al-qarn 8AH/14CE).* Rabat: Wizarat al-Thaqafa, 2011.

Arabi, Oussama, David S. Powers, and Susan A. Spectorsky, eds. *Islamic Legal Thought: A Compendium of Muslim Jurists.* Leiden: Brill, 2013.

Arbuh, Zuhur. *Awdaʿ al-Marʾa bi al-Gharb al-Islami min khilal Nawazil "al-Miʿyar li al-Wansharisi."* Rabat: Dar al-Iman, 2013.

Ávila, María Luisa. "Las mujeres sabias en al-Andalus." In *La Mujer en Al-Andalus: reflejos históricos de su actividad y categorías sociales,* edited by María Jesus Viguera, 139–84. Seville: Ediciones de la Universidad Autónoma de Madrid; Editoriales Andaluzas Unidas, 1989.

Awass, Omer. *Fatwa and the Making and Renewal of Islamic Law: From the Classical Period to the Present.* Cambridge: Cambridge University Press, 2023.

al-Bahi, Muhammad al-'Alawi. *'Ulama' Taza wa Majalisihim al-'Ilmiyya: Muqaraba Tarikhiyya*. Mohammedia, Morocco: Matba'a Fadala, 2004.

Beattie, Cordelia, and Matthew Frank Stevens. *Married Women and the Law in Premodern Northwest Europe*. Woodbridge, Suffolk: Boydell Press, 2013.

Benchekroun, Mohamed B. A. *La vie intellectuelle marocaine sous les Merinides et les Wattasides (XIIIe XIVe XVe XVIe siecles)*. Rabat: [s.n.], 1974.

Benmira, Omar. *Al-Nawazil wa al-Mujtama: Musahima fi Dirasat Tarikh al-Badia bi al-Maghrib al-Wasit (al-Qarnan al-Thamin wa al-Tasia / 14 wa 15)*. Rabat: Kulliyat al-Adab wa al-Ulum al-Insaniyya, 2012.

Berkey, Jonathan. *The Transmission of Knowledge in Medieval Cairo: A Social History of Islamic Education*. Princeton, NJ: Princeton University Press, 1992.

Bowring, Bill. "Law: Customary: Central Asia." In *Encyclopedia of Women & Islamic Cultures: Volume II: Family, Law and Politics*, edited by Suad Joseph, 416–18. Leiden: Brill, 2005.

Brockopp, Jonathan E. "Sahnun B. Sa'id." In *Islamic Legal Thought: A Compendium of Muslim Jurists*, edited by Oussama Arabi, David S. Powers, and Susan A. Spectorsky, 65–84. Leiden: Brill, 2013.

Brown, Jonathan A. C. *Hadith: Muhammad's Legacy in the Medieval and Modern World*. Oxford: Oneworld Publications, 2009.

Bourqia, Rahma and Susan Gilson Miller, eds. *In the Shadow of the Sultan: Culture, Power and Politics in Morocco*. Cambridge, MA: Harvard University Press, 1999.

Burke, Edmund III. *The Ethnographic State: France and the Invention of Moroccan Islam*. Oakland: University of California Press, 2014.

Burke, Edmund III and David N. Yaghoubian. "Middle Eastern Societies and Ordinary People's Lives: Rethinking Middle Eastern History." In *Struggle and Survival in the Modern Middle East*. Second edition, edited by Edmund Burke III and David N. Yaghoubian, 1–32. Berkeley/Los Angeles: University of California Press, 2006.

al-Burzuli, Abu al-Qasim ibn Ahmad. *Fatawa al-Burzuli: Jami' Masa'il al-Ahkam li ma Nazala min al-Qadaya bi al-Muftin wa al-Hukkam*, edited by Muhammad al-Habib Hila. 7 vols. Beirut: Dar al-Gharb al-Islami, 2002.

Buskens, Leon, "Recent Debates on Family Law Reform in Morocco: Islamic Law as Politics in an Emerging Public Sphere." *Islamic Law and Society* 10, no. 1 (2003): 70–131.

Chahboun, Nassima. "Taza, the Medina of Shimmering Words and Pale Stones." *Patrimoine d'Orient*, June 10, 2021. https://patrimoinedorient.org/index.php/en/2021/06/10/taza-the-medina-of-shimmering-words-and-pale-stones/.

Chamberlain, Michael. *Knowledge and Social Practice in Medieval Damascus, 1190–1350.* Cambridge: Cambridge University Press, 1994.

Cornell, Rkia E. "Introduction: As-Sulami and His Sufi Women." In Abu 'Abd al-Rahman al-Sulami, *Early Sufi Women: Dhikr al-Niswa al-Muta'abbidat as-Sufiyyat,* translated and edited by Rkia E. Cornell. Louisville: Fons Vitae, 1999.

Cornell, Vincent J. *Realm of the Saint: Power and Authority in Moroccan Sufism.* Austin: University of Texas Press, 1998.

Cuno, Kenneth M. *Modernizing Marriage: Family, Ideology, and Law in Nineteenth- and Early Twentieth-Century Egypt.* Syracuse, NY: Syracuse University Press, 2015.

Cuno, Kenneth M. and Manisha Desai, eds. *Family, Gender, and Law in a Globalizing Middle East and South Asia.* Syracuse, NY: Syracuse University Press, 2009.

Dunn, Caroline. *Stolen Women in Medieval England: Rape, Abduction and Adultery, 1100–1500.* Cambridge: Cambridge University Press, 2013.

Dunn, Ross E. *The Adventures of Ibn Battuta: A Muslim Traveler of the 14th Century.* Berkeley: University of California Press, 1986.

El Bouhsini, Latifa. "La Place Reservée aux Femmes dans Les Ecrits et L'Historiographie Marocains Relatifs au Moyen-Âge (De la Fin du Xe à La Fin du XIVe Siècle)." PhD diss., Université de Toulouse - Le Mirail, 1996.

Esposito, John L., with Natana J. DeLong-Bas. *Women in Muslim Family Law,* 2nd ed. Syracuse, NY: Syracuse University Press, 2001.

Fadel, Mohammad. "The Social Logic of Taqlid and the Rise of the Mukhtasar." *Islamic Law and Society* 3, no. 2 (1996): 193–233.

Fatha, Muhammad. *al-Nawazil al-Fiqhiyya wa al-Mujtama': Abhath fi Tarikh al-Gharb al-Islami (min al-Qarn 6 ila 9H /12–15M).* Casablanca: Manshurat Kulliyat al-Adab wa al-'Ulum al-Insaniyya Ain Shock, 1999.

Fierro, Maribel. *The Almohad Revolution: Politics and Religion in the Islamic West during the Twelfth–Thirteenth Centuries.* Surrey: Ashgate, 2012.

Fierro, Maribel. "Ill-Treated Women Seeking Divorce: The Qur'anic Two Arbiters and Judicial Practice among the Malikis in al-Andalus and North Africa." In *Dispensing Justice in Islam: Qadis and Their Judgments,* edited by Muhammad Khalid Masud, Rudolph Peters, and David S. Powers, 323–47. Leiden: Brill, 2006.

Fierro, Maribel. "Mujeres Hispano-arabes En Tres Repertorios Biograficos: Yadwa, Sila y Bugya." In *Las Mujeres Medivales y Su Ambito Juridico,* 177–82.

Madrid: Servicio de Publicaciones de la Universidad Autónoma de Madrid, 1983.

Fierro, Maribel. "Proto-Malikis, Malikis, and Reformed Malikis in al-Andalus." In *The Islamic School of Law: Evolution, Devolution, and Progress*, edited by P. J. Bearman, Rudolph Peters, and Frank E. Vogel, 57–76. Cambridge, MA: Islamic Legal Studies Program, Harvard Law School, 2005.

Fromherz, Allen James. *The Almohads: The Rise of an Islamic Empire*. London: I.B. Tauris, 2010.

Gannun, ʿAbdullah. *Al-Nubugh al-Maghribi fi al-Adab al-ʿArabi* [The Moroccan Genius in Arabic Literature]. 3 vols. Beirut: al-Maktaba al-Madrasa wa Dar al-Kitab al-Lubnani, 1975.

Garulo, Teresa. "Desde Siria a al-Andalus: El Viaje de Sara al-Halabiyya." *Hesperia Culturas del Medeterráneo* 1 (2008): 43–53.

Garulo, Teresa. "Una Poetisa Oriental en al-Andalus: Sara al-Halabiyya." *Al-Qantara* 6, no. 1 (1985): 153–77.

Geertz, Clifford. *Islam Observed: Religious Development in Morocco and Indonesia*. New Haven: Yale University Press, 1968.

Global Rights: Partners for Justice. "Conditions, Not Conflict: Promoting Women's Human Rights in the Maghreb through Strategic Use of the Marriage Contract," 2008. Accessed December 21, 2024, http://www.globalrights.org/sites/default/files/docs/Conditions_not_Conflict_Marriage_Contract.pdf.

Global Rights (translator). "The Moroccan Family Code (*Moudawana*): An Unofficial English Translation of the Arabic Text." Accessed March 24, 2016. http://www.wluml.org/sites/wluml.org/files/moudawana-english.pdf.

Haddadi, Ahmad. *Rihlat Ibn Rushayd al-Sabti Abi ʿAbd Allah Muhammad ibn ʿUmar* [The Travels of Ibn Rushayd al-Sabti Abi ʿAbd Allah Muhammad ibn ʿUmar]. Rabat: Wizarat al-Awqaf wa al-Shu'un al-Islamiyya, 2003.

Hajji, Muhammad. *Nadharat fi al-Nawazil al-Fiqhiyya*. [Rabat?]: al-Jamʿia al-Maghribiyya lil-Talif wa al-Tarjama wa al-Nashr, 1999.

Hallaq, Wael B. *An Introduction to Islamic Law*. Cambridge: Cambridge University Press, 2009.

Hallaq, Wael B. "From *Fatwas* to *Furuʿ*: Growth and Change in Islamic Substantive Law." *Islamic Law and Society* 1, no. 1 (1994): 29–65.

Hallaq, Wael B. *Shariʿa: Theory, Practice, Transformations*. Cambridge: Cambridge University Press, 2009.

Hallaq, Wael B. "Was the Gate of Ijtihad Closed?" *International Journal of Middle East Studies* 16, no. 1 (1984): 3–41.

Hamitu, Abd al-Hadi. *Qira'at al-Imam Nafi' 'and al-Maghariba min Riwayat Abi Sa'id Warsh.* 5 vols. al-Mamlaka al-Maghribiyya: Manshurat Wizarat al-Awqaf wa al-Shu'un al-Islamiyya, 2003.

Hardwick, Julie. *Sex in an Old Regime City: Young Workers and Intimacy in France, 1660–1789.* New York, NY: Oxford University Press, 2020.

Hassan, Mona. "Reflections, Narrations, and Judgments: The Scholarly Contributions of an Early Female Muslim Jurist." *Islamic Law and Society* 22 (2015): 323–51.

Hendrickson, Jocelyn. *Leaving Iberia: Islamic Law and Christian Conquest in North West Africa.* Cambridge, MA: Harvard University Press, 2021.

al-Hilali, Muhammad Yasir. "Masadir Tarikh al-Mar'a al-Maghribiyya khilal al-'Asr al-Wasit." *Daouat al-Haq* 399 (2011): 117–27.

al-Hilali, Muhammad Yasir. "Mujtama' al-Maghrib al-Aqsa khilal al-Qarnayn 8–9AH, 14–15CE: Musahima fi Dirasat ba'ad Mafahim al-Nidham al-Ijtima'i al-'Aama al-Khasa al-Tabaqa al-Martaba." PhD diss., Kulliyat al-Adab wa al-'Ulum al-Insaniyya, Rabat, 2000.

al-Hilali, Muhammad Yasir. "Nadharat al-Mujtama' lil Mar'a fi Maghrib al-Qarn 8–9AH/14–15CE: Musahimat fi Tarikh al-Dhihiniyyat." *Amal: al-Tarikh, al-Thaqafa, al-Mujtama'*, no. 13–14 (1998): 76–98.

Hirschkind, Charles and Saba Mahmood. "Feminism, the Taliban, and Politics of Counter-Insurgency." *Anthropological Quarterly* 75, no. 2 (2002): 339–54.

Hooker, M. B. *Indonesian Islam: Social Change through Contemporary Fatawa.* Honolulu: University Of Hawai'i Press, 2003.

Ibn Hosni, Abd al-Karim. "Jamia' al-Qarawiyyin." In *Jamia' al-Qarawiyyin fii Dhikrha al-Mia baad al-Alf,* 158–72. Muhammedia: Matbaa Fadala, 1960.

Ibn Rushayd, Muhammad ibn Umar, and Abd al-Latif ibn Muhammad al-Jilani. *Istida'at al-ijazah.* Rabat: Wizarat al-Awqaf wa-al-Shu'un al-Islamiyya, al-Mamlaka al-Maghribiyya, 2007.

Idris, Hady Roger. "Le Mariage en Occident Musulman: D'après un Choix de Fatwas Médiévales Extraites du 'Mi'yar' d'al-Wansarisi." *Studia Islamica* no. 32 (1970): 157–67.

Idris, Hady Roger. "Le Mariage en Occident Musulman: Analyse de Fatwas Médiévales Extraites du 'Mi'yar' d'al-Wansarisi." *Revue de L'Occident Musulman et de la Méditerranée* 12 (1972): 45–62.

Idris, Hady Roger. "Le Mariage en Occident Musulman: Analyse de Fatwas Médiévales Extraites du 'Mi'yar' d'al-Wansarisi." *Revue de L'Occident Musulman et de la Méditerranée* 17 (1974): 71–105.

Idris, Hady Roger. "Le Mariage en Occident Musulman: Analyse de Fatwas Médiévales Extraites du 'Mi'yar' d'al-Wansarisi." *Revue de L'Occident Musulman et de la Méditerranée* 25 (1978): 119–38.

Iluri, Adam Abdullah. *Al-Islam fi Nigeria wa al-Shaykh Uthman bin Fodio al-Fulani*, edited by Abd al-Hafidh al-Awladusu. Alexandria: Maktab al-Iskanderiyya, 2014.

Imber, Colin. "'Involuntary' Annulment of Marriage and its Solutions in Ottoman Law." *Turcica* 25 (1993): 39–73.

Imber, Colin. "*Zina* in Ottoman Law." In *Studies in Ottoman History and Law*, 175–206. Istanbul: Isis Press, 1996.

Jenkins, Dafydd and Morfydd E. Owen, eds. *The Welsh Law of Women: Studies Presented to Professor Daniel A. Binchy on his Eightieth Birthday, 3 June 1980.* Cardiff: University of Wales Press, 1980.

Jennings, Ronald C. "Women in Early 17th Century Ottoman Judicial Records: The Sharia Court of Anatolian Kayseri." *Journal of the Economic and Social History of the Orient* 18, no. 1 (1975): 53–114.

Kably, Mohamed. "Legitimacy of State Power and Socioreligious Variations in Medieval Morocco." In *In the Shadow of the Sultan: Culture, Power and Politics in Morocco*, edited by Rahma Bourqia and Susan Gilson Miller, 17–29. Cambridge, MA: Harvard University Press, 1999.

Kara, Hayat. *al-Nisa' fi Fida' al-Bahr al-Abyad al-Matawassit: al-Thaqafa wa al-Mujtama' fi al-'Asr al-Wasit.* Rabat: Dar Bouregreg li al-Taba'a wa al-Nashr, 2011.

Katz, Marion Holmes. *Women in the Mosque: A History of Legal Thought and Social Practice.* New York: Columbia University Press, 2014.

Khaneboubi, Ahmed. *Les Premiers Sultans Mérinides (1269–1331): Histoire Politique et Sociale.* Paris: L'Harmattan, 1987.

Kim, Jisoo M. *The Emotions of Justice: Gender, Status, and Legal Performance in Chosŏn Korea.* Seattle: University of Washington Press, 2015.

Kugle, Scott Alan. *Rebel between Spirit and Law: Ahmad Zarruq, Sainthood, and Authority in Islam.* Bloomington: Indiana University Press, 2006.

Lagardère, Vincent. *Histoire et Société en Occident Musulman au Moyen Age: Analyse du Mi'yar d'Al-Wansarisi.* Madrid: Casa de Valázquez, 1995.

Laroui, Abdallah. *The History of the Maghrib: An Interpretive Essay.* Translated by Ralph Mannheim. Princeton, NJ: Princeton University Press, 1977.

Latif, Muhammad. *al-Usra fi Maghrib al-'Asr al-Wasit.* Marrakesh: Mu'assasa Afaq, 2021.

Latif, Riyaz Mansur. “Ornate Visions of Knowledge and Power: Formations of Marinid Madrasas in Maghrib al-Aqsa.” PhD diss., University of Minnesota, 2011. ProQuest (3457099).

Le Tourneau, Roger. *Fez in the Age of the Marinides.* Translated by Besse Alberta Clement. Norman: University of Oklahoma Press, 1961.

Linant de Bellefonds, Y. “Hadana.” *Encyclopaedia of Islam, Second Edition,* edited by P. Bearman, Th. Bianquis, C. E. Bosworth, E. van Donzel, and W. P. Heinrichs. Brill Online, 2015. University of Illinois at Urbana-Champaign. July 22, 2015. http://www.brillonline.nl/entries/encyclopaedia-of-islam-2/hadana-SIM_2583.

Lutfi, Huda. “Manners and Customs of Fourteenth-Century Cairene Women: Female Anarchy versus Male Shar‘i Order in Muslim Prescriptive Treatises.” In *Women in Middle Eastern History: Shifting Boundaries in Sex and Gender,* edited by Nikki R. Keddie and Beth Baron, 99–121. New Haven: Yale University Press, 1991.

Mahmood, Saba. *Politics of Piety: The Islamic Revival and the Feminist Subject.* Princeton, NJ: Princeton University Press, 2005.

Makdisi, George. *The Rise of Colleges: Institutions of Learning in Islam and the West.* Edinburgh: Edinburgh University Press, 1981.

al-Manouni, Mohammed. *Waraqat ‘an Hadarat al-Mariniyyin.* Rabat: Manshurat Kulliyat al-Adab wa al-‘Ulum al-Insaniyya, 2000.

Marín, Manuela. “Derecho Islámico Medieval y Fronteras de Género: Reflexiones Sobre Textos de al-Burzuli (m. 841/1438) [Medieval Islamic Law and Gender Boundaries: Reflections on the Texts of al-Burzuli (d. 841/1438)].” *Revista Clepsydra* 9 (2010): 21–40.

Marín, Manuela. *Mujeres en Al-Ándalus.* Estudios Onomástico-Biográficos de al-Andalus, XI. Madrid: Consejo Superior de Investigaciones Científicas, 2000.

Martin, B. G. *Muslim Brotherhoods in Nineteenth-Century Africa.* Cambridge: Cambridge University Press, 1976.

McClanan, Anne L. and Karen Rosoff Encarnación. *The Material Culture of Sex, Procreation, and Marriage in Premodern Europe.* New York: Palgrave, 2002.

Meriwether, Margaret L. “The Rights of Children and the Responsibilities of Women: Women as *Wasis* in Ottoman Aleppo, 1770–1840.” In *Women, the Family, and Divorce Laws in Islamic History,* edited by Amira El Azhary Sonbol, 219–35. Syracuse, NY: Syracuse University Press, 1996.

Mernissi, Fatema. *The Veil and the Male Elite: A Feminist Interpretation of Women's Rights in Islam.* Translated by Mary Jo Lakeland. Reading, MA: Addison-Wesley Publishing Company, 1991.

Messier, Ronald A. *The Almoravids and the Meanings of Jihad.* Santa Barbara: Praeger, 2010.

Mir-Hosseini, Ziba. *Marriage on Trial: A Study of Islamic Family Law: Iran and Morocco Compared.* London: I.B. Tauris, 1993.

Mir-Hosseini, Ziba. "Muslim Legal Tradition and the Challenge of Gender Equality." In *Men in Charge?: Rethinking Authority in Muslim Legal Tradition*, edited by Ziba Mir-Hosseini, Mulki Al-Sharmani, and Jana Rumminger, 13–43. London: Oneworld, 2015.

Mir-Hosseini, Ziba, Mulki Al-Sharmani, and Jana Rumminger, eds. *Men in Charge? Rethinking Authority in Muslim Legal Tradition.* London: Oneworld, 2015.

Munson, Henry Jr. *Religion and Power in Morocco.* New Haven: Yale University Press, 1993.

Muqirr, Muhammad. *al-Libas al-Maghribi: min bidayat al-Dawla al-Mariniyya ila al-'Asr al-Sa'adi*. Rabat: Wizarat al-Awqaf wa al-Shu'un al-Islamiyya, 2006.

Nadwi, Muhammad Akram. *Al-Muhaddithat: The Women Scholars in Islam*. Oxford: Interface Publications Ltd, 2007.

Naji, Lamine. *Abu al-Hassan al-Sughayyir: Ra'id al-Madrasa al-Malikiyya bi al-Maghrib al-Aqsa.* Rabat: Al-Rabita al-Muhammadiyya lil Ulama, 2010.

Najmabadi, Afsaneh. "Beyond the Americas: Are Gender and Sexuality Useful Categories of Analysis?" *Journal of Women's History* 18, no. 1 (2006): 11–21.

Peirce, Leslie. *The Imperial Harem: Women and Sovereignty in the Ottoman Empire*. New York: Oxford University Press, 1993.

Peirce, Leslie. *Morality Tales: Law and Gender in the Ottoman Court of Aintab.* Berkeley: University of California Press, 2003.

Peirce, Leslie. "'She Is Trouble . . . and I Will Divorce Her': Orality, Honor, and Representation in the Ottoman Court of 'Aintab." In *Women in the Medieval Islamic World: Power, Patronage, and Piety*, edited by Gavin R. G. Hambly, 269–300. New York: St. Martin's Press, 1998.

Peters, Rudolph. *Crime and Punishment in Islamic Law: Theory and Practice from the Sixteenth to the Twenty-First Century.* Cambridge: Cambridge University Press, 2005.

Phipps, Teresa, and Deborah Youngs, eds. *Litigating Women: Gender and Justice in Europe, c.1300–c.1800.* Abingdon: Routledge, 2022.

Powers, David S. "Four Cases Relating to Women and Divorce in al-Andalus and the Maghrib, 1100–1500." In *Dispensing Justice in Islam: Qadis and their Judgments,* edited by Muhammad Khalid Masud, Rudolph Peters, and David S. Powers, 383–409. Leiden: Brill, 2006.

Powers, David S. *Law, Society and Culture in the Maghrib, 1300–1500.* Cambridge: Cambridge University Press, 2002.

Powers, David S. "Women and Divorce in the Islamic West: Three Cases." *Hawwa* 1, no.1 (2003): 29–45.

Quraishi, Asifa. "Her Honor: An Islamic Critique of the Rape Laws of Pakistan from a Woman-Sensitive Perspective." *Michigan Journal of International Law* 18, no. 2 (1997): 287–320.

Quraishi, Asifa. "What if *Sharia* Weren't the Enemy? Rethinking International Women's Rights Advocacy on Islamic Law." *Columbia Journal of Gender and Law* 22, no. 1 (2011): 173–249.

Rapoport, Yossef. "Legal Diversity in the Age of Taqlid: The Four Chief Qadis under the Mamluks." *Islamic Law and Society* 10, no. 2 (2003): 210–28.

Rapoport, Yossef. *Marriage, Money and Divorce in Medieval Islamic Society.* Cambridge: Cambridge University Press, 2005.

Rapoport, Yossef. "Matrimonial Gifts in Early Islamic Egypt." *Islamic Law and Society* 7, no.1 (2000): 1–36.

Rausch, Margaret. "Ishelhin Women Transmitters of Islamic Knowledge and Culture in Southwestern Morocco." *The Journal of North African Studies* 11, no. 2 (2006): 173–92.

Roded, Ruth. *Women in Islamic Biographical Collections: From Ibn Sa'd to Who's Who.* Boulder, CO: Lynne Rienner Publishers, 1994.

Rosen, Lawrence. *The Anthropology of Justice: Law as Culture in Islamic Society.* Cambridge: Cambridge University Press, 1989.

Ruggiero, Guido. *The Boundaries of Eros: Sex Crime and Sexuality in Renaissance Venice.* New York: Oxford University Press, 1985.

Ruggles Fairchild, D., ed. *Women, Patronage, and Self-Representation in Islamic Societies.* Albany: State University of New York Press, 2000.

al-Sa'adi, Hoda, and Omaima Abou-Bakr. *al-Mar'a wa-al-Hayat al-Diniyya fi al-'Usur al-Wusta.* Cairo: Women and Memory Forum, 2001.

Sadiqi, Fatima. "The Central Role of the Family Law in the Moroccan Feminist Movement." *British Journal of Middle East Studies* 35, no. 3 (2008): 325–37.

Sal, Uthman. "Qadaya al-Mar'a al-Taziyya khilal al-'Asr al-Wasit" [Issues of the Tazan Woman during the Middle Ages]. In *Hadirat Taza wa Nahiyatuha Abr al-Tarikh: al-Dhakira wa al-Turath,* edited by Khadija al-Yaqubi al-Qabaqabi and Sabah Awinati, 159–75. Rabat: Manshurat al-Mandubiyya al-Samiyya l-Qudama' al-Muqawamin wa Ada' Jaysh al-Tahrir, 2022.

Sayeed, Asma. "Muslim Women's Religious Education in Early and Classical Islam." *Religion Compass* 5, no. 3 (2011): 94–103.

Sayeed, Asma. *Women and the Transmission of Religious Knowledge in Islam.* Cambridge: Cambridge University Press, 2013.

Scott, Joan W. "*AHR Forum:* Unanswered Questions." *American Historical Review* 13, no. 5 (2008): 1422–29.

Scott, Joan W. "Gender: A Useful Category of Historical Analysis." *The American Historical Review* 91, no. 5 (1986): 1053–75.

Semerdjian, Elyse. *"Off the Straight Path": Illicit Sex, Law, and Community in Ottoman Aleppo.* Syracuse, NY: Syracuse University Press, 2008.

Serrano Ruano, Delfina. "La Lapidación como Castigo de las Relaciones Sexuales No Legales (zina) en el Seno de la Escuela Malikí: Doctrina, Práctica Legal y Actitudes Individuales Frente al Delito (ss. XI y XII)." *Al-Qanṭara* 26, no. 2 (2005): 449–73.

Shatzmiller, Maya. *The Berbers and the Islamic State: The Marinid Experience in Pre-Protectorate Morocco.* Princeton: Markus Weiner, 1999.

Shatzmiller, Maya. *Her Day in Court: Women's Property Rights in Fifteenth-Century Granada.* Cambridge, MA: Harvard University Press, 2007.

Shatzmiller, Maya. "Les Premiers Mérinides et Le Milieu Religieux de Fès: L'introduction des Médersas." *Studia Islamica* 43 (1976): 109–18.

Sonbol, Amira El Azhary. "A History of Marriage Contracts in Egypt." In *The Islamic Marriage Contract: Case Studies in Islamic Family Law,* edited by Asifa Quraishi and Frank E. Vogel, 87–122. Cambridge, MA: Harvard University Press, 2008.

Sonbol, Amira El Azhary, ed. *Women, the Family, and Divorce Laws in Islamic History.* Syracuse, NY: Syracuse University Press, 1996.

Soulaimani, Dris. "Writing and Rewriting Amazigh/Berber Identity: Orthographies and Language Ideologies." *Writing Systems Research* 8, no. 1 (2016): 1–16.

Spectorsky, Susan A. *Women in Classical Islamic Law: A Survey of the Sources.* Leiden: Brill, 2010.

Tazi, Abdelhadi. "Fii Tarikh Taza [On the History of Taza]." *Daouat al-Haq* 241 (October 1984). https://www.habous.gov.ma/daouat-alhaq/item/6284.

Tazi, Abdelhadi. *Jami' al-Qarawiyyin: al-Masjid wa al-Jami' bi Madinat Fez* [The Qarawiyyin Mosque: The Mosque and the Congregational Mosque in the City of Fez]. 3 vols. Beirut: Dar al-Kutub al-Lubnani, 1972–73.

Tazi, Abdelhadi. *al-Mar'a fi Tarikh al-Gharb al-Islami*. Casablanca: Nashr al-Finik, 1992.

al-Terrab, Samirah. *Taza wa Iqlimuha Fi 'Asr Bani Marin, 609–916H/1212–1510M*. Rabat: Eventus Dar Bouregreg li al-Taba'a wa al-Nashr, 2020.

Titaou, Hamid. *al-Harb wa al-Mujtama' bi al-Maghrib khilal al-'Asr al-Marini 609–869AH/1212–1465CE: Isham fi Dirasat In'ikasat al-Harb 'ala al-Binyat al-Iqtisadiyya wa al-Ijtima'iyya wa al-Dhihniyya*. Casablanca: Fondation du Roi Abdul-Aziz, 2009.

Titaou, Hamid. "Jabrut al-Qadi wa Fatat Taza." *Zamane* 2 (2013): 64–67.

Toledano, Ehud R. "Shemsigul: A Circassian Slave in Mid-Nineteenth-Century Cairo." In *Struggle and Survival in the Modern Middle East*, second ed., edited by Edmund Burke III and David N. Yaghoubian, 48–63. Berkeley/Los Angeles: University of California Press, 2006.

Toledano, Henry. *Judicial Practice and Family Law in Morocco: The Chapter on Marriage from Sijilmasi's* al-'Amal al-Mutlaq. Boulder, CO: Social Science Monographs, 1981.

Trouillot, Michel-Rolph. *Silencing the Past: Power and the Production of History*. Boston: Beacon Press, 1995.

Tucker, Judith E. "'And God Knows Best': The *Fatwa* as a Source for the History of Gender in the Arab World." In *Beyond the Exotic: Women's Histories in Islamic Societies*, edited by Amira El-Azhary Sonbol, 165–79. Syracuse, NY: Syracuse University Press, 2005.

Tucker, Judith E. *In the House of the Law: Gender and Islamic Law in Ottoman Syria and Palestine*. Berkeley: University of California Press, 1998.

Tucker, Judith E. "Questions of Consent: Contracting a Marriage in Ottoman Syria and Palestine." In *The Islamic Marriage Contract: Case Studies in Islamic Family Law*, edited by Asifa Quraishi and Frank E. Vogel, 123–35. Cambridge, MA: Harvard University Press, 2008.

Tucker, Judith E. *Women, Family, and Gender in Islamic Law*. Cambridge: Cambridge University Press, 2008.

University of Ibn Tufayl. *Pour une Histoire des femmes au Maroc*. Kenitra: Kulliyat al-Adab wa al-'Ulum al-Insaniyya, 2001.

University of Ibn Tufayl. *Tarikh al-Nisa' al-Maghribiyyat: al-Iqsa' wa Rudud al-Fa'il—Histoire des femmes au Maghreb: Réponses à l'exclusion*. Kenitra: Kulliyat al-Adab wa al-'Ulum al-Insaniyya, 1999.

Vidal Castro, Francisco. "Ahmad al-Wansarisi (m. 914/1508). Principales aspectos de su vida." *Al-Qantara* 12, no. 2 (1991): 315–52.

Vidal Castro, Francisco. "El *Mi'yar* de al-Wansarisi (m. 914/1508). I: Fuentes, Manuscritos, Ediciones, Traducciones." *Miscelánea de Estudios árabes y Hebraicos, Sección de árabe—Islam* 42–43 (1994): 317–61.

Vidal Castro, Francisco. "El *Mi'yar* de al-Wansarisi (m. 914/1508). II: Contenido." *Miscelánea de Estudios árabes y Hebraicos, Sección de árabe—Islam* 44 (1995): 213–46.

Vidal Castro, Francisco. "Ibn Rushayd." In *Encyclopaedia of Islam*, Three, edited by Kate Fleet, Gudrun Krämer, Denis Matringe, John Nawas, and Everett Rowson. Accessed: August 24, 2022. http://dx.doi.org/10.1163/1573-3912_ei3_COM_32193.

Vogel, Frank E. *Islamic Law and Legal System: Studies of Saudi Arabia.* Leiden: Brill, 2000.

Wadud-Muhsin, Amina. *Qur'an and Woman.* Kuala Lumpur: Penerbit Fajar Bakti Sdn. Bhd., 1992.

Yacoob, Saadia. "Women and Education in the Pre-modern Middle East: Reconstructing the Lives of Two Female Jurists (*Faqihat*)." Master's thesis, McGill University, 2006. ProQuest (MR32574).

al-Zarakshi, Muhammad Ibn Ibrahim, *Tarikh al-Dawlatayn al-Muwahhidiyya wa al-Hafsiyya,* edited by Muhammad Madur. Tunis: al-Maktaba al-Atiqiyya, 1966.

Zilfi, Madeline C. "'We Don't Get Along': Women and *Hul* Divorce in the Eighteenth Century." In *Women in the Ottoman Empire: Middle Eastern Women in the Early Modern Era,* edited by Madeline C. Zilfi, 264–96. Leiden: Brill, 1997.

Zomeño, Amalia. "Abandoned Wives and their Possibilities for Divorce in al-Andalus: The Evidence from the Watha'iq Works." In *Writing the Feminine: Women in Arab Sources,* edited by Randi Deguilhem and Manuela Marín, 111–26. London/New York: I.B. Tauris, 2002.

Zomeño, Amalia. *Dote y Matrimonio en al-Andalus y el Norte de África: Estudio Sobre la Jurisprudencia Islámica Medieval.* Madrid: Consejo Superior de Investigaciones Científicas, 2000.

Zomeño, Amalia. "The Islamic Marriage Contract in al-Andalus (10th–16th Centuries)." In *The Islamic Marriage Contract: Case Studies in Islamic Family Law,* edited by Asifa Quraishi and Frank E. Vogel, 136–55. Cambridge, MA: Harvard University Press, 2008.

Zomeño, Amalia. "*Kafa'a* in the Maliki School: A *Fatwa* from Fifteenth-Century Fez." In *Islamic Law: Theory And Practice,* edited by R. Gleave and E. Kermeli, 87–106. London: I.B. Tauris, 1997.

Index

Rosemary Admiral is assistant professor of history at the University of Texas at Dallas. Her research interests include Islamic legal studies, premodern North African history, and histories of women and gender.

www.ingramcontent.com/pod-product-compliance
Lightning Source LLC
Chambersburg PA
CBHW060602120825
30778CB00002B/2
9780815611844